Cinema of the
Psychic Realm

ALSO BY PAUL MEEHAN

*Tech-Noir: The Fusion of Science Fiction
and Film Noir* (McFarland, 2008)

Cinema of the Psychic Realm

A Critical Survey

PAUL MEEHAN

McFarland & Company, Inc., Publishers
Jefferson, North Carolina, and London

LIBRARY OF CONGRESS CATALOGUING-IN-PUBLICATION DATA

Meehan, Paul.
    Cinema of the psychic realm : a critical survey / Paul Meehan.
        p.   cm.
    Includes bibliographical references and index.

    ISBN 978-0-7864-3966-9
    softcover : 50# alkaline paper ∞

    1. Psychic ability in motion pictures.   2. Motion pictures—
Psychological aspects.   I. Title.
PN1995.9.P7825M44   2009
791.43'67—dc22   2009020194

British Library cataloguing data are available

©2009 Paul Meehan. All rights reserved

No part of this book may be reproduced or transmitted in any form or by any means, electronic or mechanical, including photocopying or recording, or by any information storage and retrieval system, without permission in writing from the publisher.

Cover photograph ©2009 Shutterstock

Manufactured in the United States of America

McFarland & Company, Inc., Publishers
    Box 611, Jefferson, North Carolina 28640
        www.mcfarlandpub.com

Table of Contents

Preface	1
ONE • A Brief History of the Paranormal in Fact and Fiction	9
TWO • Early Paranormal Films	26
THREE • ESP in Drama, Comedy and Children's Films	37
FOUR • Paranormal Crime and Melodrama	59
FIVE • The Dark Side of ESP: Horror and Fantasy	75
SIX • Alien ESP	106
SEVEN • Psi-Fi: Psychic Science Fiction Blockbusters	141
EIGHT • Remote Viewing, Black Psi-Ops and Paranoia	177
Conclusion	206
Filmography	211
Chapter Notes	219
Bibliography	221
Index	223

Preface

Since the beginning of recorded history, humankind has had a fascination with individuals thought to possess seemingly miraculous powers of mind that enabled them to see the future, have visions of faraway events, read minds and perform other feats that defy ordinary explanation. In ancient Greece the oracles of the gods foretold future events, while in the Old Testament, prophets of the Lord counseled Biblical kings. In the 21st century, science has replaced magic and religion as an explanation for these unusual abilities, talents the public continues to regard with a mixture of awe, fear and skepticism.

What, exactly, is meant by the term "psychic"? The word derives from the classical Greek word *psyche*, meaning the soul, the spirit, or the mind. Webster's dictionary defines psychic as both an adjective ("lying outside the sphere of physical science or knowledge") and a noun ("a person apparently sensitive to nonphysical forces"). These definitions describe the psychic realm as an occult territory existing apart from our everyday world of logic and science, and individuals who function within this realm as "sensitives" with special powers of mind.

The word psychic evokes a variety of cinematic icons, from wizened, Old World fortune-tellers to high-tech Jedi Knights. In the movies, psychics are usually portrayed as tormented, misunderstood loners whose paranormal powers make them unable to fit into mainstream human society. Sometimes the psychic individual is even an inhuman, extraterrestrial being. The world of movie-psi is overlaid with supernatural imagery and is frequently presented in terms of ghosts, demons and other denizens of the netherworld. Fiction films about the psychic realm do not constitute a separate genre, but are culled from the ranks of the horror, science fiction, film noir and dramatic genres (although the vast majority of them are to be found in a horror/sci-fi vein).

This is in stark contrast to the pursuit of psi in the real world, where scientists strive to bring the light of reason and the scientific method to the study of the paranormal. The term psi (rhymes with I) is derived from a letter of the Greek alphabet that is used by parapsychologists to describe anomalous phenomena such as precognition, clairvoyance, telepathy and psychokinesis. It came into usage in the 1950s to replace the word "psychic," which had fallen into scientific disrepute. Contrary to popular belief, individuals with augmented psychic abilities are in most cases not significantly different from the normal human population. Additionally, the most advanced psi research suggests some degree of psychic ability resides within everyone. Parapsychologists have focused on researching four principal psychic abilities:

- *Precognition*: the ability to perceive future events before they occur
- *Clairvoyance*: the visualization of objects or events at a distance
- *Telepathy*: the power to send or receive information from another person's mind
- *Psychokinesis*: the ability to affect the physical world using thought alone

The most dramatic and cinematic of these psi abilities is psychokinesis (sometimes abbreviated as PK). Movie psychics routinely wield great powers of mind-over-matter in blockbusters and cult favorites such as *The Medusa Touch, Carrie, Scanners, Star Wars* and *X-Men*, where they are able to hurl large objects around with their PK abilities without breaking much of a sweat. In the real world this level of psychic energy is only manifested in cases involving poltergeists, which occur in "the field" and are not generally amenable to laboratory study. Demonstrations of the existence of PK in the lab have proven elusive, but this hasn't stopped Hollywood from exploiting the more sensational implications of psychokinesis. As for clairvoyance, precognition and telepathy, these psi powers are not as visually dramatic but have featured in memorable films in a variety of genres such as *The Night Has a Thousand Eyes, Resurrection, The Eyes of Laura Mars, Don't Look Now, The Last Wave, The Dead Zone, The Green Mile, The Gift* and *Minority Report*.

The medium of film is ideally suited to render the fantastic world of psi visible. A technique as simple as an off-screen voice-over can simulate mental telepathy. Unusual lighting, set design, fades, dissolves and other optical tricks can conjure clairvoyant visions. The advent of ultra-sophisticated computer graphics and other exotic cinematic techniques have made it possible to picture any conceivable visionary state, no matter how unusual or bizarre.

There is, to be sure, a negative aspect to the study of psi. Carny hucksters, confidence men, fortune tellers and phony mediums have exploited a credulous belief in psychic powers, from time immemorial to the more recent depredations of Uri Geller and the Psychic Friends Network. The skeptical/cynical view of ESP (extrasensory perception) is represented in a number of films about bogus psychics, swamis and magicians involved in criminal schemes. Examples include *Nightmare Alley, The Amazing Mr. X, Man on a Swing, Family Plot* and *Seance on a Wet Afternoon*. These films explore the potential psychological dangers of an uncritical belief in these poorly understood phenomena.

Throughout its history, parapsychology has been considered a "fringe" subject unworthy of serious scientific inquiry. The dubious academics portrayed in the *Ghostbusters* films by Bill Murray, Dan Aykroyd and Harold Ramis, who are hounded out of their ivory tower by skeptical university administrators, present a comic take on reality. Despite decades of research, the scientific establishment remains hostile to the existence of ESP because of their attitude of "It can't be, therefore it isn't." Despite the acceptance of the Parapsychological Association as a valid discipline by the American Association for the Advancement of Science in 1969, institutional science continued to turn up its collective nose at the notion of psi.

Then, in the late 1960s, reports began to filter out of the Soviet bloc that the Communists had developed a sudden interest in psychic phenomena. Russian and Eastern European psi research programs, geared toward intelligence gathering and mind control were reportedly serious and well-funded by their Communist sponsors. The implications for American national security were ominous, especially if the Reds were to make breakthrough discoveries in parapsychology. In order to counter this perceived threat, beginning in the early 1970s the U.S. intelligence services began funding psychic research at the esteemed Stanford Research Institute (SRI) in Palo Alto, California. The SRI psi research went underground by the end of the decade, and the existence of an American psychic espionage unit of "remote viewers" was not revealed to the public until the late 1990s, by which time the psi-spy outfit had been disbanded. Although the track record of the psychic spies in deciphering enemy secrets was decidedly mixed, there were reportedly some spectacular successes, including the discovery of a downed Soviet bomber on the African continent by an American remote viewing team in 1978 that was later confirmed by former president Jimmy Carter.

Psi and the Occult

From the time of prehistoric shamans to the 21st century, psychic functioning has had a whiff of the supernatural about it despite the best efforts of the science-minded to bring psi out of the darkness of the occult. Individuals endowed with psychic powers are frequently demonized in horror/sci-fi flicks in order to exploit the darker aspects of the psi phenomenon at the box office. This is perfectly illustrated in Brian de Palma's psychic thriller *Carrie* (1976), in which a sensitive, innocent teenager (Sissy Spacek) with telekinetic powers is instantaneously transformed, via a sadistic prank, into a psychotic, blood-soaked avenger who brutally murders her high school classmates before stalking off to her own death. On the other end of the spectrum are suave, *veddy* British psychotronic killers such as Michael Rennie in *The Power*, Richard Burton in *The Medusa Touch* and Ben Kingsley in *Suspect Zero*. Somewhere in between are sinister American psychic villians like Michael Ironside in *Scanners* or Andrew Stevens in *The Fury*. Needless to say, these psi-powered assassins have little if any basis in reality.

While the mechanics of psychic functioning are still not clearly understood, researchers have taken pains to separate psi from the supernatural world of ghosts and spirits. There is one phenomenon, however, that defies easy categorization: the poltergeist. Derived from a German word that means "noisy ghost," poltergeists constitute the most extreme and dramatic manifestation of psychic power; however parapsychologists are divided as to the true nature of the poltergeist. Some researchers postulate that the phenomenon is the result of "recurring spontaneous psychokinesis" (or RSPK), while others believe that spirit beings are responsible for the effect. As the RSPK theory is currently in vogue among parapsychologists, films about poltergeists can be considered a part of the psychic continuum.

Psi and Mysticism

Some ESP-themed films emphasize a mystical or religious approach to psi. In the *Star Wars* films, for instance, the Jedi Knights derive their paranormal powers from "the Force," a thinly-veiled substitute for God, and their organization constitutes a neo-pagan order of psychic warriors devoted to "bringing peace and justice to the Galaxy." Similarly, in *Dune* the protagonist's extraordinary psi powers inspire a futuristic Islamic messiah cult to perpetrate a galactic jihad. In dramatic treatments of the theme such as *Resurrection* and *The Gift*, psychics living in conservative rural communities are persecuted by zealous religious individuals who believe their powers derive from demonic sources. Obeying the Old Testament dictum "Thou shalt not suffer a witch to live," the religionists plot murder against psychics.

Psychics and Crime

Psychics have frequently been associated with criminal behavior in movies, either as criminals or as paranormal sleuths. Films noir of the 1940s tended to portray psychics and mediums as slick crooks and manipulative swindlers in films like *Nightmare Alley* and *The Amazing Mr. X*. This theme was later carried forward in thrillers such as *Séance on a Wet Afternoon* and *Family Plot*. In addition to perpetrating thievery, psychics used their powers to commit homicide in *The Power*, *Patrick*, *Psychic Killer*, *Dreamscape* and *The Medusa Touch*.

As in real life, where psychics are sometimes called upon to aid the police in solving murders, individuals gifted with psi powers have been involved in bringing killers to justice in a number of films. The standard plot formula involves a psychic (usually female) who inadvertently begins receiving visions of a murder or series of murders being committed in the vicinity. Information essential to solving the crime is passed along to detectives, who are generally skeptical and even suspicious about the psychic's visionary evidence, but who come around to a grudging acceptance of psi by the last reel. This is the basic (and by now clichéd) plotline of such psi-oriented fare as *The Psychic, The Dark, Man on a Swing, In Dreams* and *The Gift*.

Alien Psi

Some of the most gifted cinematic psychics are non-human or partly human extraterrestrials. Psychic aliens in films have been around from the early 1950s, and have been endowed by screenwriters with paranormal powers of telepathy, telepathic hypnotism and psychokinesis. Oddly, telepathic aliens have also been reported in real-world cases of alien abduction. These psi abilities enable them to exert their will over the non-psychic general population of humankind and to visit all manner of mischief on hapless homo sapiens. Like superior intelligence, psi powers are a hallmark of the E.T.'s superior mental capabilities. The only defense lies in using earthling psychics to counter them. In the alien invasion blockbuster *Independence Day*, for instance, the President of the United States (played by Bill Pullman) has a psychic exchange with one of the aliens and uncovers their motivations. Not all extraterrestrials use their powers for evil, however. Some of them, like the beneficent aliens of *Starman* and *E.T.* use their powers for healing and other good deeds, while everybody's favorite spaceman, *Star Trek*'s Mr. Spock, is well-known for his use of the telepathic "Vulcan mind meld" to help the crew of the starship *Enterprise* out of some very tight spots.

Sci-Fi Psi

While movie aliens seem to be generously endowed with psi, other science fiction films also explore the ramifications of psi talents in human individuals. The most well-known example is, of course, in the *Star Wars* series, in which psychic individuals are recognized, recruited and trained by the organization of the Jedi Knights to function as a corps of paranormal paramilitary troops who enforce the dictums of a galactic empire. Similarly, in *Dune*, guilds exploiting various ESP powers vie with each other for dominance of a star-flung imperial culture. In *Starship Troopers* human psychics use their talents to hunt and destroy fearsome alien arachnids, while in *Minority Report* a group of psychic "precogs" visualize murders before they happen.

Drama and Comedy

Outside the realm of melodrama, psi phenomena have also been featured in a number of films that are primarily dramatic, including *The Clairvoyant*, *Resurrection*, *The Green Mile* and *Premonition*. These films tend to treat the theme in a more serious and thoughtful fashion. Paranormal themes also crop up occasionally in dramatic films that are not fundamentally about psi. Examples include *Juarez*, *8½*, *Fanny and Alexander* and *Shadow of a Doubt*. The psychic world can also provide material for comedy, as evidenced in such varied fare as *Wilder Napalm*, *Ghostbusters* and *What Women Want*, and in kiddie fare like *Escape from Witch Mountain*, *Matilda* and *The Last Mimzy*.

Psychic Paranoia

During the 1980s, news reports detailing CIA malfeasance against U.S. citizens and rumors about clandestine government ESP programs inspired a flurry of movies in which well-funded espionage agencies, staffed by a corps of evil bureaucrats, conducted unholy experiments that produced homicidal psychic warriors with terrifying paranormal powers. Your tax dollars were hard at work on psychic black ops projects in films like *Dreamscape*, *Scanners*, *The Lawnmower Man*, *The Fury* and *Firestarter*. These films served to create paranoia about psi, which was shown in a negative, even demonic light, while at the same time exploiting paranoid anxieties about a "secret government" wielding quasi-occult powers designed to subjugate the populace.

Into the Psychic Wilderness

These are some of the themes running through popular films that have served to inform public attitudes about ESP. For the most part, they have tended to exploit the negative aspects of the phenomenon and portray psychics as threatening monstrosities, marginal schizoid individuals, and even aliens, characterizations that grossly distort the nature of psi and minimize its positive aspects. On one level this is due to the greed of Hollywood film-makers eager to exploit the more fantastic implications of psi, but on another level this also represents a visceral uneasiness about the nature of ESP itself. The very idea of psi defies our commonsense view of reality and challenges us on the level of phenomenology and epistemology; this disquieting mental undertow is reflected in the mirror of cinema. This uneasiness about psi is especially true of psychics themselves, who must live with the disturbing implications of their extraordinary experiences.

This, then, is a journey into another realm, a dimension, as Rod Serling used to say, not only of sight and sound, but of mind. It is a trip one step beyond the Twilight Zone, a voyage over the threshold into a brave new world of dazzling filmic possibilities.

• ONE •

A Brief History of the Paranormal in Fact and Fiction

Although there are no written records, psychic phenomena have been part of human culture since prehistory. In analyzing the nature of still-existing pre-industrial societies, anthropologists have documented the role of individuals they refer to as shamans. They are, in essence, "witch doctors" who utilize apparently paranormal abilities for the benefit of the tribe. Shamans are reportedly able to locate lost objects, foretell future events and heal illnesses, and are usually highly respected within their societies. Cave paintings thought to represent shamans dating back to the Paleolithic period attest to their great antiquity. Shamanic practices have survived into the modern world, as depicted in Peter Weir's apocalyptic thriller *The Last Wave* (1977).

Divinatory techniques were commonplace in the emerging civilizations of Egypt, China, India and Mesopotamia, where written records of such practices date back to the Second Millennium B.C. In ancient Sumeria, the first civilization in history, the will of the gods was ascertained in dreams and in the interpretation of the size and shape of the livers of sacrificed animals. Bronze Age China developed a system of fortune-telling based on a book called the *I Ching*, which is still used in the East (and West) in modern times. Texts such as *The Leyden Papyrus* have preserved the divinatory formulas of ancient Egypt.

The Delphic Oracle

In Classical Greek and Roman times, divinely-inspired oracles delivered prophecies of future events. The most famous of these was the Oracle at Delphi, where a prophetess called the Pythia foretold the future while in an altered state of consciousness induced by vapors rising from a deep cleft in the earth. The oracle was consulted on matters of war by emperors and kings, and had a profound effect on the history of the Western World. In a famous story recounted by the Greek historian Herotodus, Croesus, the wealthy ruler of the gold-rich kingdom of Lydia, was contemplating an attack on the Persian Empire and decided to test the various oracles to ascertain which was the most accurate. He sent messengers to the seven most prominent oracles to query them about what King Croesus was doing at that exact moment. Only the oracle at Delphi conveyed the correct answer, namely that the king was boiling a lamb and a tortoise together in a cauldron made of brass. On the basis of this contest, Croesus decided to ask the Pythia if he would be victorious if he attacked the Persian Empire. The oracle replied, in typically opaque fashion, that if he attacked the Persians, a great empire would fall. Unfortunately, when Croesus acted on this advice, it was his own empire that fell. Croesus's contest between the oracles is considered the first test of remote viewing recorded in history.

Another famous incident from Greek history also highlights the importance of Delphi. As depicted in the film *300* (2007), the Persian King Xerxes I launched an invasion of Greece in 480 B.C., which was opposed chiefly by King Leonidas of Sparta and the fearsome warriors of his city-state. The Oracle was consulted regarding the prospects for a Greek victory, and the answer came back that Sparta could only be saved from destruction by the death of one of its kings. On the basis of this prophecy, Leonidas decided on a suicidal defense of the pass of Thermopylae accompanied by 300 of his best warriors against overwhelming odds. Although the Persians ultimately prevailed at Thermopylae and Leonidas was killed in battle, Xerxes was later defeated when the Greeks united, having been inspired by the resistance of the 300 Spartans.

Psi in the Bible

In the Old Testament of the Bible, divinely-inspired prophets foretold future events and provided clairvoyant information about the enemies of Israel. The word "prophet" derives from the Greek word "prophetes," meaning "to speak before" or "proclaim." In Hebrew the term is *nabi*, meaning "to utter." Like the Delphic Oracle, the Hebrew prophets functioned as psychic mediums who received messages and visions from a higher power and provided information that enabled rulers to make important decisions. The first *nabi* is generally considered to be the patriarch Moses; other important prophets wrote books of the Old Testament, including Samuel, Jeremiah, Isaiah, Daniel and Ezekiel.

According to the prophet Daniel, the holy seer "reveals deep and secret things; he knows what is in the darkness and light dwells within him" (Dan. 2:22). These powers of divination were frequently used to provide vital information in times of crisis. For instance, the prophet Elisha instructed King Joash to throw two arrows through a window in order to determine whether the king would be victorious in battle (2 Kings 13:14–19). Elisha also used his clairvoyant abilities to baffle the king of Syria during a military campaign by reporting the Syrian's location to the Hebrew king. One of the Syrians explained to his king that "Elisha, the prophet that is in Israel, telleth the king of Israel the words that thou speakest in thy bedchamber" (2 Kings 6–12).

In addition, another method of divination discussed in the Bible involved the use of the "Urim and Thummin," sacred stones or gems that were manipulated by both prophets and priests to foretell the future. The Old Testament also mentions similar divinatory techniques practiced by contemporary cultures in the ancient Near East. In Ezekiel 21:21 we read: "For the King of Babylon stands at the parting of the road, at the fork of the two roads, to use divination. He shakes the arrows, he consults the images, he looks at the liver."

While legitimate prophets of the Lord were highly esteemed by the Israelites, anyone else practicing divination outside of the approved religious framework was subject to severe censure or even death. The book of Deuteronomy, one of the books of Jewish law attributed to Moses, clearly spells out these penalties: "But that prophet or dreamer of dreams shall be put to death because he has spoken in order to turn you away from the Lord your God" (Deut. 13:5). The book also states more explicitly, "There shall not be found among you anyone who makes his son or his daughter pass through the fire, or one who practices witchcraft, or a soothsayer, or one who interprets omens, or a sorcerer, or one who conjures spells, or a medium, or a spiritist, or one who calls up the dead. For all who do these things are an abomination to the Lord, and because of these abominations the Lord your God drives them out from before you." (Deut 18:10–12). The most succinct and oft-quoted passage on the subject is found in Exodus 22:18, which states flatly, "Thou shalt not suffer a witch to live." These ultra-strict religious injunctions would negatively affect attitudes toward psychics and ESP for millennia, and they continue to have repercussions on the study of psi in the present day.

In the New Testament, Jesus is reported to have performed many miracles, including healings and levitation on water. After the death of Jesus, some of these divine powers were bestowed upon his disciples, notably Peter, who travelled to Rome to spread the gospel of Christianity as related in the Book of Acts. One of Peter's rivals was a famous magician named Simon Magus, who sought to duplicate or hoax the miracles of Jesus in order to establish a cult of personality around himself that would rival the Christian faith.

The story of Simon Magus is dramatized in the fiction film *The Silver Chalice* (1954), in which Paul Newman (in his screen debut) plays Basil, a Greek slave and artisan who is commissioned by Christian leaders to fashion a chalice to hold the cup from which Jesus drank during the Last Supper. When he embraces Christianity, Basil runs afoul of the flamboyant pagan sorcerer Simon Magus (Jack Palance), who claims to have powers greater than those of Christ. Believing his own hype, Simon arranges for a public display of his supernatural talents. Claiming that he has the ability to fly, he jumps from a tall tower and promptly plummets to his death, while onlookers shake their heads in bafflement at the spectacle and scornfully observe, "He didn't fly."

This story illustrates the attitude of the Christian church toward those who claim to have paranormal powers. While proof of Jesus's divinity rests upon the miraculous feats as reported in the Gospels, anyone else claiming to have preternatural talents is regarded as a heretical "false Christ." Later church doctrine introduced the concept of the "Antichrist," a demonic analog of Jesus who Christian prophecies foretold would appear in the last times before Judgment Day to confound the faithful with false miracles accomplished through the power of Satan. Thus anyone demonstrating psi powers outside of the approved religious framework would be considered dangerous and diabolical, and perhaps even be branded as the Antichrist.

Rome, Christianity and the End of the Ancient Prophetic Traditions

Like the Greeks before them, the Romans practiced forms of pagan divination. Roman seers known as *augurs* were authorized to interpret the will of the gods according to their observations of the skies. By the late Republic period there were sixteen official augurs who looked at lightning flashes, cloud formations and flights of birds to issue edicts that decided the election of Roman magistrates, dictated military tactics, and judgments about important legal matters. Many lesser seers and soothsayers also plied their trade in the city, typified by the sayer of sooth who famously warns Caesar to "Beware the Ides of March" in Shakespeare's *Julius Caesar*. Also popular were the *haruspices*, individuals who practiced a form of divination based on the inspection of the liver and entrails of sacrificed animals.

All this would change abruptly as Christianity began to replace the pagan cults as the state religion of the Empire in the fourth century A.D., which culminated in the declaration of the new faith as the official Roman religion under the Emperor Constantine. Once in power, the Christians suppressed the ancient pagan ways by imposing strict penalties on their practice. While paganism was for the most part tolerant of the various and sundry cults contained within the vast mosaic of the Empire, Christianity would accept no other gods and ruthlessly destroyed all of its divine competitors. In A.D. 398 the Temple of Apollo at Delphi was torn down, and an oracular legend of great antiquity faded into obscurity. Similarly, prophetic traditions among the Hebrews had also lapsed and were entirely non-existent by the time of Christ in the first century A.D. With injunctions against psychics and seers embedded in their scriptures, priestly castes among both Jews and Christians replaced prophets and oracles, declaring them anathema. This situation prevailed for the next 1400 years of Western civilization, exacerbated by the witch hunts of the Middle Ages in

Europe and the forced conversion of "heathen" religious practitioners as Christianity was spread by the sword. Charismatic seers like Joan of Arc usually wound up being burned at the stake for practicing witchcraft. In spite of this persecution, folk healers and "dowsers" (psychics who use a forked stick to locate water and other objects underground) continued to ply their trade in rural areas.

The Return of the Paranormal

Things did not begin to loosen up until after the Enlightenment, when the absolute authority of religion began to be questioned. By the 19th century, a number of popular movements had arisen that would lead to the development of parapsychology as a scientific discipline. One of these was Mesmerism, a movement started by the Viennese doctor Franz Mesmer in Paris in the late 1700s. Mesmer was basically a quack who submerged his patients in baths filled with iron filings and stared directly into their eyes in order to induce trance states. It was observed that certain entranced persons, referred to as "somnambules" or "clairvoyants," seemed to exhibit paranormal skills and became renowned psychic celebrities. By Mesmer's death in 1815, Mesmeric salons had emerged all over Europe. Some of his techniques eventually developed into the modern practice of hypnotism.

Another popular psi-oriented movement of the time was Spiritualism, which had its genesis in 1847 when two sisters, Margaretta and Catherine Fox, reported a series of strange rapping noises on the farm where they lived in Hydesville, New York. These anomalous raps were allegedly communications from spirit beings, who could in this way answer "yes" or "no" to questions. Later, the sisters devised a code to correspond to individual letters of the alphabet in order to facilitate more elaborate communications from the spirit world. The rapping spirits soon spread from the Fox household to the surrounding communities, as people set up their own séance groups and found that they could produce similar phenomena. Spiritualism, as the new movement was called, soon spread throughout America and Europe as psychic "mediums" supposedly summoned spirits in hundreds of darkened séance parlors. Spiritualist practitioners believed that mediums could speak with the dead, levitate and materialize objects, clairvoyantly reveal hidden information and produce writings penned by spirit beings.

The heady world of Spiritualism was delightfully satirized in David Lean's film version of Noël Coward's play *Blithe Spirit* (1945). In the film, a dotty bogus medium played by Margaret Rutherford (best known for her screen portrayal of Agatha Christie's dowager sleuth Miss Marple in a series of British comedy/mysteries), holds a séance where she attempts to summon the spirit of Rex Harrison's deceased wife. To everyone's surprise the wife's ghost (Kay Hammond) promptly materializes, much to the chagrin of Harrison's current spouse (Constance Cummings), and a living/dead love triangle ensues. This supernatural bedroom farce pokes gentle fun at Spiritualism, although it turns out that there is a true medium, a humble servant girl, in the household.

The proliferation of spirit mediumship led to widespread fraud and abuse, as bogus mediums bilked the credulous out of their life savings. Despite the fact that Margaretta Fox had recanted and declared the Fox family medium to be fraudulent in 1888, the belief in spirits in séances remained popular and had become something of a social problem by the late 19th century. In an attempt to separate the psychic wheat from the chaff, the first paranormal research organization, the Society for Psychical Research (SPR), was formed in London in 1882. Founding members of the SPR included luminaries such as physicists Sir Oliver Lodge and Sir William Crookes, Cambridge philosopher Henry Sidgwick, psychologist Fredrick Myers, Nobel prize–winning physiologist Charles Richet, the poet William Butler Yeats and Sir Arthur Conan Doyle, the creator of Sherlock Holmes. This august assemblage of scientific and literary talent was charged with the mission of "making an organized and systematic attempt to investigate the larger group of phenomena designated by such terms as mesmeric, psychical, and spiritualistic." An American offshoot, the American Society for Psychical Research (ASPR), was formed in Boston in 1885. The scientific search for psi had begun.

Despite their lofty pedigree, the SPR and ASPR failed to establish the study of the paranormal as a valid scientific discipline. Part of the problem was with the questionable nature of mediumship itself, which was rife with fraud and abuse. The famed magician and escape artist Harry Houdini conducted a personal crusade against these bogus mediums that was covered extensively in the press. As depicted in George Pal's 1953 biopic *Houdini*, the magician had become obsessed with the afterlife after the death of his mother and briefly fell under the sway of mediums, only to discover that it was all a sham. Afterward, Houdini employed his skills as an illusionist to uncover the trickery that created the mirage of the supernatural in the séance room. These revelations did nothing to bolster the case for psychic phenomena in the public mind. Additionally, the paradigms of the material world as understood by turn-of-the-century science were unable to accommodate psi phenomena within any scientifically recognized framework. Author Jim Schnabel observes in his book *Remote Viewing*, "It became increasingly fashionable among scientists to portray psi as a primitive, retrograde fantasy which modernity was swiftly leaving behind."[1]

Mental Radio

The development of radio technology in the late 19th century led to the formulation of the concept of telepathy, or mind-to-mind thought transference. The term was coined in 1882 by F.W.H. Myers, one of the founders of the SPR.

Telepathy was believed to function in a manner analogous to radio, in which a "sender" broadcast a signal through the ether to a "receiver" using ultra-low frequency radio waves. In the 1930s this idea was popularized by the respected American novelist Upton Sinclair in his remarkable book *Mental Radio*. Sinclair, who would win a Pulitzer Prize, was best known for his hard-hitting journalistic novels such as *The Jungle*, an exposé of the American meat packing business.

Mental Radio was a nonfiction account of a series of telepathy experiments Sinclair conducted with his wife of fifty years, Mary Craig Sinclair, and other psychics during the 1920s. Sinclair's pioneering work concentrated on sending and receiving pictorial information via telepathy. His experiments revealed an important insight: psychic information exchange was primarily visual in nature rather than verbal. In fact, attempts to build a conceptual, language-based framework around the images actually interfered with the telepathic process. Sinclair's insights regarding the visual nature of psi were independently validated by a contemporary, French chemist and parapsychologist René Warcollier, who also noted a visual basis for psi. Unfortunately, Warcollier's 1946 book *Mind to Mind* was not widely available in English translation, and his work fell into obscurity.

Sinclair and Warcollier's work provided valuable clues into the image-based nature of psychic functioning, but the significance of their research would not become apparent until decades later, when their insights would be instrumental in formulating basic remote viewing theories during the 1970s. The notion that telepathy functioned through the action of radio waves or via some other form of electromagnetic energy would prove to be a blind alley for Soviet and Western psi researchers, who would spend decades conducting experiments that ultimately disproved this hypothesis.

Parapsychology in the Laboratory

A different approach to psi research was advocated by J. B. Rhine, a scientist who had become interested in the phenomenon in the 1920s. Rhine, a botanist by training, founded the Parapsychology Laboratory at Duke University in North Carolina in 1930, where he attempted to study psi under controlled conditions. Taking a statistical approach, he conducted hundreds of thousands of laboratory trials in order to prove that his results were greater than those that could be expected by chance alone. Rhine employed a specially designed deck of cards, called "Zener cards," which were imprinted with five symbols: a star, a cross, a square, a circle and a pair of wavy lines. Picking a card, a "sender" would attempt to transmit the correct design to a telepathic "receiver," and the results were recorded. This process is depicted in an amusing scene in *Ghostbusters* (1984), in which psychic researcher Dr. Venkman (Bill

Murray) dispenses electric shocks to student volunteers for incorrect Zener card guesses during an ESP experiment.

Rhine coined the term "extrasensory perception," abbreviated as ESP, to bring precognition and telepathy within the orbit of perceptual psychology and out of the shadows of the séance room. Similarly, in order to de-mythologize the concept of mind-over-matter, Rhine invented the word "psychokinesis" (or PK), and conducted statistical tests with dice-throwing to measure this psychic ability. After several years of experimentation at the Duke Lab, Rhine summarized his findings in a book entitled *Extra-Sensory Perception*, published in 1934. The book was well received in the American press and was followed by a sequel, *Extra-Sensory Perception After 60 Years*, in 1940. Rhine's books were instrumental in bringing the concepts of psi to the attention of the general public.

Despite Rhine's scientific rigor, the study of ESP continued to be denounced as a pseudoscience by the academic establishment, and psychic research once again fell into obscurity. The Duke Lab's statistical methodologies and experimental protocols were called into question as the conservative scientific establishment scrambled to debunk psi. Rhine's best evidence for the existence of ESP and PK was in the statistical analysis of a large number of Zener card and dice-throwing trials, which showed positive guessing results that were only very slightly higher than chance. These dry stat tables did not appear to offer compelling proof for the claimed wonders of the paranormal realm. Additionally, later psi studies would determine that Rhine's bean-counter approach to ESP research was so mind-numbing that it was actually antithetical to psychic functioning.

Rhine and the Duke Parapsychology Lab continued to soldier on for decades, but ESP research became permanently marginalized, existing on the far fringes of orthodox science. Parapsychologists were ostracized, deprived of funding and forced to make do with private contributions from philanthropists, while publishing the results of their research in the *Journal of Parapsychology* and other obscure technical journals with a negligible readership.

Psychic Poltergeists

The most controversial, dramatic, and cinematic of psychic phenomena is the poltergeist. Derived from the German, the word means "noisy ghost," a reference to the pandemonium caused by the phenomenon. A poltergeist causes objects (even large, heavy ones) to move around by themselves as if directed by invisible hands. Sometimes strange noises, raps or mysterious voices are heard. It can even cause *apports*, the de-materialization and re-materialization of solid objects. Ghost-like apparitions have also been reported, but are rare. Like psychic phenomena such as clairvoyance and precognition, accounts of poltergeists have been reported since antiquity. Perhaps the earliest case on record dates to 858 B.C., when a farmhouse near Bingen on the Rhine River was pelted with showers of stones from an unseen source; the "evil spirit" even caused the walls of the house to shake.

Unlike a conventional haunting, which is confined to a specific place (i.e., the "haunted house"), a poltergeist seems to attach itself to a specific person and will manifest itself wherever that person happens to be. In psychic terms, this individual is referred to as the "focus" of the poltergeist. Invariably the focus is a young person, in an age-range from early puberty to young adulthood. Researchers theorize that the poltergeist somehow feeds off of the intense psychosexual energies generated by adolescents and young adults. The phenomenon is believed to be caused by "unconscious" psychokinetic forces on the part of the focus individual, and is commonly referred to as "recurrent spontaneous psychokinesis," or RSPK, by paranormal researchers.

The RSPK hypothesis is an attempt to remove the phenomenon from the realm of the occult and transform it into a scientific anomaly that could be studied in the physical world. Unfortunately, researching the poltergeist in a laboratory setting proved to be highly problematic. The phenomenon prankishly refused to manifest itself under controlled conditions, and had to be studied in the field at the location where the psychic outbursts occurred. Furthermore, the manifestations were frequently so complex that the idea they were caused or directed by the focus person strained credulity. Some researchers have noted similarities between the poltergeist phenomenon, multiple personality disorder and so-called "demonic" possession, all of which produce psychokinetic effects. While the precise nature of the poltergeist remains elusive, the RSPK hypothesis is still the prevailing one among ESP researchers and serves to bring the phenomenon out of the domain of the supernatural and into the light of scientific inquiry.

No matter what its ultimate nature, the poltergeist has provided inspiration for a number of psychic thrillers, including *Poltergeist* (1982) and its three sequels. William Friedkin's seminal horror classic *The Exorcist* (1973) was based on a real-life case that a number of psi researchers think was more probably a poltergeist manifestation than an example of demonic infestation, and the film presents a number of instances of PK and telepathy. In the disappointing sequel, *Exorcist II: The Heretic* (1977), Linda Blair's preternatural abilities are studied in a psychic laboratory setting. The notion that poltergeist-like PK effects could be harnessed and directed by individuals with psychic powers found its way into many a movie script, and would inspire a new generation of Scanners, Jedi Knights, X-Men and assorted psychic characters who came equipped with major-league PK.

Into the Sixties

As the paradigm-shifting Age of Aquarius moved into high gear in the 1960s, psychic researchers anticipated that the esoteric study of psi might finally achieve a higher level of scientific respectability. Although there was some movement toward acceptance within the scientific community, ESP research would remain a fringe discipline on the edge of pseudoscience throughout the decade. While popular belief in psi had risen to new heights, fueled in part by the use of psychedelic drugs during the swingin' 60s, the conservative scientific establishment remained unconvinced. In 1969, at the urging of the esteemed anthropologist Margaret Mead, the American Association for the Advancement of Science admitted the Parapsychological Association into its group of approved scientific disciplines. In spite of this apparent victory, psi research continued to languish in a netherworld of academic non-respectability. Things would change in the following decade, however, as the U.S. Government secretly became involved in psychic research.

Spurred by reports of Soviet developments in psychic spying, the CIA decided to conduct their own experiments into psychic functioning in the early 1970s. These studies were carried out at the Stanford Research Institute in Palo Alto, California, by physicists Russell Targ and Hal Puthoff. The two scientists designed a series of trials to test the psi talents of individuals under strict scientific protocols. The CIA-sponsored project in what came to be known as "remote viewing" was code-named "Project Scannate," a term derived from the phrase "scanning by coordinate." In 1976 the project graduated from research to applications when it was adopted by a unit of the U.S. Army's Intelligence and Security Command (INSCOM) based at Ft. Meade, Maryland. Although much information about the project remains classified, the remote viewers were reportedly able to achieve upwards of 65 percent accuracy when run against hard espionage targets in the real world. One of the most spectacular of the program's known successes came in 1978, when two SRI-trained remote viewers managed to locate a Soviet TU-22 bomber that had gone down in the African nation of Zaire before the KGB could get to it. This extraordinary incident was later publicly verified by former president Jimmy Carter.

The Army/CIA remote viewing project kept a very low profile for most of its existence, not only because its intelligence operations were classified, but also because of the embarrassment that would follow should the U.S. government's dabbling in the paranormal ever become known to the public. Then in 1995 the government was forced to admit the existence of the project in connection with a lawsuit brought against the Army by a former viewer, David Morehouse, who claimed that he had suffered mental and emotional damage from his involvement with the Ft. Meade unit. Faced with having to reveal details of the psi-spy project, the CIA quickly issued a disclaimer. In September 1995, the agency's Public Affairs Bureau issued a statement admitting the involvement of the U.S. military/intelligence communities with remote viewing, but claiming that psychic espionage had proven ineffective and was being discontinued immediately. Despite this official denial, many former psi-spies believe that the program has not been shelved, but has merely gone underground and faded into a deeper shade of black. The psychic cat, however, was already out of the bag. The results-oriented techniques developed for the program offered strong evidence for the reality of psi and pointed the way toward further avenues of research.

Although the U.S. Government is officially out of the psychic business, parapsychologists continue to probe the mysteries of psi. Current thinking has attempted to link ESP functioning to the topsy-turvy world of quantum physics. Scientists have observed that matter behaves differently on the quantum level, that is, on the level of the tiniest sub-atomic particles. In the quantum world matter can exist as both a wave and a particle simultaneously, and an object can be in two places at the same time as the familiar world of classical physics collapses. Paranormal researchers theorize that precognitive, telepathic or clairvoyant perception takes place on the quantum level, where the commonsense rules of the physical world no longer apply.

While scientists continue to argue about the existence and nature of psi, the concept of ESP has taken root in an entirely different realm: in the fantastic alternate worlds of science fiction literature.

Psi as a Literary Device

ESP-related themes appear in works dating back to the beginning of literature. In the Sumerian *Epic of Gilgamesh*, which was composed in the Third Millennium B.C., the hero Gilgamesh has a precognitive dream about the coming of his fellow demigod Enkidu. Similarly, in a hymn to the deity Dumuzi from the Ancient Near East, the god dreams of the future circumstances of his own death.

Tales from Classical Greek mythology are also replete with prophecies and oracles. One of the most dramatic is the story of the prophetess Cassandra, who had been granted the gift of prophecy by her lover, the god Apollo. When Cassandra later spurned the god, Apollo could not rescind the gift, so he laid a curse upon her so that no one would believe her predictions. In the tragedy *Agamemnon* by the Greek playwright Aeschylus, the Greek king Agamemnon returns to his homeland victorious after the Trojan War, with Cassandra in tow as his spoils. While the king is unaware that his wife and her lover are planning to murder him and seize the throne, Cassandra has already "seen" the regicide with her prophetic sight, and screams in terror as she is led into the royal palace, where she knows she is soon to be dispatched by the queen.

Ancient Norse literature contains many references to precognitive and clairvoyant phenomena. As recounted in the Norse *Eddas*, the principal deity Odin trades one of his eyes for the power of the second sight. The hero of *Njal's Saga* is an Icelandic Viking who possesses precognitive vision and is haunted by the prophetic revelation of his future death inside a burning house. Similarly in the Arthurian cycle of tales from medieval Britain, the magician Merlin employs his magical powers of prognostication to advise King Arthur.

While these myths and tales reflect a belief in psychic functioning held within these societies, it is also possible to view the idea of psi as a literary device used to increase dramatic tension. Consider, for instance, the use of the technique of the *presentiment,* in which characters experience a fleeting vision of future events in the plot. A memorable example of this occurs in Dennis Hopper's 1960s hippie anthem *Easy Rider* (1969), in which Peter Fonda's character experiences brief flash-forwards of his own death during the fiery climax of the film. These glimpses of the future are not provided in the interest of showing that Fonda's character is psychic, but rather to create a mood of sadness and inevitability about the proceedings. Thus the portrayal of psi in literature and film can sometimes have more to do with the generation of dramatic *frisson* than with a portrayal of the reality of psychic phenomena.

Science Fiction Psychics

As literary science fiction emerged as a distinct genre in the early part of the 20th century, writers found inspiration for their fantastic adventures in the emerging realm of the psychic as explicated by the scientific studies of the Society for Psychical Research and the Duke Parapsychology Lab. Science fiction writers in this formative period tended to concentrate on exploring the provocative implications of telepathy rather than other paranormal abilities such as precognition, clairvoyance or psychokinesis. The notion of telepathy, with its radical possibilities, provided fertile ground for the exploration of human consciousness and speculation about the evolution of society. Sci-fi writers coined the term "psionics" to describe the industrial application of psi in futuristic societies. Alfred Bester's 1953 novel *The Demolished Man,* for instance, posits a future world in which an elite corps of mind-reading "Espers" pervades every institution of business and government. ESP abilities were usually portrayed as a positive force within society and, like atomic energy, computers or space travel, an emerging technology with transformative possibilities for humankind. Psi was the province of advanced, superior beings: aliens, mutants and supermen and women of every stripe.

Not all assessments of psi by the sci-fi crowd were positive, however. Some writers theorized that telepathic functioning might constitute a retrograde ability that may have had a negative survival value for our ancestors. Neanderthal Man in particular, whose cranial equipment was wired differently than the brains of modern humans, is sometimes depicted as an ESP-enabled loser in the evolutionary lottery. In Nobel Prize–winning author William Golding's 1963 novel *The Inheritors,* a kindly race of telepathic Neanderthals is driven to extinction by a group of non-psychic Cro-Magnons who, deprived of a genetic

ESP advantage, are forced to develop language and technology to compensate. A similar theme was explored more recently in John Darnton's 1997 novel *Neanderthal*, in which two relict groups of Neanderthals are discovered in a remote area of the former Soviet Union, one of which possesses telepathic abilities: here too the more aggressive, non-telepathic tribe dominates the gentler, telepathic group. In science fiction terms, a telepathic hive mind also carries the potential danger of the surrender of one's individuality to a collective consciousness.

Science fiction writers exploited some of the more sensational implications of psi in a manner similar to that adopted by Hollywood decades later, albeit in a much more thoughtful fashion. Their works explored the conflict between "normal" humans and ESP-equipped *Übermensch*, and the consequences of this alienation. The protagonists of these paranormal fables are typically alien or mutant psychic individuals who are brought into conflict with the majority population of normals.

Odd John

British SF writer Olaf Stapledon's 1935 novel *Odd John* is arguably the first serious treatment of the psi theme in science fiction literature. The title character, John, is a mutant superman who is gifted not only with a superior intellect but with telepathy and other powers of mind. Presented as a story related by a semi-anonymous human narrator, the narrative begins in England, where the precocious John slowly matures into a child prodigy. Upon reaching adulthood and undergoing a series of intense, self-imposed trials, Odd John sets out on a quest to find other oddities like himself. He is aided in this task by his telepathic powers, which enable him to mind meld with other "supernormals" around the world.

John is driven by a vision of creating a sanctuary where he and his ilk can form a society entirely free from the influence of *homo sapiens*. Toward this end, he invents a saucer-shaped, atomic-powered seagoing yacht equipped with a high-tech airplane and goes in search of other members of the *homo superior* species. Guided by his telepathy, Odd John manages to locate a number of his fellow mutants in various exotic places around the globe, and he transports them to a remote, uncharted island in the South Seas. The mutants then use their psychic powers to induce the entire indigenous population of the island to commit suicide in an act of inter-species ethnic cleansing. John and his followers establish the first *homo superior* colony in Earth's history and (if allowed to breed) will represent the next evolutionary step beyond ordinary humankind.

The supernormal members of the Colony establish a utopian collective and engage in various spiritual, artistic, scientific and psychic pursuits. They frolic naked in their tropical Eden, living in telepathic union, where their paranormal abilities are enhanced to include a limited form of psychokinesis and the hypno-telepathic control over human minds. Strangely, these assembled specimens of *homo superior* are described as freakish-looking, even deformed in appearance, and they mature much more slowly than normal humans do, giving them a sort of juvenile quality. Unfortunately there's trouble brewing in paradise when a British naval vessel discovers the Colony, and despite the best efforts of the mutants to psychically alter the memories and perceptions of the sailors, their existence becomes known and *homo sapiens* come to realize that they cannot tolerate a competitor. After several attacks by human shore parties, John and his followers opt to destroy the island in a nuclear conflagration rather than be killed or enslaved by an inferior species.

In *Odd John*, Stapledon links psi abilities with an assortment of grotesque, inhuman beings rather than with everyday people. Those who possess ESP powers are mutants, different, odd; in fact, they constitute an entirely different species. The "supernormals," obsessed with surviving in a world dominated by an inferior race, are amoral in their dealings with *homo sapiens*. As a child John murders a policeman, and in adulthood he kills two sailors in order to protect the secret of the Colony. Under his leadership, the mutants use their mind control powers to perpetrate mass genocide upon the hapless humans on the island, treating them like so many vermin to be exterminated on a piece of coveted real estate. Stapledon loads the novel with John's wry observations about the foibles and limitations of humankind while presenting enhanced intellect and psychic abilities as advanced evolutionary attributes of *homo superior*. Their telepathic abilities enable them to construct a truly democratic, utopian society of linked superminds.

Slan

Another early SF novel that featured a telepathic race of superbeings was A.E. van Vogt's *Slan* (1946). Set hundreds of years in the future, the novel follows the exploits of young Jommy Cross, who is a *slan*, a mutant with physical and mental abilities that are superior to those of *homo sapiens*. True slans possess two hearts and have a head endowed with a mass of tendrils that enable telepathy in place of hair. The word *slan* is based on a contraction of the name of their discoverer and patron Samuel Lann, who first recognized them as a distinct race and groomed them to dominate humankind. After years of warfare between man and slan, the slans were decisively defeated and went underground, their remnants hunted down and killed by humans. To complicate matters further, a second mutation has taken place producing a race of "tendrilless" slans who look completely human but lack the telepathic abilities of true slans. These tendrilless mutants have covertly infiltrated human society, and are also actively stalking their tendrilled brethren.

After Jommy's mother and father are brutally killed by humans, the young mutant goes on a quest to find other true slans and to develop high-tech inventions devised by his father. Going underground among the humans, Jommy works on perfecting his father's technology while being hunted by both humans and tendrilless slans. His superior offensive and defensive weapons and his telepathic powers enable him to stay one step ahead of both races. In spite of being subjected to blasts of pure mental hatred from the minds surrounding him, Jommy consistently shows compassion toward his enemies. The freewheeling pulp fiction plot careens through futuristic cities on Earth and Mars as Jommy seeks his elusive slan birthright and finally brings reconciliation to the three races.

Written during the "golden age" of magazine science fiction, the basic narrative of *Slan* seems derived from plot elements of *Odd John*. Again there is a gifted young genius/telepath who scours the globe in search of other members of his hidden mutant race. However, unlike the amoral, aristocratic John, Jommy's telepathy serves to make him more compassionate and makes it possible for him to gain perspective on non-slan minds from the inside. This empathic sensitivity extends to those who hate him and wish him harm. Once more psychic powers are portrayed as being possessed not by humans but by a race of superhuman mutants. The slans have even evolved specialized anatomy for this purpose. There is also a persistent warlike enmity between mankind and a telepathic race. The final triumph of the true slans over the tendrilless slans seems to suggest that telepathy has a higher evolutionary survival value than enhanced intelligence.

More Than Human

In Theodore Sturgeon's novel *More Than Human* (1953), an itinerant halfwit with telepathic abilities named Lone hooks up with a number of children who also possess psychic powers: Janie can telekinetically move objects with her mind; the twins, Bonnie and Beanie, are able to teleport themselves through space; Gerry is another telepath who can hypnotically influence people's minds; while Baby is superintelligent but infantile. These cast-offs from society eke out a feral existence in an isolated backwoods area, living on the fringes of our society where they develop a special kinship and begin to function as a team by using their special abilities to help the group survive.

In their totality this group of freaks begins to meld into something resembling a complete being, a "gestalt organism" whose potential as a whole exceeds that of its individual parts. This psychic unity is enabled through a psi process called "bleshing" (a combination of the words blending and meshing), which allows the members to function as a greater whole. It soon becomes obvious that *homo gestalt*, as this unitary being is referred to, is on a collision course with *homo sapiens*. Wishing only to develop their psychic abilities in solitude, the individual members of the gestalt must use their psi powers to the fullest to keep their existence a secret from humankind. While *homo gestalt* may represent the next step in human evolution, it is unrestrained by human morality. Its members commit murder and other crimes in their struggle to survive, but in the end strive to develop an ethos that will guide the actions of the new species.

Sturgeon exhibits some familiarity with concepts found in ESP research, although bodily teleportation and hyperintelligence are not truly within the realm of psi. The notion of a group of psychic geeks who represent the next step in the evolution of the human race living in isolation seems to have been lifted from *Odd John*. Although the novel contains evocative descriptions of the subjective experience of telepathy, the concept of "bleshing" is not developed fully, and seems confusing because not all of the members of the gestalt group are telepathic. Once again, individuals possessing psychic powers are depicted as grotesque misfits living on the margins of human society. In fact, it is their psi abilities that make them different and serve to marginalize them, an idea that would later be taken up in ESP-oriented movie thrillers such as *Scanners, The Fury* and *Firestarter*. No explanation is given as to why this motley crew are gifted with psychic abilities, although the author implies that psi occurs naturally during childhood and gradually fades away as we get older.

The Demolished Man

The most acclaimed SF novel on the psychic theme from science fiction's "golden age" is Alfred Bester's *The Demolished Man* (1953), which won the very first Hugo Award for a novel (sci-fi's equivalent of an Oscar). Hundreds of years in the future when telepathy has become an applied science, a minority of the human population who possess telepathic abilities are organized into an elite corps of "Espers." Derided as "peepers" by the general public, the telepaths are nonetheless tolerated and grudgingly appreciated for their unique and valuable abilities. Members of the Espers Guild pervade all professions in human society, commercial and administrative, including the police. Mind-reading Esper cops have all but eliminated the simple art of murder.

Super-rich industrialist Ben Reich thinks otherwise. He plans to murder a commercial rival to secure a business advantage and beat the rap by defeating the Esper's mental probes. In order to accomplish this, Reich makes use of an insipid pop song that centers on the meaningless phrase, "tenser, said the tensor," which will flummox all attempts to meld with his mind. Going on the lam after committing the homicide, Reich successfully uses the rhyme to deflect Esper telepathy, and uses his vast resources to stay one step ahead of the law. He is pursued by the peeper Prefect of Police Lincoln Powell, and despite the Esper's telepathic edge, Reich's wits and money frustrate the police as they relentlessly pursue him around the Solar System. Reich is eventually brought to justice only when the Espers as a group employ mass telepathy to alter his subjective reality and cause him to be "demolished" in an ESP-induced mental breakdown.

Unlike the other science fiction treatments of psi, *The Demolished Man* departs from portraying psychic individuals as mutants and freaks secretly living apart from humankind. Bester's Espers are fully integrated into the human world, which makes full commercial use of their abilities; but they remain a breed apart, living in a closed, elite society where their telepathic exchanges and communications are not accessible or comprehensible to the vast majority of the population. In addition, Espers are only allowed to marry and breed with others of their kind. The novel suggests that the development of natural psi talents into a commercial science of psionics would have positive benefits for all mankind, including the eradication of serious crimes. Although psi is shown in a positive light, the reader's sympathies are frequently with Reich as he strives to outwit the Esper's mental intrusions and avoid his seemingly inevitable demolition.

ESP Real and Unreal

These four science fiction novels represent the most seminal and highly regarded treatments of the psi theme during this early period of literary science fiction. In most of them, ESP abilities are associated with grotesque, quasi-human mutants, members of *homo superior, homo gestalt* or the snake-headed slan race. Only in *The Demolished Man* is psi talent presented as a naturally-occurring attribute in otherwise normal humans. All of the novels portray ESP as a potent force with the potential to enrich humankind and even propel *homo sapiens* to the next evolutionary level. But at the same time they all hint at a darker side to psi and posit telepaths who have the power to probe and manipulate human minds at will. The emphasis on telepathy over other forms of ESP reflects the gadget-oriented emphasis of this early phase of "hard" science fiction, in which the idea of thought exchange was viewed as a type of "mental radio" existing in the physical realm of electromagnetic phenomena. Fortunately or unfortunately, the sci-fi notion of psionics, or the large-scale practical application of psi in society at large, has never been realized.

While the scientists assembled their stat tables and the science fiction writers spun their tales of the paranormal, psi remained in the limbo of fringe scientific publications and sci-fi pulp magazines. But there was another domain where the paranormal not only existed, but even flourished: the cinema. The mysterious shadow world of visions, mind-reading and prophecy would find its most popular expression in the medium of film.

• TWO •
Early Paranormal Films

The subject of psychic phenomena did not immediately lend itself to cinematic treatment. Early films dealing with psi were typically clouded over by association with the supernatural realm. These films emerged during the period of Expressionist cinema in Germany between the two world wars, when the Teutonic psyche was haunted by the spectres and shadows of the Great War, when all manner of ghosts, devils, golems, grim reapers and vampires inhabited darkened movie theaters. Films of this period tend to emphasize a single psychic ability above any others, namely the use of hypnotic telepathy to control the minds of groups or individuals.

In Robert Weine's *The Cabinet of Dr. Caligari* (1919), for instance, the evil hypnotist Dr. Caligari (Werner Krauss) exerts his mind control powers over Cesare (Conrad Veidt), who is reduced to a somnambulistic state wherein he lies asleep in a coffin until roused to do the murderous bidding of the monstrous doctor. The hypnotized Cesare recalls the psychic "somnambules" who were so prominent in the Mesmerist movement of the late 18th Century. With its highly stylized Expressionist sets, which represented the interior worlds of madness and dreams, *Caligari* was an international sensation that launched the German Expressionist cinema movement and is today considered a classic of the silent era.

Nosferatu (1922), an unauthorized screen adaptation of Bram Stoker's novel *Dracula* lensed by the esteemed director F.W. Murnau, featured Max Schreck as the gnome-like "Count Orloc." Like the many vampires who would follow him, the Count possessed hypno-telepathic abilities that enable him to impose his will on his victims from a distance. *Nosferatu*, like *Caligari*, was critically well-received at the time, but lawsuits from the Stoker estate prevented the film from being widely shown outside Germany for many years.

The great Austrian director Fritz Lang created the first truly psychic film character in Dr. Mabuse, an arch-villain who was the brainchild of novelist Norbert Jacques. In Lang's four-hour silent epic *Dr. Mabuse, the Gambler* (1922), the evil Mabuse (Rudolf Klein-Rogge) uses his hypnotic powers to manipulate the minds of those around him in a bid to control the world's economy. In one

Mesmerist Dr. Caligari (Werner Krauss, left) displays his somnambulistic slave, Cesare (Conrad Veidt), to Lil Dagover in *The Cabinet of Dr. Caligari* (1919).

scene Mabuse creates an elaborate, cinema-like illusion of a procession of horses that is witnessed by the entire audience at a theater, while at the same time giving a policeman a telepathic command to shoot himself. Brought to justice at the end of the film, the criminal genius returned in Lang's sound-era sequel, *The Testament of Dr. Mabuse* (1933), in which Mabuse (Klein-Rogge) again uses his preternatural abilities in a bid to conquer the world. Unlike *Caligari* and *Nosferatu*, which were both set in earlier historical periods, the two Mabuse films take place in contemporaneous Germany and eschew the trappings of the supernatural in favor of real-world science fiction.

Due to a materialistic mindset that was skeptical of all "supernatural" subjects, American film audiences were not partial to psychic themes during Hollywood's silent era, and few films dealing with this topic were produced at this time. This would change in the early-talkie period, when the supernatural horror film came to America with the twin Universal Studios hits *Dracula* and *Frankenstein* in 1931. In particular, Bela Lugosi in *Dracula* ably exhibited the vampire's powers of hypnotic telepathy that enabled him to control his victims from a distance.

Early Psi Films

In the wake of the Universal monster hits, other studios scrambled to cash in on the horror craze. One early effort was Warner Brothers' *Svengali* (1931), featuring the great John Barrymore in the title role. Based on George du Maurier's 1894 novel *Trilby*, the film tells the story of the hypnotist and musical impressario Svengali, who possesses the ability to mesmerize and control women. In an early scene one of Svengali's students and romantic conquests, the talentless Madame Honori (Carmel Myers), announces that she has left her husband for him and is now penniless, whereupon Svengali uses his hypnotic powers to compel her to commit suicide. Soon afterward he meets the beautiful young model Trilby (Marian Marsh) and becomes instantly infatuated with her. Trilby, however, is in love with a young artist named Billee (Bramwell Fletcher). One day while Svengali is treating Trilby for a headache, he uses his powers to place her in a hypnotic trance. "You shall see nothing ... hear nothing ... dream nothing ... but Svengali," he drones, as his eyes glow with an unholy light. Once she is under his control, he erases her memory of Billee, fakes her suicide and transports her away from Paris under cover of night. Svengali then transforms her into an operatic diva of immense talent, but in spite of their artistic relationship his love for her remains unrequited.

The "Great Profile" John Barrymore as the telepathic hypnotist in *Svengali* (1931).

The couple embark on a tour of Europe, with the newly-minted singing sensation Trilby now billed as "Madame Svengali." After entertaining the crowned heads of Europe on an extended tour, Svengali and Trilby return to Paris for a much-heralded concert; but when Trilby recognizes Billee in the crowd, her love for him makes her personality re-assert itself. As Svengali's mental control of the diva begins to wane, Trilby starts to lose her singing talent and must ultimately choose between her love and her art.

The Great Profile plays the role of the malevolent maestro with considerable verve, sporting a Rasputin-like appearance complete with a baroque beard, long hair and flowing operatic robes. In one semi-comic scene, he attempts to force Trilby into his bed with hypnotism, but when she responds to him, he abruptly dismisses her, saying, "But it is only Svengali, talking to himself again." Another sequence conveys Svengali's hypno-telepathic powers in a distinctly cinematic fashion. It begins with a closeup of Barrymore's magnetic eyes as the camera slowly pulls backward, through a window and out into the street, then travels over the rooftops of Paris, finally penetrating Trilby's bedroom. This type of moving camera technique was rare in early sound-era films that tended to employ static camera setups. Director Archie Mayo deserves kudos for working with the notoriously difficult Barrymore while serving up gobs of mysterioso visual atmosphere and deftly mixing comedy, horror and romance into a highly diverting whole.

Svengali was the first film of the sound era to portray an individual with psychic powers. Although Barrymore's histrionic portrayal paints psi in an occult light, there is no clearly supernatural element to the plot. The transformative potential of psi is suggested in Trilby's psychically-induced metamorphosis from shallow model to musical genius under her master's paranormal tutelage. Oddly, *Svengali*'s hypno-telepathic domination of women would find a parallel in eerily similar psi experiments conducted in the Soviet Union in the 1960s. According to the 1970 book *Psychic Discoveries Behind the Iron Curtain*, male telepathic senders would attempt to render young female students unconscious and hypnotize them, sometimes over long distances.

Actor Claude Rains, who had his first starring role in James Whale's riotous screen version of H.G. Wells' *The Invisible Man* (1934), travelled back across the pond to England to star in Maurice Elvey's paranormal thriller *The Clairvoyant* (1935). Rains plays Maximus, a small-time music hall mentalist who has a modestly successful act with his wife and assistant, Rene (Fay Wray). The couple use an elaborate system of code words to simulate clairvoyance until Maximus begins to experience real psychic visions. Unfortunately his gift is only enabled when he is in the presence of newspaper heiress Christine Shaw (Jane Baxter), a situation that leads to complications in his marriage.

His first major premonition comes when he is travelling on a train with Rene, Christine and her newspaper mogul father Lord Southwood (Athole Stewart). After having a vision that the train will crash, Maximus pulls the emergency cord and stops the train, lessening the impact of the inevitable collision and saving their lives. When the event is widely reported in Lord Southwood's newspapers, the clairvoyant becomes a media celebrity, signs a lucrative contact with the publishing magnate and lands a theatrical booking at the Palladium. Maximus goes on to predict a 100 to 1 winning horse in the Derby, but his next premonition gets him in big trouble. He predicts a massive cave-in in the nearby Humber Shaft, an enormous mine being excavated by hundreds of workers, and even goes to the mine in person to beg the miners to discontinue their work. The miners reject his pleas, and when the cave-in occurs as predicted, Maximus is ordered to stand trial for having caused the disaster in the

Svengali (John Barrymore) puts the hypnotic eye on his apprentice, Trilby (Marian Marsh), in *Svengali* (1931).

manner of a self-fulfilling prophecy. The court marshals strong evidence against him, and Maximus is only exonerated when he correctly predicts that a large number of the men are alive and have escaped through a side tunnel. In the happy ending, the rescued miners come marching into the courthouse and Maximus is persuaded to give up his gift along with his relationship with Christine.

Ad copy for the film proclaimed, "The Invisible Man makes the future visible," in this modest Gaumont Studios production. In his first visible starring role, Rains delivers a strong performance as the tortured psychic Maximus and is ably assisted by Fay Wray (who had only recently escaped from the grasp of *King Kong*) and a fine British cast. Ably directed by Maurice Elvey, the film recycles footage from Elvey's sci-fi production *The Transatlantic Tunnel* (1935) for the Humber Shaft cave-in sequences. The screenplay by Charles Bennett, who co-wrote the classic Hitchcock thriller *The 39 Steps* (1935), steers clear of the supernatural while exploring the mystery of psychic premonition, although the script provides no clues as to why Christine's presence is necessary for Maximus's psi powers to function. Maximus's paranormal gift brings him equal measures of fame and grief, and in the end is rejected in favor of normalcy. The film also plays on the tendency of everyday people to blame the psychic messenger when bad things happen according to their predictions, and to brand their mysterious ESP abilities as demonic and therefore subject to righteous punishment. Historically, *The Clairvoyant* (also known under the alternate title *The Evil Mind*) represents the first notable feature film on the subject of psychic phenomena, and has affinities with another early essay on precognition, John Farrow's *film noir The Night Has a Thousand Eyes* (1948).

Like *Svengali*, Paramount's *Peter Ibbetson* (1935) was based on a turn-of-the-century novel by George du Maurier, and had previously been lensed during the silent period as *Forever* (1921). As the story opens, two children, Peter and Mary, are childhood sweethearts who develop the ability to "dream true"—to visit each other in their dreams. Separated in childhood, they are re-united as adults when Peter (Gary Cooper), now an architect, is hired to do a restoration job for the Duke of Towers (John Halliday). Mary (Ann Harding), who is now the Dutchess of Towers, is still carrying the flame for Peter. Learning of his wife's attraction, the jealous Duke pulls a gun on Ibbetson, who kills the nobleman in self-defense. Put on trial for murder, Peter is convicted of murdering the Duke and sentenced to life in prison. For the rest of their lives, Peter and Mary can only meet inside the mutual dream world they share.

Director Henry Hathaway, best known for his action-oriented productions, is more restrained in his treatment of this sentimental, romantic material, but *Peter Ibbetson*'s uneasy blend of fantasy and costume romance did lukewarm business at the box office. Even though the emphasis is on the romantic aspect of the story, what is really being described here is the psychic phenomenon known as *dream telepathy*, in which thoughts or experiences can be exchanged between two minds in a dreaming state. This phenomenon has been documented as occurring between psychotherapists and their patients in Elizabeth Lloyd Mayer's book *Extraordinary Knowing* (2007) and has been extensively researched by ex-military remote viewer Dale Graff in *Tracks in the Psychic Wilderness* (1998).

Psychics, Mediums and Cynics in Film Noir

The term *film noir* was coined in France but refers to a body of American crime thrillers produced roughly between 1942 and 1953 that were characterized by a world-weary fatalism, a profound social cynicism and a stylish eroticism. *Film noir* heroes, typically hard-boiled private eyes like Sam Spade and Philip Marlowe, exist in a shadow world where they confront sadistic hoods, deadly *femmes fatales*, big-time gangsters, psychotic criminals and other perverse characters caught in a web of fear, violence and intrigue. Some of the inhabitants of this dark and sinister milieu are bogus mediums and psychics who use their illusory paranormal powers to further their criminal schemes.

By the early 1940s, the *noir* metropolis of Los Angeles in particular had become home to a sizable assortment of kooks, quacks and weirdos who made their way into mystery fiction and Hollywood *films noir*.

In Raymond Chandler's mystery novel *Farewell, My Lovely* (1940), Chandler's private detective Philip Marlowe is menaced by a sinister phony psychic named Jules Amthor. The author acidly describes the "Psychic Consultant" thus: "Give him enough time and pay him enough money and he'll cure anything from a jaded husband to a grasshopper plague. He would be an expert in frustrated love affairs, women who slept alone and didn't like it, wandering boys and girls who didn't write home, sell the property now or hold it for another year, will this part hurt me with my public or make me seem more versatile?" Chandler further notes that most of Amthor's clientele consists of women, "fat women that panted and thin women that burned, old women that dreamed and young women that thought they might have Electra complexes, women of all sizes, shapes and ages, but with one thing in common — money."[1] In Edward Dmytryk's 1944 screen adaptation entitled *Murder, My Sweet*, Marlowe (Dick Powell) squares off against Amthor (Otto Kruger), who is using information gleaned from his rich lady clients to perpetrate a series of jewel heists. In one scene, Marlowe gets roughed up by the jewel thieves inside the psychic's elegant apartment. Later Amthor turns up dead when he is double-crossed by one of his fellow criminals. Slick, dapper and sinister, Amthor personifies the archetype of the phony psychic within the cynical, hard-boiled universe of *film noir*.

One of the darkest and most acclaimed of the classic *films noir* also revolves around the character of a phony psychic. Edmund Goulding's *Nightmare Alley* (1947) cast handsome leading man Tyrone Power against type as Stanton Carlisle, a small-time carnival hustler who obtains the secret of a fake mentalist act from Zeena (Joan Blondell), one of the other carnies. The mind-reading trick involves the use of an elaborate system of code words to emulate clairvoyance. He takes the act on the road with his wife Molly (Colleen Gray), billing himself as "The Great Stanton," and as their telepathy act becomes a hit they are booked into larger and larger venues. They soon get a high-class gig at an upscale nightclub in Chicago, where the Great Stanton wows the urban sophisticates with his carny fakery masquerading as ESP.

Stanton has ambitions that go beyond show business, however. He takes up with unscrupulous psychologist Dr. Lilith Ritter (Helen Walker), with whom he hatches a scheme to defraud wealthy Chicagoans. Using information taken from the confidential files of Dr. Ritter's patients, he makes it appear that he has obtained intimate knowledge of their personal lives via clairvoyance or telepathy. With his victims in awe of his apparently paranormal powers, Stanton bilks them out of a fortune while assuming a false piety that makes them believe he is a godly man. When he enlists Molly to impersonate the ghost of an industrialist's dead sweetheart, she rebels and deliberately spoils the illusion.

Two • Early Paranormal Films   33

Bogus psychic "The Great Stanton" (Tyrone Power, center) wows Chicago society with his phony ESP in *Nightmare Alley* (1947).

Discredited by this debacle and cheated out of his money by the wily Lilith, Stanton separates from his wife and descends into the carny life once more. He hits rock bottom when he becomes a carnival "geek," a grisly attraction who bites the heads off live chickens, before he is finally redeemed by his wife's love.

This offbeat melodrama is critically viewed today as one of the most unusual works in all of *film noir*. *Nightmare Alley*'s blend of carny exploitation, white-collar criminality, obsession, degradation and psychic chicanery is perfectly realized by director Goulding and cinematographer Lee Garmes. Tyrone Power, in the most far-out role of his career, carries the film as the sociopathic Stanton and delivers a powerful portrayal of one man's descent into a private hell. The screenplay, adapted by Jules Furthman from a novel by William Lindsay Gresham, exposes the seamy world of psychic charlatanism with unblinking candor and explores the gullibilities that enable bogus mentalists to manipulate their victims.

This cynical view of psi, emerging through the jaded prism of *film noir*, offers a compelling presentation of the skeptical position regarding ESP. The debunkers believe that all psychic functioning is a fraud perpetrated on gullible believers by clever fakers, and *Nightmare Alley* illustrates people's willingness to believe in fortune telling. In one carny spiel, repeated twice in the film, the seer supposedly has a vision of a little boy running through a field with a dog at his side. Most shills fall for this psychic con job, but the trick is that every boy has a dog and the situation is common in almost every lad's childhood. Stanton's bogus clairvoyance convinces even wealthy, educated people by manipulating their will to believe in the preternatural. Ironically, Zeena is given to fortune-telling with a deck of arcane Tarot cards, and correctly predicts both her husband's death and Stanton's eventual downfall.

Another *noir* that explored the world of phony occultism was *The Amazing Mr. X* (1948). Rich widow Christine Faber (Lynn Bari), who lives in a beautiful mansion overlooking the Pacific, is haunted by ghostly visions and by the voice of her recently deceased husband calling to her from the sea. With her sanity on the line, she meets a mysterious man named Alexis (Turhan Bey) who claims to have psychic powers and offers to put her in touch with her dead spouse. Alexis seems to know intimate details about Christine's personal life, which bolsters her belief in his ESP abilities. Her new fiancé, Martin (Richard Carlson), and her sister (Cathy O'Donnell) are appalled as she falls under the sway of the suave psychic.

Christine visits Alexis in his spooky digs, which are adorned with weird statuary, a crystal ball and a trained raven. The audience is shown the elaborate mechanical devices that Alexis uses to simulate his paranormal powers, including one-way mirrors, secret chambers, sliding doors and a turban containing a radio headset. It soon becomes evident that the psychic is involved in a plot to defraud Christine's estate, and that reports of her husband's death have been greatly exaggerated.

Directed by Bernard Vorhaus from a screenplay by Crane Wilbur, *The Amazing Mr. X* is enlivened by the camera work of ace *noir* cinematographer John Alton, who stylishly evokes a mysterioso paranormal world of light and shadow. Like *Murder, My Sweet* and *Nightmare Alley*, the film exposes the machinations of bogus "psychic consultants" who cynically manipulate wealthy women with grand larceny in mind. Stolen photographs are used to simulate the faces of deceased loved ones in the séance room, while sophisticated devices like a concealed TV camera and a radio-equipped turban enable the illusion of the psychic's omniscience. Alexis describes the appeal of his vocation as "feeding people's desire to escape the present," and *The Amazing Mr. X* goes out of its way to examine the elaborate mechanisms of fakery, both psychological and technological, that are used to manipulate gullible believers.

While most *films noir* of the period portrayed psychics as criminal frauds, there was one case of genuine ESP among them. John Farrow's *The Night Has a Thousand Eyes* (1948), adapted from a haunting novel by Cornell Woolrich, stars *noir* icon Edward G. Robinson as John Triton, a carnival mentalist who discovers he has genuine precognitive and clairvoyant powers. While performing his act one night, he tells a woman that her house is on fire and her son is in danger, which proves to be the case. In the weeks that follow Triton makes several more predictions that come true, but they all involve death and destruction. The reluctant prophet becomes consumed with guilt by the implications of his psychic visions, and laments, "I had a crazy feeling I was making the things come true." One tragic prediction involves his former sweetheart, Jenny (Virginia Bruce), who he has foretold will die in childbirth, and when this comes to pass Triton is crushed and goes into seclusion.

Years later, Triton moves to Los Angeles to be near Jenny's daughter Jean (Gail Russell), whose father is the rich industrialist Whitney Courtland (Jerome Cowan). Courtland becomes apprised of Triton's psychic prowess, and uses the seer to make money at the racetrack and on the stock market; however the prophet's fateful visions return as he successfully predicts Courtland's death in a plane crash. Triton then has an even more disturbing vision, that of Jean lying dead at the feet of a lion, but at this point Jean's fiancé Elliott (John Lund) suspects foul play and calls the police. Triton is arrested and the psychic goings-on are investigated by Lt. Shawn (William Demarest), but the seer convinces the detective of his powers by correctly predicting the suicide of a prisoner. Released from custody, Triton has a premonition of his own death, and races to save Jean by taking a bullet meant for her fired by one of her father's criminal associates. Trading fates with Jean, Triton expires at the feet of a stone lion, under the thousand eyes of the fateful stars.

Departing from the usual *noir* formula of depicting psychics as slick, manipulative grifters pretending to have psi abilities, *The Night Has a Thousand Eyes* ponders the melancholy destiny of an individual who possesses true paranormal gifts. Farrow's film is infused with a mood of brooding gloom and mystery that are associated with Triton's eerie abilities, as the psychic believes that his visions are somehow linked to his very existence. While Triton is not himself a criminal, his real ESP powers are even darker, and are associated with supernatural dread, night and fate. The film has affinities with *The Clairvoyant* (1935) and *The Medusa Touch* (1978) in its depiction of a psychic prophet tormented by the perverse gift of foreknowledge of disastrous events, and is unusual in its presentation of the uncanny within the hard-boiled realism of the *film noir* universe.

Crime, Skepticism and ESP

All of these early films on the subject of ESP involve a connection between psi and crime in some fashion. Even when psychics are blameless of any criminality, as in *The Clairvoyant, Peter Ibbetson* and *The Night Has a Thousand Eyes*, they are indicted by society at large because of the strangeness and "otherness" of their paranormal powers, and by the odd belief that they are somehow responsible for the dire events that follow in the wake of their visions. An association between psychics and criminality was established during the period of classic *film noir* in *Farewell, My Lovely*, *Nightmare Alley* and *The Amazing Mr. X*, and this connection would re-establish itself in later psi-oriented crime thrillers such as *Séance on a Wet Afternoon* (1964), *Man on a Swing* (1974) and *Family Plot* (1976).

The gritty realism of *noir* provided a context for the skeptical view of the paranormal. American "I'm-from-Missouri" hard-headedness had no room for spiritualists, mentalists or mediums. The psychic racket was portrayed as preying upon human gullibility and religiosity, with most of the victims of Jules Amthor, The Amazing Mr. X, and Stanton Carlisle being of the supposedly more irrational female gender. There are also associations between ESP and religious transgression, especially in *Nightmare Alley*, where a psychic swindler invokes God in order to further his criminal schemes, and in *The Night Has a Thousand Eyes*, in which the seer is tormented, Job-like, for the sin of possessing the second sight. Both ultra-rational skepticism and religious bias would continue to limit the appeal of psi-themed movie fare in years to come.

• THREE •

ESP in Drama, Comedy and Children's Films

While the majority of movies on paranormal themes are consigned to the science fiction, fantasy and horror genres, there are a number of films that are primarily dramatic in focus. These films concentrate on emotional interactions between the characters, and while ESP is an important element in the narrative, it is not the soul of the plot. This reflects the experience of the paranormal in people's everyday lives, when it may emerge spontaneously during a life crisis situation. There are many anecdotal accounts of spontaneous ESP manifesting itself in ordinary, non-psychic individuals on a single-event basis: the mother who knows that her son has been killed on the battlefield before the letter arrives from the war department; the time you thought about someone you hadn't heard from in a while just before the phone rang with a call from that person; the identical twins who can read each other's minds at a great distance. These films explore the dramatic implications of life inside a psychic universe without reverting to melodrama.

An early example is *The Rocking Horse Winner* (1949), a British film directed by Anthony Pelissier and adapted from a short story of the same name by D.H. Lawrence. The narrative centers around the Grahame family, upper-class Londoners who have fallen on hard financial times. Their economic woes are solely the result of the family's profligate lifestyle. Father Richard Grahame (Hugh Sinclair) persistently loses money at the track, while mother Heather (Valerie Hobson) continues to squander the family's remaining cash on expensive clothes, jewelry and other luxuries they can't afford. Things get paranormal when their adolescent son, Paul (John Howard Davies), discovers he can predict winners at the racetrack while riding on his wooden rocking horse. Colluding with servant Bassett (John Mills) and his uncle Oscar (Ronald Squire), Paul begins to turn his hunches into hard cash at the track, secretly bringing in money to support his mother and father in the style to which they have become accustomed. But Paul's precognitive powers have their price, and picking the winners to fund his parent's compulsive materialism begins to diminish the boy's life force, with ultimately tragic consequences.

Director Pelissier imbues Lawrence's parable of British mores and materialism with an otherworldly gloss, as homey scenes of upper-class English domestic life are contrasted with the sequences in which Paul rides his haunted hobby-horse, where skewed camera angles and expressionistic lighting setups are employed to give the proceedings an atmosphere of the occult. POV shots of Paul's subjective vision as he rocks himself into a precognitive altered state are especially jarring. Although the child's prophetic powers are never explained, the dark-eyed rocking horse becomes a talisman of dread and symbolic of the dangerous ESP abilities that ultimately consume Paul. Like many later films, *The Rocking Horse Winner* correlates paranormal functioning with childhood or adolescence. A fine cast, solid direction and classy source material distinguish this production. Lawrence's story was remade as a short film by Michael Almereyda in 1997 with the locale moved to Southern California.

Another British paranormal drama is Jerzy Skolimowski's offbeat feature *The Shout* (1979). Alan Bates stars as the enigmatic Charles Crossley, a man who believes he possesses preternatural shamanic powers. As the film opens, Crossley is a patient in a mental hospital who relates the actions leading to his commitment in a flashback — or is it a hallucination? The plot unfolds against the bleak backdrop of a small seaside village in North Devon, England, where Anthony (John Hurt) lives an idyllic existence with his wife Rachel (Susannah York). Anthony is an electronic musician who uses sophisticated equipment to record exotic sounds such as the amplified buzzing of a fly or the magnified sound of stroking a dog's fur.

Enter the mysterious Crossley, who forces his way into the lives of the couple using his charismatic powers and takes up residence in their cottage. Crossley explains to Anthony that he has lived among the aborigines of the Australian Outback for eighteen years in complete isolation from white society. During this time he claims to have learned a technique called the "terror shout," a cry that will kill all who hear it, from an aboriginal sorcerer. When Anthony expresses skepticism, Crossley arranges a demonstration of his power. He advises Anthony to stop his ears with wax in order to blunt the full power of the terror shout as the two of them hike to a remote spot out on the dunes. Believing them to be alone, Crossley unleashes the shout, which shocks Anthony into unconsciousness while inadvertently killing a nearby shepherd and his sheep.

Now convinced of Crossley's paranormal powers, Anthony is fearful of asserting himself against the interloper, even when Crossley seduces Rachel. For his part Anthony has been seduced by the shout, and wishes to capture the sound the way he samples the noises of nature with his electronic gear. Pushed to the breaking point, Anthony fights back by finding a way to use Crossley's aboriginal powers against him, which presumably leads to his commitment to the mental institution. The story then builds to an enigmatic climax as the nuthouse's lunatics go crazy during a sudden thunderstorm and the power of Crossley's shout is unleashed once more.

This lurid material could have been the basis for a melodrama or horror movie, but Skolimowski's glacial pacing, naturalistic setting and emphasis on the interactions of a small number of characters keep *The Shout* entirely within the realm of the dramatic film. Derived from a story by mytho-poetic writer Robert Graves, the screenplay by Skolimowski and Michael Austin is crafted into the story of a love triangle between a group of isolated people set against a compelling backdrop of madness and shamanic mystery. In open-ended fashion, the issue of whether Crossley is insane or possesses psychic powers is never fully settled. The bleak North Devon landscape of tufted sand dunes and ragged seashore is employed to build the film's mood of sterility and loneliness. Acclaimed British thesps Bates, Hurt and York turn in sincere, intense performances in this character study.

Dressed in a thick, black overcoat and sporting a mop of shoulder-length black hair for most of the film, Bates's Crossley presents a dour, threatening figure who stands outside normal societal conventions and destroys the lives of an otherwise happily married couple. His psi powers make him an alien figure devoid of any human morality who is walking along a knife-edge of madness. In addition to the "terror shout" (which sounds like the combination of a human cry and a jet plane taking off), it is implied that Crossley also possesses telepathic and psychokinetic powers, although this is downplayed. An unusual art-house take on the paranormal, *The Shout* is a unique take on the dangerous potential of psi in the hands of an amoral and/or mentally disturbed individual. The mysteries of Australian aboriginal shamanism had previously been explored in Peter Weir's apocalyptic horror melodrama *The Last Wave* (1977).

Back in the States psychic drama was also taking hold with movie audiences. In *Resurrection* (1980), ordinary housewife Edna McCauley (Ellen Burstyn) undergoes a mystical near-death experience when she is involved in a car accident that kills her husband. Crippled from the waist down after the accident, she returns to her parents' home in rural Kansas to recuperate. Although her doctors have told her she will never walk again, Edna manages to cure herself through a newfound ability of psychic healing. When she spontaneously stops the bleeding of a hemophiliac girl at a family picnic, matriarch Grandma Pearl (Eva LaGallienne) tells Edna that she now possesses preternatural healing powers. Her abilities are put to the test when she cures local ne'er-do-well Cal Carpenter (Sam Shepard) of serious injuries sustained in a knife fight. After his healing, the child-like Cal strikes up a romantic relationship with Edna and the two move in together and seem to be deeply in love.

Edna becomes a local phenomenon, conducting healing sessions in revival-type tent meetings where she affects seemingly miraculous cures. Her powers

Ellen Burstyn as psychic healer Edna McCauley in *Resurrection* (1980).

eventually come to the attention of psychic researchers, who arrange to study her ESP in the lab. Edna performs an act of healing in the parapsychology laboratory under controlled conditions. Trouble starts brewing back home, however, when some of the Kansas farmers begin to voice religious objections to Edna's healings. Even Cal, who has had a strict Christian upbringing, becomes alienated and begins to think that her abilities come from the Devil. When the non-religious Edna acknowledges that she believes her gift does not come from God but from profound love and understanding instead, the stage is set for a violent confrontation. In the end Edna is forced to continue her healing work in secret, apart from our scientific and religious establishments.

One of a very few films to portray the paranormal in a positive light, *Resurrection* is a serious essay on the enigma of ESP that avoids melodramatic treatment. The film contains perhaps the first screen depiction of a near-death experience (or NDE), a phenomenon that can enable psi functioning and affect other profound lifestyle changes. There are affinities with David Cronenberg's *The Dead Zone* (1983), in which a man emerges from a coma with psi powers. The notion of psychic healing goes back to antiquity, and today is thought to be a variety of psychokinesis in which the healer's mind works on a biological organism rather than an inanimate object. *Resurrection* also reflects the tradition of shamans as "wounded healers" who emerge from a serious illness with

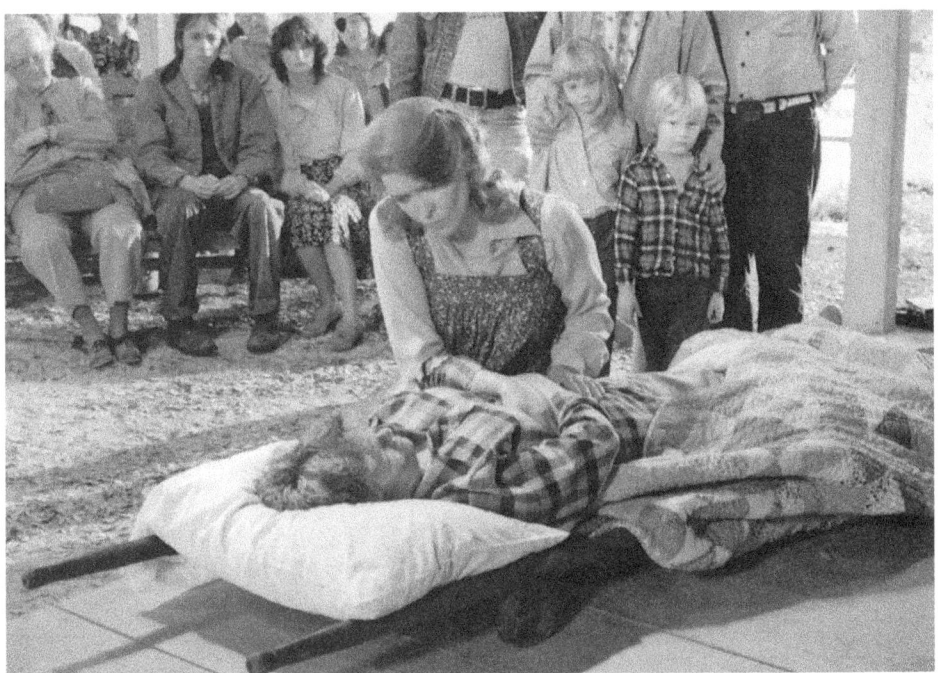

Edna (Ellen Burstyn) demonstrates her paranormal healing powers in *Resurrection* (1980).

curative powers, and the film-makers reportedly employed Rosa Bruyere, a healer affiliated with California's Healing Light Center, as a technical consultant on the film.

While the film emphasizes the positive therapeutic potential of psi, it also takes aim at the narrow-minded religious bigotry against the paranormal that prevails in many parts of Middle America, as Cal takes the Biblical dictum "Thou shalt not suffer a witch to live" literally. In their book *The Mind Race*, parapsychologists Russell Targ and Keith Harary observe, "The film also offers an accurate though depressing view of what can result from publicly admitting to having psychic abilities.... The heroine is a normal, happily married housewife who appears to have no unusual psychic talents. She is then transformed into a powerful psychic healer, which leads eventually to her becoming a peculiar old woman who lives alone in an isolated gas station in the Southwest American desert."[1] Despite its New-Agey positivism, *Resurrection* can be read as a cautionary tale about the dangers of being psychic in a close-minded society.

Whatever its ambiguities, *Resurrection* is a serious-minded, non-exploitive treatment of a potentially melodramatic theme. Director Daniel Petrie lends a good deal of dignity to the material with an assist from Lewis John Carlino's

Top: Mary Steenburgen, left, and Lance Henriksen, right, escort psychic teen Sean Patrick Flanery to a foster home in *Powder* (1995). *Bottom:* Powder (Sean Patrick Flanery, left) gets words of encouragement from sympathetic teacher Donald Ripley (Jeff Goldblum) in *Powder* (1995).

script, but the film is sometimes a little sappy and tends to take itself a bit too seriously. The film garnered a Best Actress nomination for Ellen Burstyn and a Best Supporting Actress nom for Eva LaGallienne, while Ms. Burstyn went on to teach psychic subjects at the New Age Omega Institute in Rhinebeck, New York, and has continued to receive critical acclaim for her acting.

Powder (1995) takes place in a tiny rural community in Texas, where a pregnant woman in the throes of labor has been hit by a bolt of lightning and rushed to the emergency room. The mother dies giving birth to a peculiar albino baby that the father rejects as a freak. Cutting forward nearly two decades, Sheriff Bob Barnum (Lance Henriksen) and social worker Jesse Caldwell (Mary Steenburgen) are called to a remote farmhouse where an old man has died of natural causes. The man's grandson, reportedly a reclusive freak who has spent his life in isolation on the farm, is hiding in the cellar. Jeremy Reed (Sean Patrick Flanery) is the abandoned albino baby grown into young adulthood as a pale-skinned, bald-headed individual who resembles a space alien or mutant human. His nickname is "Powder" because of the whitish appearance of his skin.

Because he is still a minor, Jeremy becomes a ward of the state and is remanded to a reformatory, where he is persecuted unmercifully by the other boys because of his unusual appearance. It soon becomes apparent, however, that Powder is not an ordinary individual. His I.Q. is off the charts, he can read minds and can perform telekinetic tricks involving metal and electricity. Jesse and science teacher Donald Ripley (Jeff Goldblum) strive to bring out Jeremy's potential, but the prejudicial attitudes of the small-minded townsfolk threaten to alienate the troubled teen permanently. Things come to a head when the boys catch Jeremy staring longingly at one of the other lads while he is undressing. Bullied, stripped and humiliated by the gang, Powder utilizes his electrical psychokinesis in self-defense, creating a pulse of force that nearly kills the bullies' ringleader (Brandon Smith) before Powder uses the same electrical energy to bring him back to life. As Sheriff Barnum arrives to take Jeremy to jail after the incident, a sudden thunderstorm blows in, leading Jeremy to escape into a field where he becomes one with the lightning that helped to create him.

Powder has much in common with *Resurrection* in its portrayal of a psychic individual with positive potential for society who is persecuted by a close-minded rural community because he is "different" and possesses inexplicable abilities. Like the earlier film, it is also a plea for tolerance, which in this case is equated with acceptance of gays in our society. The film also references Brian de Palma's horror thriller *Carrie* (1976) in its mixture of teenage angst and psychokinesis. While making its case for tolerance, however, *Powder* seems to exploit the grotesque appearance of its main character for dramatic purposes, with the electrical theme suggesting the life-bringing lightning from *Frankenstein* (1931) and its many sequels. Jeremy's unusual origin and departure, heralded by thunderbolts, are kept deliberately ambiguous and suggest that he may actually be an extraterrestrial or supernatural being. Fortunately, the film seldom strays into melodrama and shows Jeremy's psi powers in a positive and even life-saving light. As in *Resurrection*, the psychic protagonist is the victim of bigoted hicks who have no use for his gift.

A fine cast of Hollywood name actors turn in warm and sincere performances, but relative unknown Sean Patrick Flanery's sensitive portrayal of the ethereal Powder dominates the film. Writer/director Victor Salva's presentation is slow-moving at times, but *Powder*'s message of tolerance was somewhat blunted by the revelation that Salva had served 15 months in prison for molesting a 12-year-old boy during production of the TV movie *Clownhouse* in 1988. Conservative groups tried to have the film banned, but *Powder* did modestly well during its release and Salva went on to helm the horror hit *Jeepers Creepers* (2001).

The John Travolta vehicle *Phenomenon* (1996) offered yet another take on the "small town psychic" theme. Travolta plays everyday joe George Malley, a humble mechanic plying his trade in a small Northern California town and a member in good standing of the rural community. Returning home late from his thirty-seventh birthday party at a local bar, George observes an anomalous light in the sky overhead that zaps him with a beam of energy. In the aftermath of his close encounter, he finds that his I.Q. has been boosted to genius level and that he can move small objects using telekinesis. "I ask it to move," he explains, elucidating his PK technique to startled witnesses. He also finds he can predict earthquakes by sensing ultra low-frequency vibrations that precede the tremor.

When George uses his newfound abilities to rescue a little boy lost in an orchard, his neighbors begin to develop a superstitious dread of his powers. He gets into more trouble when he unscrambles encrypted signals from a nearby military base picked up by his buddy, ham radio enthusiast Nate Polk (Forest Whitaker), and broadcasts a reply back to the base. When George and Nate are arrested and detained by the FBI, they are accused of violations of national security. Government scientists subject George to a battery of tests, but can find no evidence of espionage and are forced to release him. Returning home, he applies his advanced intellect to solving practical problems in the small community by inventing alternative fuels, perfecting solar power generators and devising innovative new fertilizers. He also attempts to institute a time-sharing barter system and other utopian social alternatives while becoming romantically involved with single mom Lace (Kyra Sedgwick).

Despite his achievements, George's apparently alien-induced powers continue to rankle the locals. Matters come to a head at the local bar when a number of the townsfolk confront him, leading George to shatter the bar's mirror in a fit of psychokinetic pique. Attempting to put things right, George agrees to a demonstration of his mental prowess at the town's annual "Library Day," but when he exhibits his telekinesis the locals are spooked, and he is mobbed

Three • *ESP in Drama, Comedy and Children's Films* 45

George Malley (John Travolta) demonstrates his ESP to Doc Brunner (Robert Duvall) in *Phenomenon* (1996).

by people demanding that he use his abilities to solve their life problems. During the stressful event, George collapses and observes the UFO returning in the sky to zap him a second time. Awakening in a hospital bed, he is confronted by the town's physician, Dr. Brunner (Robert Duvall), who tells him that his augmented intellect and psi powers are due to a malignant brain tumor that is killing him. George chooses to spend his last moments with Lace, and a year after his death the town holds a posthumous birthday party for him on the anniversary of his close encounter.

Like *Resurrection* and *Powder*, *Phenomenon* deals with a psychic individual who is confronted with the prejudices of a group of small-minded, small-town bigots. Despite George's efforts to use his ESP to save lives and solve the town's problems, the townsfolk's superstitious dread of the paranormal serves to alienate him from them. He becomes an outcast, an object of dread and scorn as traditional small-town intimacy collapses in the face of the uncanny, and is only restored to social legitimacy by his death. George acquires his psychic abilities from an encounter with a UFO, and while this may seem far-fetched, a number of alien abductees have reported similar psi-enhancing effects in connection with their experiences. The controversial Israeli psychic Uri Geller also claims that his ESP and PK come from an extraterrestrial source. *Phenomenon*'s warm-hearted drama plays well against the unusual subject matter under Jon Turtletaub's deft direction and Gerald DiPego's intriguing screenplay, while

King-sized psychic John Coffey (Michael Clark Duncan) is escorted to death row by Tom Hanks, left, and David Morse, right, in *The Green Mile*, (1999).

the well-seasoned cast of Travolta, Whitaker, Duvall and Sedgewick turn in strong, thoughtful performances.

Horror novelist Stephen King and writer/director Frank Darabont, who had previously teamed for the prison drama *The Shawshank Redemption* (1994), collaborated once more on another jailhouse epic, *The Green Mile* (1999). Set in Cold Mountain Penitentiary, Louisiana, during the Depression year of 1935, the film stars Tom Hanks as Paul Edgecomb, head of the prison's death row unit, dubbed the "Green Mile." One of the condemned is John Coffey (Michael Clarke Duncan), a "monstrous big" African-American man who has been convicted of raping and murdering two young girls. Contrary to his fearsome reputation, the simple-minded Coffey is a good-natured, gentle giant, and Edgecomb, who knows violent men, begins to have second thoughts about Coffey's guilt. It soon becomes apparent that the prisoner also possesses extraordinary psychic powers when he spontaneously cures Edgecomb of a painful urinary infection. Coffey's method of psychic healing involves making physical contact with the sick person and literally taking the illness into his own body, after which it is expelled from his mouth like a swarm of black insects. His power can make light bulbs explode and cause earthquake-like tremors and strange light phenomena. After the healings Coffey becomes sick for a time and must recuperate.

When Edgecomb and the other guards watch Coffey bring an inmate's pet mouse back to life, they hatch a plot to smuggle Coffey out of the prison in the dead of night in order to cure the warden's wife (Patricia Clarkson) of an inoperable brain tumor. Despite the fact that the healing succeeds, the warden (James Cromwell) is still unable to commute Coffey's death sentence. Using mental telepathy, Coffey perceives that one of the other prisoners, the psychotic "Wild Bill" Wharton (Sam Rockwell), is the real murderer of the two girls Coffey was convicted of killing. Upon obtaining this knowledge, he utilizes his psychic powers to compel a sadistic guard, Percy Wetmore (Doug Hutchinson), who has been brutalizing the inmates, to shoot Wharton dead in his cell, and in the aftermath puts Wetmore into a permanent catatonic state. Before his execution, Coffey telepathically transmits the mental vision of Wharton's awful crime to Edgecomb, explaining that he used his ESP abilities to punish the two evil men. To enable the mind meld, Coffey passes some of his psychic power to Edgecomb, who afterward becomes abnormally long-lived and at 108 years old considers his dreary longevity a curse for having destroyed "God's miracle," John Coffey.

With a runtime of over three hours, the film explores a number of subplots and interactions between the various characters that sometimes push the psychic goings-on into the background. *The Green Mile* is basically a gritty prison picture that is as much about racial prejudice and capital punishment as it is about the paranormal. On a dramatic level, the film is earnestly acted and ably directed, although Darabont's script sometimes descends into bathos about "Mr. Jingles" the pet mouse and suchlike. The film was nominated for four Academy Awards, including Best Picture and Best Supporting Actor for Michael Clarke Duncan, whose dignified, understated performance drives the film.

Despite its extensive length, little in the way of backstory about John Coffey is revealed, obscuring the source or nature of his mystifying powers. He is portrayed as a simpleton with little memory of the events of his life. Bearing the initials "J.C.," Coffey is meant to suggest Jesus Christ, who was also an innocent miracle-worker put to death by the power structure. Like many screen psychics, Coffey's outward appearance is unusual, even menacing, and marks him as being "other." The workings of his paranormal powers are attended by arcing electric lights, the trembling of the earth and other melodramatic events. During his execution, confronted by the victims' families for a murder he did not commit, he tells them, "I'm sorry for what I am"—a common lament for screen psychics. Horror maven Stephen King, whose serial novel provided the source material for the film, had previously expressed ambivalent attitudes about ESP phenomena in his books *Carrie*, *The Dead Zone* and *Firestarter*. In this context, it should be noted that Coffey's powers are not all sweetness and light, as he uses his abilities to compel one man to shoot another dead.

Premonition (2007) stars Sandra Bullock as suburban mom Linda Hanson, whose cozy domestic life is shattered by a string of inexplicable events.

Julian McMahon and Sandra Bullock watch future storm clouds approach in *Premonition* (2007).

First, her husband Jim (Julian McMahon), who is away on a business trip, leaves a cryptic message on the answering machine. Next, the local sheriff shows up at her door to announce that Jim has been killed in a car accident that occurred the previous day, meaning that he could not have sent the phone message. Shattered by her loss, Linda is surrounded by grieving family members who seem oddly antagonistic. Upon awakening the next day, Linda is astounded to find that Jim is alive again, and that she has been transported back in time to the day before the accident. Things get even more confusing when she wakes up the following day to find Jim dead once more. After seesawing back and forth through several live Jim/dead Jim episodes, it appears that she is having lucid precognitive dreams about her husband's demise. Armed with detailed foreknowledge of the fatal event, Linda strives to change destiny.

Scenarist Bill Kelly and director Mennan Yapo appear to be trying to emulate the work of the popular horror film writer/director M. Night Shyamalan in this moody, low-key drama, employing Shyamalan's signature hand-held camerawork and confining indoor settings. *Premonition* also borrows from the jumbled narratives of films like *Groundhog Day* and *Memento* in its repetition of inexplicable events, making its story line confusing at times. The eerie paranormal happenings frequently take a back seat to middle–American domestic soap opera in this Bullock vehicle. Little is offered in the way of explanation of Linda's precognitive insights. A lapsed Roman Catholic, she visits her parish priest (Jude Ciccolella) for advice, and is told that these types of premonitions happen to people who have lost their religious faith, a belief that equates ESP with ungodliness.

There are also a number of dramatic films in which psychic phenomena appear but are only incidental to the main thrust of the narrative. In William Dieterle's historical biopic *Juarez* (1939), for instance, Bette Davis plays the role of Empress Carlotta von Hapsburg, wife of the "Emperor of Mexico" Maxmilian (Brian Aherne), who has been installed as the puppet ruler of Mexico in the 1860s by Napoleon III (Claude Rains). When the Indian leader Juarez (Paul Muni) leads a revolution against the foreign dictator, Maxmilian sends his wife back to Paris for safekeeping. Unfortunately, Maxmilian's forces are defeated and he is sentenced to be executed by firing squad. During the execution he requests that a folksinger perform the Mexican folk song "La Paloma," a favorite of his and Carlotta's, which tells of a sailor drowned at sea whose soul returns to his lover as a white dove. Back in Paris, Carlotta knows that her husband is dead when she hears the strains of "La Paloma" clairvoyantly playing inside her head.

Federico Fellini's *8½* (1963) is considered a classic of world cinema, and also contains a psychic interlude. The main character is film director Guido Anselmi (Marcello Mastroianni), who is experiencing a fit of "director's block" while lensing a science fiction picture, causing him to enter a fantasy-prone state where it is difficult to distinguish fantasy from reality. In one sequence, Guido attends a raucous party that includes a performance by stage magician Maurice (Ian Dallas), who is assisted by a psychic named Maya (Mary Indovino). Tasked with reading Guido's mind during the performance, Maya correctly perceives the seemingly nonsensical phrase, "ASA NISI MASA," which is unintelligible to everyone but Guido. The phrase relates to an episode from the director's childhood in which he and his cousin would use the expression as a magic chant designed to make the eyes of a wall portrait move until they point to the location of a secret treasure. One possible interpretation of the scene is that the thought process of the creative artist is so enigmatic that it is impenetrable even to a mind-reader.

In acclaimed Swedish director Ingmar Bergman's last fully realized film, the family saga *Fanny and Alexander* (1983), a theatrical clan, the Ekdahls, have fallen on hard times after the death of their patriarch. The matriarch (Ewa Froling) is forced to wed the town's Bishop (Jan Malmsjö), and the Ekdahl family must move into the clergyman's gloomy estate. Ten-year-old Alexander Ekdahl (Bertil Guve) has a nephew named Ismael (Stina Ekblad), who possesses psychic powers and is therefore kept inside a locked room in the house of one of Alexander's uncles. Ismael (who is, inexplicably, played by a girl) uses clair-

Wacko parapsychologists Dr. Venkman (Bill Murray, left), Dr. Stanz (Dan Aykroyd) and Dr. Spengler (Harold Ramis) display their paranormal detection gear in *Ghostbusters* (1984).

voyance to see inside the Bishop's house, where he correctly remote-views the Bishop's death by fire. As in Fellini's *8½*, the line between reality and unreality becomes blurred, and the film ends with the recitation of a passage from Strindberg's *The Dream Play* that seems to sum up a philosophy of the paranormal: "Anything can happen, anything is possible and likely. Time and space do not exist. On a flimsy ground of reality, imagination spins out and weaves new patterns."

ESP and Comedy

While the great majority of films on psychic themes approach the subject seriously, ESP can sometimes be played for laughs. The most notable example of paranormal comedy is also one of the most popular and acclaimed comedy films in Hollywood history, *Ghostbusters* (1984). The titular characters are a trio of psychic researchers who run a paranormal studies laboratory at prestigious Columbia University in New York. The group includes the brilliant physical scientist Dr. Egon Spengler (Harold Ramis), paranormal historian Dr. Raymond Stantz (Dan Aykroyd) and suave con man Dr. Peter Venkman (Bill Murray). When the dean of the university pulls the group's funding grant, they decide to continue their activities in the private sector. Setting up shop in an abandoned firehouse, they become the "Ghostbusters" and offer a paranormal elimination service that exorcises pesky spooks. As business picks up, the Ghostbusters hire a fourth member of the team, non-scientist Winston Zeddmore (Ernie Hudson). The boys are soon up to their necks in paranormal trouble as an ancient Babylonian god opens a portal in the space-time continuum and lets loose all manner of supernatural mayhem, climaxing in a battle with a humongous marshmallow man atop a New York City skyscraper.

Inspired comic performances by Murray, Aykroyd and Ramis, ably assisted by Sigourney Weaver and Rick Moranis, make *Ghostbusters* a preternatural delight. Director Ivan Reitman moves the comic action along breathlessly, while Richard Edlund's nifty special effects provide the fantasy element and necessary suspension of disbelief. The film was conceived and co-scripted by Aykroyd, who has an intense interest in the paranormal. His brother, Peter, is a practicing parapsychologist, and Dan would later host the investigative TV series *The Psi Factor* in 1996. Dan has also become active in the UFO field, producing the documentary DVD *Dan Aykroyd Unplugged on UFOs* (2005), and he currently serves as the "Hollywood Consultant" for America's premier research organization, the Mutual UFO Network (MUFON).

While *Ghostbusters* quickly veers into supernatural territory, some of the early scenes comically illustrate the plight of parapsychological researchers within the scientific establishment. The ghost-busting scientists are depicted as a group of jokers, oddballs and borderline charlatans existing on the far fringes of science. For instance, Venkman's questionable methodology is illustrated in a previously-cited scene in which he conducts an experiment designed to measure "the effect of negative reinforcement on ESP ability" by giving electric shocks to two student volunteers for incorrect guesses at Zener cards. The joke is that Venkman is more interested in wooing the cute co-ed volunteer, and rewards her wrong guesses while dispensing shocks to the male student who is guessing the cards correctly. "You're no fluke, Jennifer," he gushes to her, "you're a legitimate phenomenon." It's no wonder the university's Dean gleefully dismantles their modest research operation and removes the last vestiges of their scientific respectability while Venkman protests, "But the kids love us!" Like action figures, the team sports bulky "proton packs" that provide energy for their ghost-breaking laser rifles, while also employing other exotic paranormal detection and containment gear. It's all funny and entertaining as hell, but at the same time it's not exactly a flattering portrait of parapsychologists.

Star-crossed lovers are the subject of the psychic romantic comedy *The Butcher's Wife* (1991). Demi Moore stars as the title character, a blonde-haired witchy-woman named Marina from a seaside town in North Carolina. A self-

Dan Aykroyd (left), Bill Murray and Harold Ramis go into action in full battle regalia in *Ghostbusters* (1984).

professed clairvoyant, she has a dream that her future husband will soon arrive, and when the lumpen butcher Leo Lemke (George Dzundza) abruptly shows up in her Carolina town on a fishing trip, the two are hastily wed. When Leo brings his new wife back to his Greenwich Village butcher shop as an assistant, it becomes apparent she has special powers when she begins to dispense psychic advice to the customers along with the veal chops. As Marina's homespun "hocus-pocus talk" serves to straighten out the tangled lives of several of George's clients, she comes to the attention of neighborhood shrink Dr. Alex Tremor (Jeff Daniels), who views her as a professional rival. As psychic and psychiatrist square off, an attraction blossoms between Marina and Alex, and the butcher's wife begins to suspect that her original vision of a happy marriage to Leo may be at fault. Things get even more complicated when hubby Leo falls for ditzy blues singer Stella Keefover (Mary Steenburgen), but predictably enough all dilemmas of the heart are happily resolved by the last reel.

ESP clearly takes a back seat to romance in this pleasant fantasy/comedy, deftly directed by Terry Hughes from a screenplay by Ezra Litvak and Marjorie Schwartz. In contrast to the depiction of most screen psychics as grotesque, maladjusted loners, Demi Moore's down-home portrayal of the wise and attractive Southern gal Marina is a refreshing change. Thematically, the equation of psychic functioning with psychiatry is the most interesting facet of the film. "We both help people, just in different ways," Marina tells Alex, but her paranormally inspired advice is clearly superior to his. One obvious paradox, however, is that Marina makes such an important mistake about her marriage by relying on clairvoyance. The film is more about the mysterious workings of fate in resolving matters of love than about ESP per se. The credits on *The Butcher's Wife* lists one Maria Papapetros as a psychic consultant for the movie.

Wilder Napalm (1993) offered a similar stab at paranormally inspired romantic comedy. The Foudroyant brothers, Wilder (Arliss Howard) and Wallace (Dennis Quaid), both possess the psychokinetic ability to create fire at will. After a childhood incident in which they accidentally roast a bum to death in a prank gone bad, Wilder vows never to use his pyrokinetic powers again, while Wallace takes the opposite approach, performing his human torch routine in a traveling circus as "Biff the Clown." While Wallace dreams of hitting the big time as the firebrand celebrity persona "Dr Napalm," Wilder works in a depressingly tiny Kwik Photo booth at a decrepit Florida shopping mall and moonlights as one of the town's volunteer firemen. Sparks begin to fly when Wallace breezes into town with the carnival and meets Wilder's free-spirited wife, Vida (Debra Winger), who quickly warms to the hottie Wallace and kindles an affair with him. When Wilder discovers his wife in the torrid embrace of his brother, the stage is set for a fiery conflagration between the incendiary siblings.

Like *The Butcher's Wife*, *Wilder Napalm* treats the paranormal within the framework of fantasy and strives for the whimsical ambience of a Tim Burton film. The film's pyrotechnics are meant to symbolize the fires of romantic passion, which are smothered in Wilder but freely expressed in Wallace. The dramatic situation is only resolved when Wilder is able to embrace his burning emotions. Despite an intriguing script by Vince Gilligan and breezy direction by Glenn Gordon Caron, critics and film-goers never warmed to *Wilder Napalm*, which remains something of a film-historical oddity. In the movie's romantic comedy/fantasy context, the pyrokinetic Foudroyant brothers are presented as normal individuals who seem to have been minimally influenced by their unusual abilities.

The most popular and memorable ESP-themed comedy is Nancy Meyers's *What Women Want* (2000), which also has the distinction of being the highest-grossing movie ever directed by a woman as of June 2008. The film stars Mel Gibson as ad exec Nick Marshall, an insensitive, womanizing lout who is forced to explore his feminine side when company head Dan Wanamaker (Alan Alda) hires rival Darcy McGuire (Helen Hunt) to work with Nick on developing an ad campaign for a line of Nike women's sportswear. As he is pondering the intricacies of feminine sales motivations, Nick accidentally falls into a bathtub while holding a hair dryer, and the resultant electric shock somehow gives him the ability to read women's minds.

Nick's newfound ability gives him an entirely new perspective on the opposite gender that enables him to get in touch with the female side of his personality. At work, he practically becomes one of the girls, gossiping and expressing women's concerns. His telepathy also enables him to reconcile sour familial relations with his estranged 15-year-old daughter, Alex (Ashley Johnson). Best of all, his mind-reading abilities give him an advantage in the advertising game, as he can tap directly into women's thought processes and understand their psychology firsthand. As Nick's psychiatrist (Bette Midler) helpfully explains, "If Men are from Mars and Women are from Venus, and you can speak Venusian, the world can be yours." Soon Nick is upstaging Darcy in knowing what women want, and he devises a killer ad campaign that nails the Nike account, while Darcy's role in the advertising company is diminished in the process. Nick abruptly loses his mind-reading powers when he is accidentally shocked once more by a downed power line, but his sensitivity to women has permanently changed his personality and made him a better human being. Confessing all to Darcy, he loses his job at the agency but begins a romantic relationship with his former colleague and competitor.

This sparkling romantic comedy showcases the talents of Mel Gibson and Helen Hunt under Meyers's able direction, and the combination struck box office gold. The screenplay by Josh Goldsmith and Cathy Yuspa revolves around the concept of the "metrosexual," an early 21st century meme that is defined as a species of urban, slightly feminized heterosexual male who is in touch with womanly sensibilities. During the 2004 presidential campaign, for instance, vice-presidential nominee John Edwards was cited as an example of a metrosexual. Protagonist Nick Marshall evolves from a Neanderthal male chauvinist pig to an enlightened metrosexual during the course of the film, his transformation enabled by the insights afforded him by his gender-specific telepathy. Of course the ESP angle is played for laughs and in the service of lighthearted romance, but even in this unserious context *What Women Want* suggests the positive transformational potential psi might hold for society.

Paranormal Kidvid

Having quasi-magical psychic abilities is a child's dream. Using these powers, psi-enabled pre-teens are able to turn the tables on the adult world and challenge its absolute authority. It's no wonder, then, that a number of kid's movies utilize paranormal themes for fantasy and adventure purposes.

Disney's *Escape to Witch Mountain* (1975) features a pair of young psychic twins, Tony Malone (Ike Eisenmann) and his sister, Tia (Kim Richards). Tony can telekinetically move small objects (with the aid of a harmonica), while Tia is clairvoyant and telepathic, especially with animals. Unfortunately the children have no clear memories of their early years, and have been shuttled in and out of orphanages and foster homes for most of their lives. The twins' psi powers come to the attention of Aristotle Bolt (Ray Milland), a ruthless multi-millionaire who is obsessed with the paranormal and the occult. Aided by his skulking henchman Lucas Deranian (Donald Pleasence), Bolt legally adopts Tony and Tia and ensconces them in his posh rural estate. At first dazzled by Bolt's wealth and lush material goodies, the kids are appalled to learn via Tia's ESP that Bolt intends to imprison them on a private island in order to extract the secrets of their powers.

Using their psychic abilities, the twins escape and are picked up on the highway by lonely retired widower Jason O'Day (Eddie Albert), who is touring the area in his Winnebago trailer. After witnessing the twins' ESP, Jason agrees to help the children flee from the clutches of Bolt and Deranian in order to reach a nearby location called Witch Mountain, which seems to have some unknown significance for the kids. A series of misadventures ensues as Jason, Tony and Tia elude Bolt's rent-a-cops on the road, but when knowledge of the kids' unusual powers reaches the local townsfolk, they become convinced that the children are evil witches and join in the hunt. In the finale, Jason's trailer is ambushed at the foot of Witch Mountain by Bolt's forces, whereupon the RV is levitated by some mysterious psychokinetic force to elude their pursuers. Up on Witch Mountain, the children are reunited with their Uncle Bené (Denver Pyle), who explains that they are extraterrestrials who possess psi powers and escorts them off the planet on a giant flying saucer.

Typical of 1970s-era Disney kidvid, *Escape to Witch Mountain* is an enjoyable piece of fluff that has darker undertones inherited from its source material, a 1968 children's sci-fi novel by Alexander Key. Although the kids are Disney-style cute and bland, they are hunted down by a wealthy adversary and later pursued even by the poor, superstitious country folk in the vicinity of Witch Mountain. Jason's airborne RV, levitated by alien psychokinetic forces to avoid capture, recalls a similar climactic scene in Spielberg's *E.T.* (1982), in which a bicycle takes flight. The film inspired a 1995 TV-movie remake, and a second theatrical version *Race to Witch Mountain* is planned for 2009.

The telekinetic twins, Tony and Tia (again played by Eisenmann and Richards), were back for the sequel, *Return from Witch Mountain* (1978). Coming back to Los Angeles for a vacation, Tony is kidnapped by the malevolent scientist Dr. Gannon (Christopher Lee) and his dowager assistant Letha (Bette Davis), while Tia escapes to fend for herself on the mean streets of L.A. Dr. Gannon and Letha surgically install a mind-control device in Tony's brain that enables them to control the youngster's psychokinetic powers and exploit them to commit crimes. They hope to harness Tony's extraordinary abilities in order to take over the world. Meanwhile, Tia takes up with a bunch of truant street kids called the "Earthquake Gang," who aid her in rescuing her brother from the clutches of the nefarious duo. This inevitably leads to a psychic showdown between Tia and Tony, who is still under the mental influence of Dr. Gannon, inside a nuclear power plant that threatens to go critical when influenced by Tony's psi powers.

While the film lacks some of the warmth and vitality of the original, it's still fun to watch screen luminaries Christopher Lee and Bette Davis interact in their scenes together. There is less reliance on special effects, and production values in general are lower in the sequel. The script by Malcolm Marmorstein deliberately references the retro-kiddie series *The Little Rascals* in its lengthy focus on the antics of the Earthquake Gang. As in the first film, wealthy parties have a vested interest in exploiting and controlling individuals with psychic powers. Despite being a children's film, *Return from Witch Mountain* touches on the serious subject of the relationship between mind control and ESP. The twins' alien identities are somewhat de-emphasized here, making them appear more like normal children.

In *Matilda* (1996), the constricting adult world is once more challenged by a psychic child. Six-year-old Matilda Wormwood (Mara Wilson) is a precocious girl with a very high I.Q. and a love of reading. Unfortunately her parents, Harry (Danny DeVito) and Zinnia (Rhea Perlman), are a couple of self-centered lowlifes who have no interest in their daughter's welfare. Harry operates an auto chop-shop and car dealership where he engages in illegal activities. Frustrated by her parents' lack of attention and insensitive cruelty, Matilda begins to annoy them with pranks. One night, when forced to stop reading and watch a mindless television show, she expresses her outrage by blowing out the cathode tube in the family's TV. This experience makes Matilda aware that she has special psychokinetic powers.

The PK-enabled child is sent to Crunchem Hall, a private school presided over by the piggish, sadistic principal Ms. Trunchbull (Pam Ferris), who totes a riding crop and whose idea of discipline is hurling children out of windows or imprisoning them in solitary confinement in a claustrophobic closet called "The Chokey." Matilda's teacher, however, is the kind and gentle Miss Honey (Embeth Davidtz), who takes the youngster under her wing and is deeply impressed by the child's prodigious intellect. This threatening environment serves to further enhance Matilda's telekinetic aptitude as she begins to use her powers to strike back at the bullying principal in a series of pranks, which lead inevitably to a battle royal that pits Ms. Trunchbull's brawn against Matilda's PK.

Adapted from a 1988 novel by Roald Dahl, the film plays upon Dahl's portrayal of the psychological terrors of childhood in a manner similar to another screen adaptation of one of his fantasy books, *The Witches* (1989). Adults, represented by Ms. Trunchbull and Matilda's parents, are scheming, threatening adversaries who wield absolute authority over the child while smothering her uniqueness, and the vulnerable girl's psychic powers are all that save her from a terrible fate. Matilda's rebelliousness leads directly to the development of her telekinesis in a manner that parallels real-world poltergeist cases, in which childish pranks escalate into paranormal activity. In contrast to the portrayal of screen psychics as evil or "other," Mara Wilson's Matilda is eminently likeable. One delightful scene shows Matilda dancing to a pop song while psychokinetically causing small objects to fly around the room in an expression of psychic joy. The underlying theme of the film is expressed in advice Miss Honey gives to Matilda: "Believe in whatever power is inside of you. Believe with all your heart." Comedian Danny DeVito, who stars along with his real-life spouse Perlman, directed this lively bit of kiddie fare.

The Last Mimzy (2001) is another family-oriented film that features a pair of psychic siblings. Seattle kids Noah (Chris O'Neil) and his younger sister Emma (Rhiannon Leigh Wryn) find a strange-looking box on a nearby beach. Inside the box are a number of equally strange "toys" that are clearly the product of a higher technology, including a stuffed bunny rabbit that Emma names "Mimzy," which communicates with the child in a kind of purring voice. Contact with the weird playthings begins to imbue the children with superior intellects and paranormal powers like telepathy, psychokinesis and levitation, which both fascinates and distresses their parents (Timothy Hutton and Joely Richardson) and Noah's science teacher (Rainn Wilson). When one of the hi-tech toys accidentally shuts down electrical power to the entire city, an FBI team managed by Special Agent Nathanial Broadman (played by Michael Clarke Duncan, the oversized psychic from *The Green Mile*) is called to investigate.

The family is taken into custody and the Feds subject Mimzy to laboratory analysis, only to discover that the toy rabbit is in reality an advanced nanotech lifeform from far in Earth's future that has been sent back in time to the 21st century. Emma learns that Mimzy is on a mission to gather DNA from our time to help the inhabitants of the future cope with an ecological disaster that has devastated their genetic material, and the kids must use their powers to escape from the FBI and send the toy bunny back to the future in order to save the world. In an epilogue, we are shown a teacher in a rosy-looking future time relating the story of Mimzy to her students via telepathy in a world where psychic abilities have become commonplace.

In contrast to other paranormally oriented kiddie fare, *The Last Mimzy* takes itself much more seriously. The action is played out against a backdrop of the War on Terror, Global Climate Change and looming ecological catastrophe without much in the way of humor or lightness. The screenplay, adapted by Bruce Joel Rubin and Toby Emmerich from a 1943 short story "Mimsy Were the Borogoves" by Lewis Padgett (a pseudonym for Henry Kuttner and his wife, C. L. Moore), is loaded down with some New-Agey pap about mandalas and Nepalese Buddhism that seem out of place in a science fiction picture. Decent special effects occasionally enliven the otherwise ponderous and serious-minded direction by Bob Shaye and the preachiness of the script. These effects also serve to render the normally invisible realm of ESP in a blaze of light and color.

The film's final scene posits a future psychic utopia in which even young children can read minds and levitate.

Without Benefit of Melodrama

Unlike the more emotionally loaded depiction of psychics in the suspense, horror and science fiction genres, in drama, comedy and children's films they are more usually portrayed as ordinary people. This is especially true of children's movies, where the pint-sized psychics in *Escape to Witch Mountain, Matilda* and *The Last Mimzy* are cute and cuddly and are made to seem just like the kids next door. Nonetheless, there are still some abnormalities, such as the alien-like psychic mutant in *Powder* and the hulking faith healer/convicted murderer in *The Green Mile*.

These films reflect spontaneous occurrences of ESP phenomena that happen in everyday life. In these homely settings, paranormal powers are shown to have positive, practical values in solving problems. Christ–like psychics heal the sick in *Resurrection* and *The Green Mile*; a kid with ESP makes money at the racetrack in *The Rocking Horse Winner*; innocent children defy evil authorities in *Matilda, The Last Mimzy* and the *Witch Mountain* movies; romantic entanglements are straightened out via psychic means in *The Butcher's Wife* and *Wilder Napalm*; an alien-inspired psychic attempts to establish a utopia on earth in *Phenomenon*. Paranormal functioning is even shown to be necessary to the future survival of humanity in *The Last Mimzy*. On the other hand, the sinister, amoral psychic in *The Shout* hints at a dark side to the application of psi.

Even outside the realm of melodrama, cinema psychics are subjected to oppression and threatened with death in *Resurrection, The Green Mile* and *Powder*, reflecting analogous religious, racial and sexual bigotries in our society as well. In *Escape to Witch Mountain*, psychic kids are hunted by a wealthy man who wishes to exploit their powers, while *Return from Witch Mountain* explored the relationship between ESP and mind control. Psychic children are pursued by the FBI in the name of homeland security in *The Last Mimzy*. A woman must struggle with clairvoyant nightmares about the death of her husband in *Premonition*. Individuals with psi powers are doomed by the negative, obsessional aspects of their wild talents in *The Rocking Horse Winner* and *The Shout*.

Without benefit of melodrama, the world of psi can be shown in a positive light as being life-affirming, problem-solving, funny, romantic and fantastical. These films, however, are in the minority. More often screen psychics are depicted as criminals, extraterrestrials, oddballs, superheroes, mutants, government agents and various other paranormal anomalies.

• FOUR •

Paranormal Crime and Melodrama

Psi and crime are a natural fit. In theory, psychic detectives would be able to solve crimes using their paranormal abilities in the manner of the ESP–enabled detectives in Alfred Bester's novel *The Demolished Man* or the mutant "pre-cogs" who predict murders in Spielberg's *Minority Report*. In practice, psychic crime-solving has had a very mixed record and limited success. The Dutch clairvoyant Peter Hurkos, who was the model for Stephen King's psychic protagonist in his novel *The Dead Zone*, reportedly solved crimes using ESP in his native country, and was even called in as a consultant on the infamous Boston Strangler and Sharon Tate murder cases. Ace U.S. government remote viewer Pat Price had formerly been the police chief of the city of Burbank, California, where he used his psychic acumen to assist in his detective work. Even cops on the beat speak of a "blue sense," of paranormal "hunches" that let them know if a perp has a gun, or is carrying drugs, or is contemplating violence. It's easy to see how this sensitivity has survival value on the mean streets that these officers must patrol.

Conversely, paranormally gifted criminals could use their abilities to commit homicide or other felonies. Although this does not seem to be reflected in real-world crimes, psychic criminals challenge the justice system in a number of movie melodramas. Criminals can also exploit their victims' superstitious beliefs in psi as part of a scam or racket, as seen in 1940s-era *films noir* such as *Murder, My Sweet* or *Nightmare Alley*.

One of the most interesting essays on criminality and ESP is Alfred Hitchcock's classic thriller *Shadow of a Doubt* (1943), reputedly one of the master's favorites of all his films. Suave lady-killer Charles Oakley (Joseph Cotten) is a serial murderer known as the "Merry Widow Murderer" because his victims are wealthy, elderly women sans husbands. On the run from a police dragnet on the East Coast, Charles decides to pay a visit to his sister Emma (Patricia Collinge) and her family in the sleepy town of Santa Rosa in Northern California. Charles sends a telegram to Emma notifying her of his impending arrival before skipping town.

Meanwhile in Santa Rosa, Oakley's niece (Teresa Wright), who is also named Charlie after her uncle, thinks that her family is in a funk and decides to wire Charles in the hopes that he will pay a visit. Decamping to the town's Western Union office, she is both stunned and delighted to find a telegram from her uncle announcing his visit. Charlie asks the telegrapher, Mrs. Henderson (Minerva Urecal), if she believes in mental telepathy, and elaborates, "Like, well, suppose you have a thought, and suppose the thought's about someone you're in tune with. And then across thousands of miles, that person knows what you're thinking about and answers you — and it's all mental." To this Mrs. Henderson wryly replies, "I don't know what you're talkin' about. I only send telegrams the normal way." Charlie is exultant over the paranormal event. "He heard me! He heard me!" she gushes on her way home.

Arriving by train a few days later, the dapper Charles charms his sister and her husband, Joseph Newton (Henry Travers), and wows the locals with his worldly ways and big bank account. Young Charlie, however, senses that her uncle has hidden depths, and that the two namesakes share a special bond. "I have the feeling that inside you somewhere, there's something nobody knows about," she claims, "because we're not just an uncle and a niece ... we're sorta like twins." Charles gives Charlie a homecoming gift, a valuable emerald ring that she discovers has the previous owner's initials engraved on the inside. Later Charlie finds herself humming the melody of Victor Herbert's "Merry Widow Waltz" without recognizing the tune. Thus she has unknowingly perceived a clue to her uncle's identity as the Merry Widow killer via a kind of musical telepathy.

Charlie's suspicions about her uncle deepen when she discovers that the initials inside her emerald ring are the same as those of one of the serial killer's victims, but when detective Jack Graham (Macdonald Carey) arrives in town on the murderer's trail, she hides this evidence from the policeman. Unable to deflect his niece's probing, Charles finally owns up to his crimes to Charlie, who continues to keep mum because she doesn't want to upset her mother. Charlie threatens to expose him unless he leaves Santa Rosa, which he agrees to do — that is, if he doesn't succeed in murdering his niece before she can reveal the truth about him.

Shadow of a Doubt is unique among Hitchcock's feature films in its use of a preternatural theme, something the director assiduously avoided because he felt it detracted from the realistic tension of the dramatic narrative. In Hitchcock's later films, paranormal phenomena are associated with fraud, manipulation and criminality. In *Vertigo* (1958), a formerly hard-boiled detective gets suckered into a murder scheme when he believes an actress to be the reincarnated persona of a dead woman. *Family Plot* (1976), Hitchcock's final film, revolves around a phony psychic's attempt to scam an elderly woman out of her fortune.

In fact, the telepathy angle is frequently omitted from plot summaries of *Shadow of a Doubt*, but in actuality the theme is central to the film's plot. The psychopathic mass-murderer Charles Oakley appears to be a pillar of the community, but only Charlie's telepathic abilities are able to penetrate the lead shield of his bogus respectability. Being privy to her uncle's deadly secrets serves to put Charlie in mortal danger. The telepathic link between the two "Charlies" is explained as a function of their familial relationship. "We're like twins," the young Charlie exclaims, referring to the well-documented mind-meld phenomenon that has long been observed between twins. Hitchcock uses a recurring shot of 1890s-era ballroom dancers waltzing to the melody of Herbert's "Merry Widow Waltz" (a shot that is unrelated to anything in the film's narrative) to convey the abstract idea of the name of the murderer transmitted telepathically by Charles's mind. *Shadow of a Doubt* was the first film to feature a natural psychic who uses ESP to uncover a murderer, a formula that would be repeated over time. Today considered one of Hitchcock's classic *film noir* thrillers, the film was scripted by Thorton Wilder (author of the famous play *Our Town*), Sally Benson and Alma Reville (a.k.a. Mrs. Hitchcock), and won an Oscar nomination for best original story for writer Gordon McDonell.

The British production *Séance on a Wet Afternoon* (1964) features the statuesque Kim Stanley as wannabe medium Myra Savage, a self-styled spiritualist who holds séances in her gloomy Victorian home in outer London. Unsure of her psychic gift, Myra conceives an audacious plot she hopes will bolster her credibility as a clairvoyant. She compels her weak-willed husband Billy (Richard Attenborough) to kidnap the 12-year-old Amanda Clayton (Judith Donner), the daughter of a London millionaire-industrialist, and imprison her in a faux hospital room concealed inside their home. In addition to collecting a ransom of 25,000 pounds sterling from the family, Myra plans to come forth and "psychically" guide the Claytons to Amanda's location, thereby gaining fame as a genuine clairvoyant. The medium believes she is in touch with the couple's deceased son Arthur somewhere in the netherworld, and rhapsodizes, "Arthur wants me to be recognized for what I am." She uses the idea of her psychic "gift" as a weapon against her husband, whom she disdains for being "ordinary and dead," and dominates him via a psychological process called *folie a deux*, in which two people share a common delusion imposed by the stronger personality on the weaker.

Billy dutifully carries out his wife's scheme, kidnapping Amanda and installing her in their phony hospital room, but the precocious child easily sees through their ruse. When Myra approaches the Clayton family in order to demonstrate her clairvoyant gift, the police become suspicious. Billy is obliged to transport Amanda around London while their home is searched, but this involves giving soporific drugs to the child. Although the couple avoid the discovery of their plot, Amanda soon becomes ill and feverish, and compassionate Billy fears she might die. Billy also takes an enormous risk by collecting the ransom money and eluding the police on the London subway. But his resolve is finally broken when Myra suggests that Arthur has told her that he wants Amanda to join him in the afterlife, and Billy is expected to murder the child.

In the unexpected climax, Myra is approached by a group of detectives who ostensibly want her to help them locate Amanda using her psychic gift. The medium then conducts an impromptu séance with the officers in which she seems to go into a genuine trance and blurts out the details of her crimes.

Written and directed by Bryan Forbes from a novel by Mark McShane, this moody, low-key thriller demonstrates the psychological perils of a belief in clairvoyance and mediumship. Myra's yearning for a psychic "gift" compromises her humanity, and leads her to contemplate the murder of a child. The medium's shadow-draped house, complete with an old-fashioned phonograph that cranks out otherworldly music, serves to externalize her morbid inner world. Gerry Turpin's stark black-and-white cinematography and location shooting on the dreary streets of London capture this eerie mood admirably while at the same time adding a documentary look to the proceedings. Bryan Forbes, who also scripted, coaxes fine performances from a distinguished British cast. Stanley's portrayal of the unhappy medium earned her an Oscar nomination for Best Actress, and is matched by Brit thesp Richard Attenborough's virtuoso performance as her mild-mannered love slave Billy.

The film explores a British preoccupation with Spiritualism, the mediumistic cult that had swept through Europe in the 19th century. Holding séances had become something of a parlor game in England, much like the use of a Ouija board. This curious practice is also depicted in other postwar British films, including David Lean's adaptation of Noël Coward's comedy *Blithe Spirit* (1945) and Jacques Tourneur's horror thriller *Curse of the Demon* (1958). The final plot twist, in which the police seek the help of a psychic to solve a crime, is the first time that this theme appears in film, with the final irony being that Myra does solve the crime and bring the perpetrators to justice during her last séance.

Moving back across the pond and from the sublime to the ridiculous, James F. Hurley's *The Psychic* (1968), a.k.a. *Copenhagen's Psychic Lovers*, attempts to combine soft-core porn with the mysteries of ESP in a confused, sleazoid mind meld. As our story opens, suburban advertising exec Dan Thomas (Dick Genola) falls off a ladder and finds he suddenly has psychic powers. Specifically, he can apprehend information about people by touching them or coming into contact with an object they own (in psi parlance this ability is known as *psychometry*). After correctly predicting the death of his boss during the following week, Dan's newfound abilities begin to wear on him. He starts drinking heavily and womanizing freely, which leads inevitably to the collapse of his marriage. One of his new girlfriends, Bobbi (Bobbi Spencer), suggests they perform in a mentalist act together, and during one performance Dan's clairvoyance dazzles tycoon Mr. Doucette (Jim Small), who offers to take him to New York and make him a star.

Unfortunately, Dan's ESP is on the wane. After dismally failing a psychic demonstration on a nationally televised TV show, his powers are put to the ultimate test when his daughter is kidnapped and he tries to help the police

Four • *Paranormal Crime and Melodrama* 63

Chief Tucker (Cliff Robertson) grills avowed clairvoyant Franklin Wills (Joel Grey) about details of the "Volkswagen Murder" in *Man on a Swing* (1974).

locate her. Again Dan's clairvoyance fails him utterly, as all of his psychic leads turn out to be bogus and his daughter is later discovered alive and well by conventional means. Distraught at the loss of his ESP, he visits psi researcher Professor Roxen (Larry Wellington), who confirms that his visionary powers are indeed fading out. In the end, Dan agonizes that the loss of his special "gift" will turn him back into a "nobody."

"He could read men's minds— and corrupt their women," blared the tag line for this strange stew of nudie exploitation and psychic crime thriller. Produced and shot by goremeister Herschell Gordon Lewis, creator of splatter fare such as *Blood Feast* (1964) and *Two Thousand Maniacs!* (1964), the film's parade of bare breasts and gratuitous simulated sex scenes serve to transform it into a sleazefest that is hard to take seriously. Dan's sudden acquisition of clairvoyance in the aftermath of a head injury recalls the real-life case of the aforementioned Dutch psychic Peter Hurkos, and his ability to "read" people by physically touching them or through handling objects would be replicated in the Stephen King novel *The Dead Zone* (1983).

Psychics and Criminals in the Seventies

In the wake of the psychedelic 60s, psychic phenomena appeared to gain a measure of popular and scientific respectability in the decade that followed. The

Psychic Franklin Wills (Joel Grey) psychs out in Frank Perry's paranormal crime thriller *Man on a Swing* (1974).

film business was quick to explore this newfound interest by producing a crop of ESP-themed movies in a number of different genres. As is their wont, moviemakers chose to exploit the more lurid and sensational aspects of the phenomenon, and many of the films of this period involve psi and criminality.

A real-life police investigation of a murder was the basis for Frank Perry's *Man on a Swing* (1974). A fictionalization of Ohio journalist William A. Clark's investigative piece *The Girl on the Volkswagen Floor*, the film begins with the brutal and senseless murder of a young girl whose body is found sprawled inside a VW. Small-town police chief Lee Tucker (Cliff Robertson) and his homicide team are baffled by the crime, but things get even creepier when an individual claiming to be a psychic phones his office and relates details of the crime known only to the police. Intrigued, Chief Tucker arranges to meet with the self-proclaimed clairvoyant, one Franklin Wills (Joel Grey), who turns out to be quite a handful. Prone to slipping into ecstatic trance states during which he dramatically re-enacts the crime, Wills's psychotic behavior and inside knowledge eventually lead Tucker to suspect that the psychic may actually be the murderer. Looking for answers, Tucker arranges to meet with parapsychologist Dr. Nicholas Holnar (George Voskovec) at a local university, but there are no easy answers as the film builds to an ambiguous denouement.

Paranormal murderer Jim Hutton (bottom) unleashes a psychic storm on this poster for *Psychic Killer* (1975).

Director Frank Perry, best known for dramatic fare like *Diary of a Mad Housewife* (1970), struggles with this unusual material and fails to generate the requisite high-octane suspense in this psi-oriented crime thriller. The staid Cliff Robertson seems to be auditioning for a block of wood in his role as Chief Tucker, while Joel Grey's leering performance as the creepy psychic Franklin Wills dominates the film. Grey, fresh from his Oscar-winning performance as the sleazy Weimar emcee in Bob Fosse's *Cabaret* (1972), delivers a scenery-chewing performance that serves to depict the psychic individual as a charismatic grotesque who may be a murderer to boot.

Psychic Killer (1975) was a modestly budgeted crime melodrama starring Jim Hutton as Arnold Masters, a mild-mannered mama's boy confined to a mental hospital for the murder of a doctor who refused to operate on his sick mother. To make matters worse, his mother has died of neglect while Arnold has been confined. In the hospital, Arnold befriends a West Indian inmate, Emilio (Stack Pierce), who confers upon Masters the powers of astral projection, telepathy and psychokinesis by means of a voodoo amulet. Unexpectedly released from the hospital when someone else confesses to the crime for which he is imprisoned, Masters uses his newfound ESP to embark on an orgy of retribution against those he holds responsible for his mother's death. First up is Dr. Paul Taylor (Whit Bissell), remotely strangled via ESP, followed by psychotic Nurse Martha Burnson (Mary Charlotte Wilcox), who gets telekinetically scalded to death while taking a shower, and shyster lawyer H.B. Sanders (Joseph Della Sorte) who is crushed to death by a cornerstone dropped on his head by a PK–controlled crane at a construction site.

These anomalous, supposedly accidental deaths come to the attention of hard-boiled homicide detective Lt. Jeff Morgan (Paul Burke), who suspects foul play and eventually connects the dots to Arnold. Morgan enlists the aid of psychiatrist Dr. Laura Scott (Julie Adams) and parapsychologist Dr. Gubner (Nehemiah Persoff) in his efforts to nail Masters, as the police stake out Arnold's digs and observe the psychic going into a deathlike trance while the killings are committed. Realizing that no jury will ever convict Masters of the murders based on paranormal evidence, Morgan takes the law into his own hands by having Arnold declared legally dead during one of his narcoleptic trances and hurriedly cremating the body.

This low-budget, ESP–themed police procedural benefits from an interesting cast, which includes Aldo Ray, Neville Brand and Della Reese in minor roles. Burke shines in his intense portrayal of the driven homicide cop puzzling over the paranormal killings, while Persoff is similarly sincere as the psi researcher Dr. Gubner. The grim narrative is relieved by occasional interludes of comedy, such as the scene in which Della Sorte gets squashed by the cornerstone while performing an operatic aria. Director Raymond Danton moves the action along nicely in this intriguing thriller, while the screenplay by Danton, Greydon Clark and Mikel Angel deliberately invokes Alfred Hitchcock's

Psycho (1960) with its mother-obsessed protagonist and the shower murder sequence.

Psi forces are depicted as malevolent and are associated with voodoo and the occult. Out-of-body experiences, telepathy and telekinesis are played as instruments of vengeance and connected to mental illness, although the film's resident parapsychologist delivers the standard spiel about the wonders of the psychic universe. Interestingly, *Psychic Killer*'s alternative title was *The Kirlian Effect*, a reference to the process of Kirlian photography, a psychic fad that was in vogue during the 60s and 70s that involved passing an electrical current across a photographic plate while taking a picture of a leaf or human body part. The resultant "Kirlian" photos purportedly showed glowing images of energy fields representing the "auras" that surround living things. It was later conclusively shown that these alleged auras were merely the result of the electrical charge used to produce the picture. The film's opening credits are displayed against a background of Kirlian photographs, and such photos are also projected during a lecture by Dr. Gubner.

Alfred Hitchcock's final film, the comedy thriller *Family Plot* (1976), strayed into psychic territory the director had not explored since *Shadow of a Doubt*. *Family Plot* opens during a séance being conducted by bogus medium "Madame Blanche" Tyler (Barbara Harris), whose head is framed inside her crystal ball in the opening shot. The séance is being held at the behest of wealthy dowager Julia Rainbird (Cathleen Nesbitt), who is obsessed with locating her sister's lost son, whom she wishes to make the heir to her fortune. She commissions Madame Blanche to find the missing heir by using her ESP for the sum of $10,000. In reality Blanche has no psi powers, but instead relies on the investigative abilities of her boyfriend, cab driver George Lumley (Bruce Dern), who digs up info on her clients by conventional means. "Without my research," George gloats, "you're about as psychic as a dry salami."

The inquisitive George manages to trace the lost heir, but unfortunately he turns out to be kidnapper/jewel thief Arthur Adamson (William Devane), who, along with girlfriend and co-conspirator Fran (Karen Black), have recently pulled off a series of daring, well-publicized heists. Arthur and Fran can't figure out why Blanche and George are prying into their affairs, but knowing that Blanche is a self-proclaimed medium, suspect that she may have come upon this knowledge via ESP. "You and I know that's off the wall," Arthur deliberates, "but can we afford to be wrong?" The couple kidnap Blanche, intending to eliminate her after their current caper is completed, but she is rescued by George and in the film's climax exhibits genuine ESP by locating a huge diamond hidden among the faux glass jewels on a chandelier.

Besides *Shadow of a Doubt*, *Family Plot* is the only Hitchcock feature film to deal with the paranormal, and the great director pokes gentle fun at belief in mediumship. Madame Blanche's trances are comic affairs wherein she speaks in husky, masculine "spirit voices" that blather absurd platitudes laced with supposedly psychic insights cynically obtained by conventional means. In one amusing scene, George must retrieve his car keys from Blanche while she is allegedly entranced during a séance. Note that a belief in the possibility of ESP on the part of Arthur and Fran serves to put George and Blanche in danger from the deadly couple. The film's plot recalls *Séance on a Wet Afternoon* in its mixture of mediumship and kidnapping. Hitch's final outing is a serio-comic romp flavored with a taste of the paranormal and is not his best film, but not his worst either. Adapted by scenarist Ernest Lehman from the novel *The Rainbird Pattern* by Victor Canning, the movie's complicated narrative sometimes seems to collapse under its own weight, and the emergence of Blanche's true psychic powers during the film's final scene are more of a plot twist than an endorsement of the reality of psi.

Horrormeister Lucio Fulci's *The Psychic* (a.k.a. *Seven Notes in Black*, 1977) is generally placed in the genre of the *giallo*, stylishly violent Italian fright films typified by the works of directors like Mario Bava and Dario Argento. As the film begins, Virginia Ducci (Jennifer O'Neill) is returning from the airport where she has seen her wealthy husband Francesco (Gianni Garko) off on a business trip, when she has a clairvoyant vision of a murder. Virginia envisions fragmentary images of a woman being killed by a man with a limp and then shut up inside a wall. Soon afterward, while inspecting a decrepit manor being renovated by her husband, she impulsively takes a pickaxe to a wall, tearing it down to reveal a skeleton. Police Inspector Luca Fattori (Marc Porel) is called in to investigate, but is highly skeptical about Virginia's vision. The skeleton is positively identified as that of a young girl who disappeared several years earlier. Upon returning from his business trip, Francesco is arrested when he admits he had had an affair with the murdered girl. Virginia strives to prove her husband's innocence, but instead has a second vision of a room inside a mirror where another murder has been committed. It becomes unclear, however, whether her vision is of the past or the future. Is Virginia destined to be the killer's next victim? And why is her husband suddenly walking with a limp?

Fulci's *giallo* is considerably more restrained than his over-the-top treatment in earlier horror fare like *Woman in a Lizard's Skin* or *Don't Torture a Duckling*. *The Psychic* comes off as a straightforward murder mystery with paranormal overtones, and is largely free of the gore and overt sadism that are the hallmarks of the genre. Jennifer O'Neil's intense performance as the psychic wife drives the film, while cinematographer Sergio Salvati serves up gobs of murky atmosphere. The titular psychic is a figure of woe, a victim besieged by dark portents and shadowy visions of death. Her clairvoyance exists in order to provide clues to a murder mystery wrapped in the shadows of preternatural intrigue.

Hannibal Lecter and ESP

The dreaded mass-murderer Hannibal "The Cannibal" Lecter first appeared as a character in Thomas Harris' 1981 novel *Red Dragon*, and so mesmerized readers that he would become the central character in Harris' sequels, *The Silence of the Lambs*, *Hannibal* and *Hannibal Rising*. Cult director Michael Mann's movie version of *Red Dragon*, entitled *Manhunter* (1986), was the first film to bring the Lecter character to the screen.

Unlike the later works featuring Lecter, *Manhunter* instead focuses on the character of Will Graham (William Petersen), a "profiler" who is working with the FBI. Profilers attempt to reconstruct the enigmatic personalities of elusive serial killers in order to con-

FBI profiler Will Graham (William Petersen) searches for an enigmatic serial killer in *Manhunter* (1986).

struct psychological profiles of the criminals that will reveal their motivations and anticipate future crimes. The wily profiler has even outfoxed the brilliant Dr. Lecter and put him behind bars, but has been deeply wounded both mentally and physically in the process. Graham is reluctantly coaxed out of retirement by FBI colleague Jack Crawford (Dennis Farina), a veteran agent on the trail of a ritual killer called the "Tooth Fairy" (Tom Noonan) who has murdered two entire families. It seems Graham has an uncanny ability to get inside the mind of his quarry, a power held in awe even by the hard-nosed Crawford.

Graham's working methods are highly unorthodox. He visits the crime scenes after dark, stalking through the rooms of the murder houses while picking up mental impressions of the perpetrator. He spends a lot of time just staring at movies and still photos of the murdered families to facilitate "seeing" the crimes. In order to "catch the scent" he even visits Lecter (here played by Brian Cox), who is ensconced in a maximum-security prison, attempting to enlist the help of one murderer to catch another before the Tooth Fairy can bite again. The profiler explains his *modus operandi* to his son thus: "I tried to build feelings in my imagination like the killer had." In the aftermath, "I still had his thoughts going around in my head," he explains, and "they're the ugliest thoughts in the world." Graham eventually nails the Tooth Fairy when he has one of his signature flashes of insight and realizes that the murderer has been watching the same 8mm home movies of the families that he has been obsessed with, and therefore must be connected to the film processing company. In the eerie climax, Graham uses his "sixth sense" to locate the killer and takes him down in a bloody shootout before he can claim his last victim.

Although the word "psychic" never comes up during *Manhunter*, Graham's working methods and deductive insights practically reek of telepathy and clairvoyance. His detective work consists of getting inside the minds of the killers and victims, a quirky talent that he alone seems to possess. The issue of Graham's ESP is addressed briefly and ambiguously in Harris's *Red Dragon*. In a scene that is not in the film, Crawford questions FBI forensic scientist Dr. Bloom about his odd behavior when he is around Graham. "One thing I've noticed — I'm curious about this: you're never alone in a room with Graham, are you?" he queries. "Why's that? Do you think he's psychic, is that it?"[1] Bloom professes to believe that Graham merely has a remarkable visual memory, but notes, "He wouldn't let Duke [University] test him — that doesn't mean anything, though."[2] After further prodding by Crawford, however, Bloom concedes that he avoids being alone with Graham because he is afraid the profiler will read his mind. Graham's prescience is also on display during the film's climactic sequence, in which Crawford and Graham are en route to the killer's house. While Graham, seemingly in a trance, is methodically loading ammunition into his pistol, a puzzled Crawford protests, "Will, you don't need that. The SWAT team's gonna take him down." But Graham continues, somehow knowing that he will be the one to locate the killer before they can call for backup. Much of the film centers on the act of seeing itself, as evidenced in the infra-red snuff movies the murderer makes for his own enjoyment, in the shattered mirrors he inserts into his victims' eyes, and in the home movies and photos of the dead families Graham constantly peruses hoping to catch clues to the crimes.

Manhunter was a box-office flop in its original release, but has since gained a cult following in the wake of Jonathan Demme's acclaimed and popular sequel *The Silence of the Lambs*. The film was remade as *Red Dragon* (2002) with Anthony Hopkins (naturally) in the Lecter role and Edward Norton playing Graham, but there are some fans of *Manhunter* who feel it is superior to all of the Lecter movies that followed. William Petersen's brooding performance as the tortured Graham brings insight and sympathy to the role, and he is ably supported by Dennis Farina as the pugnacious Crawford and Tom Noonan as the chilling serial killer. Michael Mann, who created the stylish TV cop show *Miami Vice*, crafts a riveting thriller using a full palette of sights and sounds. Dante Spinotti's stark cinematography and looming shadows create an eerie mood of fear and tension, while a moody synthesizer score by Michael Rubini and The Reds adds a disquieting undertow to the proceedings. Mann, who also scripted, delivers a fine adaptation of Harris's novel, with the book's original ending changed much for the better.

It should be noted, however, that the real-life FBI profilers upon whose exploits *Manhunter* is based do not employ empathic or psychic techniques in their efforts to profile and apprehend murderers and other dangerous criminals. Instead of ESP, the profilers rely on proven forensic deductive procedures and sophisticated psychological models to catch the perps. Seen in this context, Graham's histrionic behavior and hinted psi abilities are entirely unrealistic.

The sequel, Demme's *The Silence of the Lambs* (1991), replicates some of the plot elements in *Manhunter*. This time it is newbie FBI analyst Clarice Starling (Jodie Foster) who is trying to pick Lecter's brains in order to get the goods on rampant serial killer "Buffalo Bill." Agent Starling has a number of tense confrontations with Hannibal the Cannibal, played to psychotic, Oscar-winning perfection by Anthony Hopkins, in the grim confines of the maximum-security prison in which he is incarcerated. During these meetings Dr. Lecter seems to have an uncanny ability to probe her mind (thereby reversing the questioner/deponent roles as established in *Manhunter*), and in one session he appears to cause a metal tray used to pass objects into his cell to move via psychokinesis. These odd, unexplained events seem to be manifestations of Lecter's inhuman evil, but are not explored further in the film.

Lady Psychics Versus Male Psychos

The mega-popularity of *The Silence of the Lambs* seems to have been very much on the mind of Neil Jordan when he directed *In Dreams* (1999). Annette Bening plays Claire (as in clairvoyant) Cooper, a rural housewife who is plagued by recurring nightmares in which she sees a long-haired murderer abducting a child. Her husband, Paul (Aidan Quinn), an airline pilot, is puzzled by his wife's odd behavior and less than sympathetic, but when their daughter, Rebecca (Katie Sagona), is kidnapped and murdered, Claire really starts to go off the deep end. She suffers a mental breakdown as her dreams and visions about the killer become more and more intense, and she forges a telepathic link with the murderer that enables the two to read each other's thoughts. In one scene he is even able to project her thoughts onto a computer screen while she is thinking them in real time, and he can exert mental control over the family dog.

After Claire attempts suicide and performs other irrational acts, Paul has her committed to the local psychiatric hospital. This only makes things worse, however, as it turns out that the killer had been incarcerated in the very same room (by coincidence?) years earlier, and has left extensive scribblings concealed behind the wallpaper. Claire learns that the psycho's name is Vivian Thompson (!), and envisions his escape from the booby hatch by cross-dressing as a nurse. Worse still, she foresees that Vivian (played by a long-haired Robert Downey, Jr.) is going to abduct another girl and lure her husband to a hotel room where he is to be murdered. Of course neither her psychiatrist, Dr.

Claire Cooper (Annette Bening) peers into the future in *In Dreams* (1999).

Silverman (Stephen Rea), and homicide detective Kay (Paul Guilfoyle) will believe her, but when the events transpire according to her prophecy she decides to take matters into her own hands. Taking her cue from the killer, she disguises herself as a nurse and escapes from the hospital, and using her psychic skills tracks Vivian to the deserted apple farm where the girl is being kept. The psychotic Vivian explains to Claire that all he wants is to form a nuclear family with her and the abducted girl (this offer comes after he has murdered her own husband and child) as he whimpers about Claire being a "bad mommy." In the final confrontation between the two psychics, both are plunged into the icy waters of a lake, from which only one will emerge alive.

In Dreams suffers from a muddled script, adapted from a novel entitled *Doll's Eyes* by Bari Wood and co-written by director Jordan and Bruce Robinson, that is often confusing and sometimes downright ridiculous. Downey's gender-bending identity as "Vivian" is never explained, for instance, nor is the basic rationale for the mind-meld between Claire and the killer ever revealed. The screenplay is also tailored as a vehicle for Ms. Bening, who is front and center in nearly every scene and whose performance, running the entire gamut of human emotions, sucks the oxygen out of every other characterization in the movie, including that of Downey's psycho-killer. With *The Silence of the Lambs* in mind, some of the scenes descend to the level of the grotesque, such as Claire's gross-out vision of the corpse of her murdered husband being devoured by the family dog. Clairvoyance is represented as a quasi-demonic

Four • *Paranormal Crime and Melodrama* 73

power as Claire, like prophets in the ancient world, is tortured by the foreknowledge of dire events over which she has no control. ESP is used by the serial killer to invade and dominate her mind, while his psychokinetic abilities are employed to further compromise her sanity. Jordan, who directed *The Crying Game* and *In the Company of Wolves*, is clearly capable of better things, but *In Dreams* bombed with the critics and at the box office.

Cate Blanchett stars as a psychic from the deep South in *The Gift* (2000). Blanchett plays Annie Wilson, a widow with three kids struggling to get by in the small town of Brixton, Georgia, by telling fortunes for her friends. This psychic "gift" runs in her family, and Annie uses a deck of Zener cards (the special ESP–measuring cards used in experiments at Duke University) to foretell the future and reveal hidden information. Annie runs afoul of "insecure redneck" Donnie Barksdale (played by a bearded Keanu Reeves), a wife-beating, bigoted bubba who thinks she's a Satan-worshipping witch and takes exception to her readings for his wife, Valerie (Hilary Swank). The brutish Donnie pays a visit to Annie's home one night and violently threatens her and her children. "You ain't no better than a Jew or n — — — r," he spits, "Messin' with the Devil's gonna get you burned."

When local rich girl Jessica King (Katie Holmes) comes up missing, Annie is approached by Sheriff Pearl Johnson (J.K. Simmons), Jessica's father Kenneth King (Chelcie Ross) and her fiancé Wayne Collins (Greg Kinnear), who want her to use her gift to help locate King's daughter. At first she is unsuccessful, due partly to the blatantly skeptical attitude of Sheriff Johnson, but later she experiences vivid visions of a murder, including a dramatic tableau of the dead Jessica floating underwater in a pond, bound with a heavy chain. Dredging the local ponds, the sheriff finds the body of the murdered girl on Donnie Barksdale's property. Donnie is accused of the crime, and during the trial the fact that the body was located using ESP becomes an issue in his legal defense. Donnie's attorney ridicules Annie's alleged psychic abilities, and notes for the jury that telling fortunes for money is against the law in the state of Georgia. Prosecutor David Duncan (Gary Cole), however, mounts a persuasive case against Donnie, who is convicted of Jessica's murder. After the trial, though, Annie's clairvoyance tells her that the wrong man has been convicted of the crime.

At the heart of this paranormal thriller is a well-plotted, sensitive screenplay by Oscar-winning actor/scenarist Billy Bob Thornton and Tom Epperson that combines mystery, horror and family drama into a tight, character-driven narrative. Director Sam Raimi, who would later go on to fame with the *Spider-Man* mega-blockbusters, wonderfully captures the ambience of small-town Southern life by shooting in rural Georgia locations in a manner that recalls the similarly themed Sun Belt mystery-thriller *Midnight in the Garden of Good and Evil*. One can almost feel the heat and smell the magnolia in Raimi's landscape of mangrove swamps, good old boys, pickup trucks, Confederate flags and those deep, dark Southern nights, an environment that is beautifully rendered by cinematographer Jamie Anderson. Ms. Blanchett's ethereal performance as the otherworldly yet down-home prophetess carries the film, and she is supported by a first-rate cast that includes Reeves, Kinnear, Swank and Holmes. *The Gift* remains one of the most thoughtful and fully realized dramatic treatments of the theme of ESP in everyday life ever made, and in addition explores the use of psi to investigate crime.

Screenwriter Thornton based the story in part on events in his own life in a rural community. His mother, Virginia, told fortunes with cards to make ends meet during lean times, and the family was subjected to harassment from their neighbors because of ESP's perceived anti–Christian associations. Like many dramatic and comedic films, such as *Resurrection, Powder, Phenomenon* and *The Butcher's Wife, The Gift* centers on the motif of a psychic individual living in a rural environment, persecuted by superstitious townsfolk who will not tolerate anything anomalous in their close-minded environment. The film's decent budget allows for the use of special effects and artful staging to render Blanchett's psychic visions in a particularly vivid cinematic fashion, such as the scene depicting the apparition of the dead Jessica floating underwater but seen through Annie's clairvoyance as floating overhead, framed against the darkened trees. As depicted in the film, in real-life criminal cases in which evidence has allegedly been obtained by psychic means, the defense has challenged its provenance and admissibility in a court of law.

The heady mix of psi and crime melodrama has produced a number of memorable works by acclaimed directors, including Hitchcock's *Shadow of a Doubt* and *Family Plot*, Mann's *Manhunter* and Raimi's *The Gift*. While a few of these films, like *Man on a Swing, Psychic Killer* and *In Dreams*, portray psychic individuals as lunatics and/or murderers, the majority of them are presented as upstanding members of society who use their abilities to bring criminals to justice and to protect themselves and their families from harm. In the majority of these films, including *Shadow of a Doubt, The Psychic, In Dreams* and *The Gift*, the psychic is a woman who must use her ESP abilities to survive when threatened by a powerful male adversary. In that sense, psi is shown to be something positive and a way to perceive reality that goes beyond societal strictures and limitations. In *Shadow of a Doubt*, for instance, young Charlie's telepathy enables her to see beyond her uncle's respectable facade and comprehend the true nature of his psychotic evil. In fact, the use of ESP in criminal investigations is the most obvious practical use for these abilities in people's everyday lives, and has sometimes been utilized as an effective law enforcement tool. It has recently been reported, for instance, that military-trained remote viewers were called on to assist the Drug Enforcement Agency in counternarcotics operations during the early 1990s, with positive results. Perhaps psi will one day be used to combat criminality and terrorism and will finally live up to its potential to be a boon to all humankind.

• FIVE •

The Dark Side of ESP: Horror and Fantasy

Paranormal phenomena have always been associated with magic, the supernatural and the irrational, and it's no wonder that these themes permeate films on the subject. The notion of ESP invokes dread on many levels and dredges up religious, philosophical and emotional issues that are enthusiastically exploited by movie makers. Horror writers, especially the ever-popular Stephen King, have created a neo–Gothic paranormal landscape that is firmly rooted in contemporary America. King's novels and their film adaptations have had a wide influence on popular attitudes about psi, and have served to color the paranormal with shades of the demonic. Likewise, the worldwide mega-success of William Friedkin's *The Exorcist* (1973) focused public attention on the enigmatic and controversial phenomenon of spirit possession and the related paranormal occurrence of the poltergeist. As previously noted, the poltergeist is the most dramatic and cinematic of all psychic phenomena, and would be explored, Hollywood-style, in movies like *Poltergeist* (1982), *The Entity* (1983) and *An American Haunting* (2005). Inspired by *The Exorcist*, a number of films, including *Carrie* (1976), *The Medusa Touch* (1978) and *Patrick* (1978), featured scary psychic mass-murderers.

Psychics and Ghosts

While mainstream scientific parapsychologists stopped studying ghosts as part of their discipline shortly after the turn of the 20th century, these two phenomena have long been linked in the public mind. Several cinematic ghost stories have featured psychics as ghostbusters who use their ESP to probe the world of the afterlife. The acclaimed director Robert Wise, who cut his directorial teeth in the 1940s working for horror producer Val Lewton on fear films like *Curse of the Cat People* and *The Body Snatcher*, concocted the Lewtonesque spookhouse story *The Haunting* (1963).

Parapsychologist Dr. Markway (Richard Johnson) pursues psychic Eleanor Lance (Julie Harris) up the spiral staircase in Hill House in Robert Wise's *The Haunting* (1963).

Hill House, a creepy old estate located somewhere in rural New England, has a fearful reputation as a haunted mansion and has stood vacant for many years. Anthropologist Dr. John Markway (Richard Johnson) considers Hill House to be the ideal environment for an ESP experiment. Seeking "the key to another world," Dr. Markway combs the records of psychic societies, newspaper morgues and parapsychological reports to locate individuals who possess genuine psi abilities, hoping that their presence "will help to stimulate the strange forces at work here." Only two of the invited sensitives finally show up to participate in the experiment, however. One is Eleanor Lance (Julie Harris), a homely neurotic spinster who has led a constipated existence taking care of her elderly, infirm mother for the past eleven years. When she was ten years old, Eleanor had a poltergeist experience when her home was pelted with showers of stones for three days, an event that was officially reported to the police. The other psychic is Theodora, "just Theodora" (Claire Bloom), an urbane, free-spirited woman who correctly guessed 19 out of 20 Zener cards during an ESP test at the parapsychology lab at Duke University.

The two female psychics are a study in contrasts, and the film quickly becomes a character study of the two women. Theodora uses her telepathic abilities to lay bare and exploit Eleanor's many vulnerabilities with a particularly feminine ruthlessness. The pathetic Eleanor, teetering on the edge of a mental breakdown, is an easy target for the self-assured, worldly-wise Theo, but Eleanor musters her own psi for a counterattack by apprehending her adversary's own secrets. "The world is full of inconsistencies," she spits at Theodora. "Unnatural things, nature's mistakes, they're called — you for instance," which is a not-so-veiled suggestion that Theo is a lesbian. As the narrative progresses, Markway, Eleanor and Theodora are joined by Luke Sanderson (Russ Tamblyn), a young cynic who is a member of the wealthy family that owns Hill House and is assigned to look after the family's interests during the experiment. Possibly stirred up by the presence of the two psychic women, the spirits of the haunted house soon manifest themselves to the experimenters and subject them to a series of terrifying ordeals that leave even the ultra-skeptical Luke a firm believer in ghosts. The supernatural manifestations particularly affect the unstable, suicidal Eleanor, who fears that she will be "absorbed" into the shadows of Hill House forever.

Wise's terror tale, adapted from the novel *The Haunting of Hill House* by Gothic writer Shirley Jackson, is a *tour de force* that is considered one of the most powerful cinematic ghost stories in screen history. Although the ghosts are never seen by either the characters or the audience, Wise skillfully uses sound and shadow to conjure the fear-drenched atmosphere of the haunted house. Beyond this, *The Haunting*'s dramatic tension arises from the conflict between the two female psychics, who are both portrayed as having severe psychological problems. The sexually repressed, self-destructive Eleanor is pathetically neurotic and unable to function in the everyday world, while the acidly cynical, manipulative Theodora is a sexual outlaw (for that time) who may harbor repressions of her own. The two women utilize their ESP in a psychic cat fight to claw each other to pieces as the film paints a less than flattering portrait of psychics as psychologically unstable individuals. *The Haunting* associates ESP with darkness, death and otherworldly spirits.

Psychic ghostbusters were back at work in *The Legend of Hell House* (1973). Again, four individuals, including two psychics, are confined to a haunted house with an evil reputation. At the behest of a wealthy benefactor who is seeking answers about the conundrum of life after death, physicist and parapsychologist Dr. Lionel Barrett (Clive Revill) is contracted to conduct an experiment inside the dread Belasco House (a.k.a. "Hell House"), known as the "Mt. Everest of haunted houses." He is accompanied by his wife Ann (Gale Hunnicutt), a "mental medium," Florence Tanner (Pamela Franklin) and a "physical medium," Ben Fischer (Roddy McDowall). In spiritualist parlance, a mental medium allows spirits to speak through her during a séance, while a physical medium exudes a substance called "ectoplasm" that is capable of interacting with physical objects. Dr. Barrett also hopes to bring the resources of science to bear on the problem, and plans to utilize an electronic machine that is designed to "exorcise" Hell House with a burst of electromagnetic radiation, thereby proving that ghosts do not exist. Predictably, spooks run wild in the haunted house and put all of the participants in mortal danger. The psychosexual forces of the ghosts are unleashed, turning Ann and Florence into raving nymphomaniacs. Even Dr. Barrett's ghostbreaking device does not work as advertised.

Scripted by horrormeister Richard Matheson from his novel *Hell House*, the film suffers greatly in comparison with *The Haunting*, from which it derives its basic plotline. Director John Hough, working with a fine British cast, fails to generate sufficient preternatural *frisson* in this haunted house thriller. The venerable Roddy McDowall turns in a particularly shoddy performance, appearing peeved and prissy during most of the film, only to erupt into histrionics and scenery-chewing fury in the last reel, where he has all the lines. While *The Haunting* harks back to Val Lewton's classy, psychologically oriented horror-chillers of the 40s, the update is inspired by the contemporaneous sex-and-violence milieu of Britain's Hammer Studios, and therefore lacks the character-driven dramatics of the earlier film. Like *Séance on a Wet Afternoon*, the film reflects an English preoccupation with Spiritualist notions such as "mental" and "physical" mediums and the séance room, but also depicts paranormal events such as precognition and poltergeist activity. The film is prefaced with a quotation from Tom Corbett, a self-proclaimed "clairvoyant and psychic consultant to European royalty," which states, "Although the story of this film is fictitious, the events depicted involving psychic phenomena are not only very much within the bounds of possibility, but could well be true."

The "Haunted Boy"

On August 20, 1949, a very strange article appeared in the *Washington Post*. "In what is perhaps one of the most remarkable experiences of its kind in recent religious history," the article proclaimed, "a 14-year-old Mount Ranier boy has been freed by a Catholic priest of possession by the devil, it was reported yesterday." The article went on to provide details of the exorcism, and included a first-hand eyewitness account by a Lutheran minister who was familiar with the case of poltergeist-like activities occurring in the boy's home. The article caught the attention of a junior at Georgetown University, who became fascinated with the notion of demonic possession. The student was William Peter Blatty, who spent years researching the phenomenon before penning his acclaimed 1970 novel *The Exorcist* and the Academy Award–winning screenplay adaptation of his book.

The details of the 1949 exorcism were kept under wraps by the Catholic Church for decades until a detailed account of the case was published as *Pos-*

sessed: The True Story of an Exorcism by Thomas B. Allen in 1993. Allen, like Blatty, had been allowed access to a diary of the event written by the priests involved in the exorcism, and he also interviewed members of the clergy who had participated. The identity of the possessed was kept secret, while some sources referred to him simply as "the Haunted Boy." The case began with the death of the boy's aunt, a Spiritualist who had taught him how to use a fortune-telling Ouija Board. Soon after her death a poltergeist that seemed intent on tormenting the unfortunate boy manifested itself in the household. Large objects such as dressers, chairs and beds were observed moving by themselves, strange scratchings and other inexplicable noises were heard, and other baffling phenomena occurred. Perhaps the most bizarre aspect of the case were the "brandings" of letters and words that would appear in bloody scratches on the victim's skin that spelled out messages like "HELL" or "SPITE." The boy was eventually taken to a Catholic psychiatric hospital in St. Louis where the grueling ordeal of exorcism was performed by a team of Jesuit priests who eventually cured the boy of his condition.

In the aftermath, Church officials conducted an inquiry into the exorcism that concluded that the Haunted Boy case was not a true instance of demonic possession, but was caused by a "psychosomatic disorder and some kinesis action that we do not understand, but which is not necessarily preternatural."[1] The reason for this conclusion is that the Church has very strict rules and indicators of what actually constitutes full-blown possession. Catholic doctrine recognizes three stages in the process: *infestation*, which corresponds to the action of poltergeist phenomena; *obsession*, where the afflicted person's body is affected; and *possession*, in which the afflicted is able to understand and converse in unknown foreign languages and demonstrates a knowledge of hidden or faraway events. In parapsychological parlance, poltergeist activities only constitute infestation and obsession, while true possession is only indicated by the manifestation of clairvoyance and telepathy. According to interviews with surviving Jesuits who were present during the exorcism, the Haunted Boy did not speak in foreign tongues, read minds or display clairvoyant abilities.

In writing the novel and screenplay for *The Exorcist*, Blatty was well aware of the Church's typology of the phenomenon. In his first draft of the screenplay, Blatty has the Jesuit priest Father Karras explain to the possessed girl's mother: "Poltergeist phenomena are pretty much accepted today, and they happen outside of possession, almost always with disturbed adolescents, in fact. Call it mind over matter. But it isn't supernatural. The same with telepathy."[2] Blatty was obliged to depart from the facts of the Haunted Boy case in order to remove *The Exorcist* from the realm of parapsychology and make it a supernatural event. For instance, in one scene the possessed girl speaks to Karras in the voice of his deceased mother in Greek, thereby evidencing knowledge of a foreign language and clairvoyance in one fell swoop.

While the Haunted Boy affair might not measure up as a legitimate case

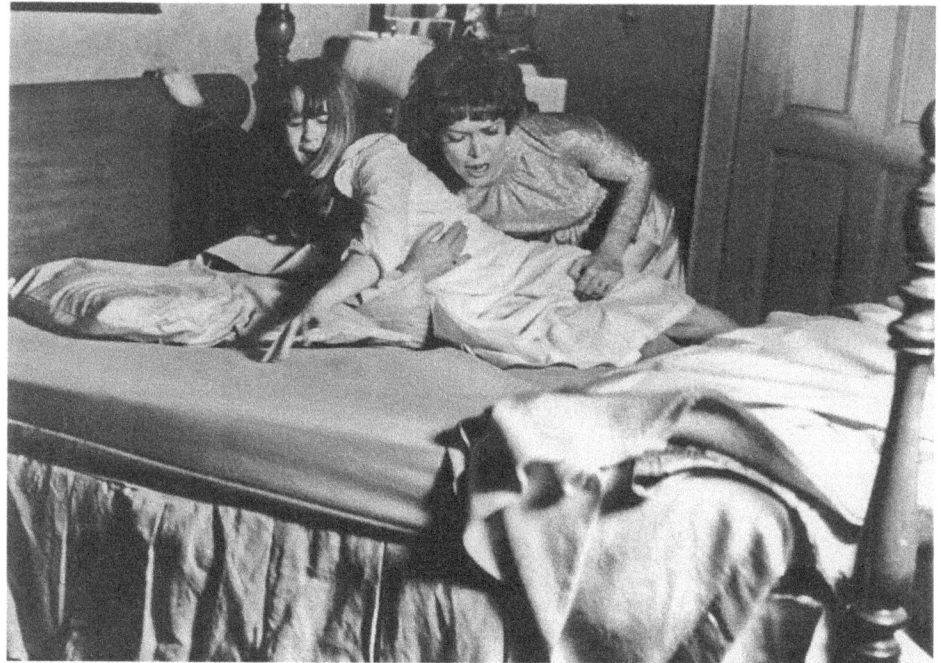

Linda Blair (left) and Ellen Burstyn contend with a levitating bed in *The Exorcist* (1973).

of demonic possession in the Church's opinion, it was, by all accounts, a spectacular poltergeist infestation. The movement of both small and large objects was observed by scores of individuals, including doctors, nurses and priests. One such observer was Karl W. Bubb, Sr., a professor of physics and mathematics at Washington University in St. Louis, who had worked on the Manhattan Project to develop the atomic bomb during World War II and had an ardent interest in parapsychology. Invited by a family member to a house where the boy was staying, the professor reportedly observed a night table in the boy's room rise into the air and levitate toward the ceiling. Bubb was shaken by the manifestation, and later observed, "there is much we have yet to discover concerning the nature of electromagnetism."[3]

Blatty's screenplay, as filmed by director William Friedkin, puts emphasis on the psychokinetic aspect of the possession. *The Exorcist* is replete with large and small moving objects, skin brandings and even the levitation of the possessed person's body in the climactic scene of the film. The plotline follows the general outline of the Haunted Boy case. Innocent adolescent Regan MacNeil (Linda Blair) is at the epicenter of a whirlwind of bizarre phenomena that include telepathy, clairvoyance, and industrial-strength telekinesis. Horrified movie-star mom Chris MacNeil (Ellen Burstyn) is forced to approach the

Catholic Church for permission to perform an exorcism after modern medical science fails to cure her daughter's condition. Jesuit priest/psychologist Damien Karras (Jason Miller) is called to evaluate the case, and finds sufficient paranormal evidence to warrant an exorcism. Grizzled veteran exorcist Father Merrin (Max von Sydow) is appointed to conduct the ceremony. The two priests struggle for their lives, their souls and their sanity as they pit their piety against the demons who are in control of Regan's body. Blatty's script adds a number of fanciful touches to the real-life incident, including having Regan's head turn 180 degrees backward and having the possessed girl commit murder, something that has never happened in any alleged case of demonic possession or poltergeist infestation.

Friedkin's directorial *tour de force* was a monster hit, grossing $82 million at the box office for a modest production cost of only $10 million. *The Exorcist* went on to become an international sensation, especially in the heavily Catholic countries of Europe and South America, where it caused reactions bordering on mass hysteria. Taking a page from Wise's *The Haunting*, Friedkin masterfully evokes a haunted domain of fear and shadow that transforms the homey MacNeil domicile into a spiritual battlefield between the cosmic forces of good and evil. But the director of *The French Connection* also utilizes documentary film-making techniques that add a much needed touch of realism to the proceedings. As in *The Haunting*, there is a particularly innovative use of sound to create a mood of horror. A fine cast, headed by Burstyn's and Miller's knockout performances, provide the dramatic framework that makes the film work. *The Exorcist*'s graphic scenes of vomit and oozing pus would exert a profound influence on the horror film, moving the genre in the direction of greater explicitness and exploitation of the degeneration of the body. It is notable that what is arguably the most influential horror film in the history of cinema is based on a parapsychological event.

In 2001 the Showtime cable TV network released a direct-to-video adaptation of Thomas B. Allen's book about the Haunted Boy affair under its own title, *Possessed*. Timothy Dalton stars as Father Bowdern, the real-life Jesuit priest who was in charge of the 1949 exorcism. Although the screenplay sticks closer to the facts of the case, it does alter many of the key elements in the interest of dramatic license. The film centers around the character of exorcist Father Bowdern, who is here transformed (inaccurately) into a volatile individual struggling with alcoholism and anger issues and tortured over his experiences as a chaplain in World War II. Bowdern's combative disposition serves him well during the exorcism, however, as he challenges the demon with lines of dialogue such as, "Fasten your seat belt, Beelzebub, it's going to be a bumpy ride." Although considerably duller than the fictional treatment in *The Exorcist*, *Possessed* does accurately re-create some of the paranormal goings-on that were observed during the actual event. One subplot concerns amateur parapsychologist Rev. Luther Schulze, the Lutheran minister the family first con-

Regan MacNeil (Linda Blair, left) establishes a telepathic link with Dr. Jean Blair (Louise Fletcher, right) using the sync machine as Father Lamont (Richard Burton) looks on.

sulted about the case, who seems more interested in documenting the poltergeist activity surrounding the boy than in helping his young charge struggle with his affliction.

The Exorcist inspired a number of sequels, but only *Exorcist II: The Heretic* (1977) contains any parapsychological content. Linda Blair reprises her role as Regan MacNeil, the formerly possessed girl whose condition is in remission. Richard Burton plays Father Lamont, a priest assigned by his superiors in the Church to conduct an investigation into Regan's exorcism and the death of Father Merrin. With her mother on location at a movie shoot overseas, Regan has been placed in the care of Dr. Jean Blair (Louise Fletcher), a child psychologist who practices hi-tech medicine at her futuristic kiddie hospital. Dr. Blair has invented a "synchronization machine" that enables mind-to-mind telepathy between two people as a psychiatric tool, which Father Lamont wants to use to probe Regan's amnesia concerning the events of the exorcism. Naturally, the padre re-opens a demonic can of worms while using the machine to mind-meld with Regan, and also receives visions of a mysterious folk healer named Kokumo (James Earl Jones) who resides in "a strange mud-hut village in Africa." Lamont takes off on a quest to find Kokumo, who knows the secrets of the dread "demon of the air, Pazuzu," and once his quest has been completed, returns to *chez* MacNeil in D.C. with Regan in tow for one last telepathy session with the sync machine. In the mind-blowing, incomprehensible climax, Regan and the good Father are locked in mortal combat, writhing on her four-poster bed amid howling winds, thunder and lightning, a swarm of locusts and an earthquake that destroys Lamont and the house of exorcism forever.

A howler of a bad movie, *Exorcist II* appears on many a "worst of" list, and its cinematic depredations have been extensively analyzed in print elsewhere. Suffice it to say Burton's way-over-the-top performance as the demon-obsessed cleric is one of the comedic high points of his illustrious career. The acclaimed British thesp adopts a laughably intent manner as he mumbles inane dialogue about "Kokumo" and "Pazuzu," while chewing on the scenery like a nest of termites. Blair, so noxious in the first movie, has been leeched of all her demonic charms in the sequel, and spends a lot of screen time wandering around her Manhattan penthouse accompanied by a flock of white doves. Nevertheless, the highly flawed screenplay by William Goodhart contains several parapsychological elements, including the telepathy-inducing synchronization machine—an affair with dual headsets, blinking lights and beeping tones that resembles an alpha-wave stimulator. In one scene Regan watches a TV documentary about psi which features a psychic bending spoons in an ESP laboratory. Regan seems to have acquired telepathic abilities in the aftermath of her exorcism, demonstrated in a scene in which she spontaneously cures a little girl of autism by using her telepathy. "First she was talking on the inside," Regan explains, "and then she started talking outside." In spite of its connection of ESP with primordial evil, in this instance the film portrays a positive application of psi in curing mental illness.

Paranormal Horror in the 1970s

The decade of the 1970s witnessed a big uptick in the number and quality of psi-oriented horror films, and the form would attract several up-and-coming directors, including Nicolas Roeg, Brian DePalma and Peter Weir. Roeg's stylish psychic thriller *Don't Look Now* (1973), derived from a story by Daphne du Maurier, was the first out of the gate. Happily married John Baxter (Donald Sutherland) and Laura (Julie Christie) suffer a tragic loss when their young daughter Christine accidentally drowns in a pond on their property in England. The child, who is wearing a bright red-plastic raincoat, is discovered by John after he experiences a premonition that she is in danger.

Cut to Venice several months later, where John is restoring a decrepit Venetian church. It is dreary wintertime in the city, where John and Laura are the only guests at their hotel during the off-season. "A city in aspic," John muses, with "too many shadows." While dining in a local restaurant, they encounter two eccentric British sisters, Wendy (Clelia Matania) and Heather (Hilary Mason). The blind Heather, who supposedly has the "second sight," tells Laura she can see the deceased Christine near her mother. Laura becomes fascinated with the blind seer and attends an impromptu séance where Heather goes into an altered state and proclaims that John is in danger as long as he remains in Venice, and also that he too has psychic abilities. "It's a curse as well as a gift," she explains to the distraught Laura.

When their son, who is still in England, is hospitalized in a minor accident, Laura flies home immediately, leaving John alone in the gloomy city. After seeing her off, he clearly observes his wife and the two sisters standing solemnly in a boat going in the opposite direction. Haunted by the thought that his wife has returned to Venice without his knowledge and fallen under the sway of the psychic, John approaches the police to ascertain Laura's whereabouts. The police, more concerned with catching a mysterious serial killer who is dumping corpses into the canals, nonetheless bring Heather in for questioning. When John receives a call from Laura telling him she is returning to Venice, he winds up escorting the blind woman back to her hotel. Upon departing to meet his wife, he encounters a strange, diminutive figure scurrying through the shadows in a hooded red raincoat. John follows the apparent apparition of his dead daughter to a deserted area, where she is revealed to be a grotesque dwarf wielding a knife. The unfortunate John is brutally killed by the serial murderer, and the film ends with his wife, Heather and Wendy standing on his funeral boat as it glides down the Grand Canal, the vision of his own death he had foreseen with his psychic prescience having come to pass.

Roeg's death-in-Venice mood piece is suffused with dread and decay in every frame, shot in drab, murky colors by cinematographer Anthony Richmond. Roeg shows us John's subjective, alien landscape as he struggles with psychic despair and impending doom. While the pacing is slow and ponderous at times and some of the camera and editing techniques date the film, *Don't Look Now* has the ambience of a ghost story or a disturbing nightmare from which there is no escape. The well-tuned screenplay by Allan Scott and Chris Bryant keeps the viewer perpetually off-balance with its procession of solemn enigmas. Ironically, the film contains a scene of lovemaking between Sutherland and Christie that was considered scandalously explicit at the time, but is tame by today's standards of cinema erotica.

The film convincingly depicts the subtle terrors of being "gifted" with the second sight. The blind psychic, Helen, recalls the sightless prophets of the classical world, such as Tiresias, and appears as a figure of dread, a harbinger of fate. Her demonstrations of prescience are accompanied by epileptic convulsions and other scary histrionics. As his own clairvoyant powers emerge, John is plunged into a maelstrom of fear and gloom where he glimpses his own death and actually envisions a funeral tableau that he will not live to see. His psychic seeing actually leads him to his death while in pursuit of what appears

Latent psychic John Baxter (Donald Sutherland) contemplates death in Venice in Nicolas Roeg's stylish psi-thriller *Don't Look Now* (1973).

to be a vision of his dead daughter. In its evocation of brooding psychic terror, *Don't Look Now* presents a tragic, highly negative portrayal of the paranormal domain.

Stephen King, the reigning god of horror fiction, is the most influential writer in this genre and has had an enormous influence on American horror films, a number of which have been adapted from his works. For his premiere novel, *Carrie* (1973), King drew upon the terrors implicit in the paranormal in his tale of a psychokinetic teenager using her powers to wreak havoc on a small New England town. The basic narrative is interspersed with quotations from pseudobibliographical works of parapsychology such as *Telekinesis: Analysis and Aftermath*, *The Shadow Exploded: Documented Facts and Specific Conclusions Derived from the Case of Carietta White* and *The White Commission Report*. These books were supposedly written in the aftermath of Carrie's psychic outburst, which is being treated as a major historical event on the level of the JFK assassination or the September 11 attacks. It's evident that King had some familiarity with parapsychological concepts of telekinesis that were incorporated into the plot of *Carrie*.

Brian de Palma's 1976 film version was the first of King's novels to be

Carrie White (Sissy Spacek, left) and her mother (Piper Laurie) hold an impromptu prayer meeting in *Carrie* (1976).

lensed, and is considered one of the best adaptations of King's work for the screen. *Carrie* opens with high schooler Carrie White (Sissy Spacek) having her first menstruation in a school shower room, where the extremely shy girl is immediately and deeply humiliated by her teen classmates. Their depredations are interrupted by feisty gym teacher Miss Collins (Betty Buckley), who takes Carrie under her wing and tries to protect her from the cruelty of the other girls. The teacher's harsh penalties over the incident only serve to further alienate Carrie from the other girls, most importantly the popular Chris Hargensen (Nancy Allen), who develops a special animus for the girl. One of the other students, Sue Snell (Amy Irving), however, is sympathetic, and arranges for her boyfriend, the handsome, wavy-haired Tommy Ross (William Katt), to take Carrie to the prom in an effort to humanize her. With the onset of menstruation, however, Carrie has acquired psychokinetic abilities that manifest themselves gradually: a lightbulb bursts, an ashtray on the principal's desk flips over by itself, and a boy is hurled from his bicycle.

Carrie's problems at school are exacerbated by her home life, where she lives in on old, dark house with her crazy religious mother, Margaret (Piper Laurie). Ma White has an extreme antipathy to sex, which she has been careful to impress upon her daughter and which explains Carrie's puzzlement over

Telekinetic teen Carrie White (Sissy Spacek, extreme upper right) unleashes her psychic fury at the school prom in Brian De Palma's *Carrie* (1976).

the onset of her period. Their house is adorned with spooky-looking religious shrines, weird biblical imagery and burning votive candles. "The first sin was intercourse," Mrs. White intones, "the curse of the blood." But Carrie begins to use her PK to back her mother off, and visits the library to read books on psychic phenomena in order to understand her abilities. In the meantime, Chris plots revenge with her lowlife boyfriend Billy Nolan (John Travolta) by arranging to dump a pail full of pig's blood on Carrie when she is elected queen of the prom.

On prom night Carrie must use her PK to physically restrain her mother so that she can attend, and after she has gone Mrs. White quotes scripture, saying, "Thou shalt not suffer a witch to live." At the event, Chris' plan comes off flawlessly, and in a matter of seconds Carrie is transformed from a naive prom queen into a blood-soaked demon of vengeance. Using her telekinetic powers, she traps the students inside the gym and methodically burns, crushes and electrocutes all of the kids and teachers to death. Chris and Billy escape, only to be burned to death in Billy's car. Returning home, Carrie is confronted by her mother, who intends to murder her and stabs her in the back. Stunned, Carrie psychokinetically crucifies her mother with kitchen knives, after which the White house collapses and burns down in a paranormal firestorm. In an epilogue dream sequence, Sue (who survived) is shown placing flowers on Carrie's grave, which is inscribed with the graffiti, "Carrie White burns in Hell," when a hand reaches out of the grave and grabs her leg.

De Palma, formerly known for his Hitchcockian crime thrillers, here ventures into preternatural horror territory for the first time and manages the transition well. The director makes extensive use of slow motion, split screen, and color filters to heighten mood, and coaxes powerful, Academy Award–nominated performances from Sissy Spacek and Piper Laurie. Lawrence D. Cohen's screenplay does a good job of fleshing out the bare bones of the King novel and adding a much-needed depth and resonance to the characters. *Carrie* was a critical and financial success, grossing nearly $34 million in its initial release against a production cost of only $1.8 mil. The film would inspire a tepid sequel, *The Rage: Carrie 2* (1999), a 2002 TV remake, and a 1988 Broadway musical (!).

Carrie paints an extremely unflattering portrait of a psychic individual. Some critics have claimed that King modeled the character on that of Eleanor from Wise's *The Haunting*, and the similarities seem obvious. Both personalities are hysterical, sexually-repressed, and dominated by their mothers. *Carrie* is really two films in one: it is a teen coming-of-age flick combined with a gory horror melodrama. The two threads of the plot don't come together until the moment Carrie is doused at the prom, when the mood abruptly shifts from teen angst to horror. It's a brilliant emotional manipulation of the audience, but Carrie White goes from being a young woman on the verge of emerging into normalcy to a psychic homicidal maniac soaked in blood and wreathed in flame. For most of the film, Carrie is a pathetic character who is forced to use her paranormal gifts to defend herself against her many enemies in a hostile world, including her own mother. Tormented by nearly everyone around her, she lashes out in blind animal fury when she is pushed beyond her emotional limits and afterward presumably burns in hell for all eternity. Yet the audience cheers when the blood-soaked telekinetic girl exacts a terrible vengeance upon her torturers. The novel and film suggest that psychic powers are dangerous to normal humans, and here they emerge in a milieu of isolation, mental and physical cruelty, and perverse religiosity.

Carrie associates paranormal phenomena with the demonic. With a nod to *The Exorcist*, the PK–enabled person is a girl just entering puberty, a detail found in real-life poltergeist cases. In *Carrie*, however, the psychic can direct the poltergeist-like psychokinetic energy at will, something not commonly found in paranormal field research, nor convincingly observed or recorded in the laboratory. However, the notion of directed PK, in which mind-over-matter can effortlessly move large objects weighing several tons, was just fine with movie audiences. In just a few years, paranormally adept Jedi Knights would perform similar feats of major-league telekinesis in the *Star Wars* movies. De Palma would go on to direct another tale of psychokinetic youngsters, *The Fury* (1978).

Five • The Dark Side of ESP

Australian director Peter Weir, who showed he had a penchant for mysterious phenomena in his enigmatic thriller *Picnic at Hanging Rock* (1975), wove another strange tale of the paranormal in *The Last Wave* (1978). The film stars American TV icon Richard Chamberlain as David Burton, an attorney practicing in Sydney, Australia, and providing legal assistance to a poor aboriginal man, Chris Lee (David Gulpilil), who is accused of murdering another aborigine. As he investigates the homicide, David is drawn into contact with aboriginal culture as he strives to understand their motivations and world view. Chris introduces him to a charismatic tribal shaman, Charlie (Nandjiwarra Amagula), who seems to think David possesses the power of prescience.

Strange happenings and anomalous weather phenomena provide an eerie backdrop to the proceedings. Rains of hail, frogs and mud, accompanied by weird-looking rainbows in the sky, seem to be portents of destruction. Perpetual downpours bathe the city in mournful waters. Soon David begins to experience odd dreams in which he sees shadowy aboriginal figures approaching him through the darkness. Shaken by these nightmares, he seeks counsel from Chris, who tells him about the aboriginal conception of the "dreamtime," the oneiric world that is more real than waking reality. Dreams are "like seeing—like hearing—like talking. They are a way of knowing things," Chris tells him. "Dream is a shadow of something real." David also experiences a waking vision as he is stopped in a traffic jam in downtown Sydney: he sees the city underwater, with drowned corpses floating by in the murk. Guided by Chris, David explores a lost aboriginal temple buried far below the city streets, where he finds wall paintings depicting a gigantic wave that has been prophesied to destroy the white man's civilization. He ponders whether his vision of the drowned city will come true.

Weir's end-of-the-world parable generates considerable unease in the viewer, and seems to anticipate current anxieties over global climate change. Burton's personal journey into the world of aboriginal shamanism is equally disquieting, and as in Roeg's *Don't Look Now*, a mood of prescient gloom and watery dissolution pervades the film. Weir's pacing is stately and dignified, and his treatment of aboriginal culture is respectful and is not played for horror. The film is dominated by the performances of David Gulpilil, who starred in Nicolas Roeg's acclaimed *Walkabout* (1971), and Nandjiwarra Amagula, an actual tribal elder who lends the film a wonderful verisimilitude. These native actors provide a striking contrast to Chamberlain's bland, whitebread screen presence. Russell Boyd's gorgeous cinematography and Charles Wain's musical score, which combines native didgeridoo sounds with electronic synthesizer tones, contribute greatly to the film's unnerving mood.

Like *Peter Ibbetson* and *In Dreams*, *The Last Wave* deals with the phenomenon of dream telepathy. David's nocturnal wanderings allow him to make aboriginal connections with native prophecy in the dreamtime. He is also prescient in his waking life, where he has even more intense visions of the watery

Producer Jon Peters, left, confers with star Faye Dunaway on location in this production still from *The Eyes of Laura Mars* (1978).

apocalypse to come. Like Skolimowski's *The Shout* (1979), *The Last Wave* explores the mysterious paranormal world of Australian aboriginal shamanism. With its apocalyptic visions, signs and portents in the skies and Fortean rains of hail and frogs, the film conjures a mood of spiritual uneasiness and possesses a disquieting undertow composed of racial guilt and fears about future survival. The screenplay by Tony Morphett and Petru Popescu was reportedly based on a real-life premonition experience of Weir's in which he had a strong feeling he would find something valuable and then unexpectedly located a buried piece of statuary in a field.

Cult director John Carpenter's first foray into big studio movies was his screenplay for a psychic thriller entitled *The Eyes of Laura Mars*, which was optioned by producer Jon Peters as a vehicle for his wife, Barbra Streisand. The pop diva reportedly rejected the role due to the film's level of violence, so Peters cast Faye Dunaway, fresh from her Academy Award–winning performance in *Network* (1976), in the title role. Carpenter's script was extensively re-written by David Goodman, and Irvin Kershner was signed on to direct the project, which was released in 1978.

Laura Mars (Dunaway) is a highly successful New York fashion photographer whose gory photo spreads feature scantily-clad models in sexually suggestive and violent poses. Life begins to imitate art when Laura has a vivid dream about the murder of her colleague, Doris Spenser (Meg Mundy), as seen through the killer's perspective stabbing Doris's eyes out with an ice pick. Calling Doris's number she gets no answer. Later she attends an exhibition of her work at a Soho art gallery, where she is questioned by good-looking stranger John Neville (Tommy Lee Jones), who seems to have a deep curiosity about her controversial work and questions her at length about her photos. The night is marred when news comes that Doris has been found murdered in the same manner Laura envisioned in her dream.

Laura begins having waking visions of other murders, and when her friends start turning up dead she is brought in for questioning by Neville, who is in reality an NYPD homicide detective. Lieutenant Neville shows her crime-scene photographs of unsolved murders never released to the public that are staged exactly like Laura's fashion spreads. It seems Laura is able to psychically tune into violent events with her precognitive/clairvoyant vision. In a similar way she is able to see the crimes subjectively, through the eyes of the murderer in a manner analogous to the way she captures her images in a camera. As the bodies pile up, suspects come into sharper focus. Is the killer her ex-husband, Michael (Raul Julia), her ex-con roadie Tommy Ludlow (Brad Dourif), or someone else? And can Neville protect Laura from becoming the ultimate victim of the serial murderer?

Many critics have compared the film to an Italian *giallo*, and it bears a particular resemblance to Lucio Fulci's *The Psychic*, which had been released a year or so earlier. Both films feature young female psychics having graphic visions of murders while being stalked by the killer. *The Eyes of Laura Mars*, however, is far removed from Euroculture and instead is immersed in the cocaine-crazed, Studio 54 disco milieu of America in the 1970s. This loopy pop ambience tends to distract the viewer from the seriousness of the theme. The redoubtable Ms. Dunaway is here reduced to mugging with her eyes bulging out of their sockets; her bug-eyed visage is meant to visually emphasize her psychic sight, and there are frequent closeups of her glaring eyeballs as she peers into the future. Peters's meddling with Carpenter's script leads to some disastrous moments, such as the film's silly ending, but despite all this *Laura Mars* does contain one important insight concerning the nature of ESP, which is that it seems to be more prevalent in individuals who have an artistic or highly visual mental orientation.

Richard Burton, fresh from his triumph as the paranormally-obsessed priest in *Exorcist II: The Heretic*, returned to the screen in another psychic melodrama, *The Medusa Touch* (1978). Burton plays eccentric British author John Morlar, who is nearly beaten to death by an assailant in the film's opening sequence. Pronounced dead by the coroner, Morlar somehow revives and is rushed to the intensive care unit of a nearby hospital, where he is swathed in bandages and hooked up to life-support machines. Inspector Brunel (Lino Ventura), a French policeman working in Britain as part of an exchange program, is assigned to investigate the attempted murder. Brunel soon discovers a tangled web of mystery surrounding the enigmatic author when he interviews Morlar's psychiatrist, the blonde, statuesque Dr. Zonfeld (Lee Remick). As the psychiatrist reveals details of her patient's past, Morlar's life unrolls in flashbacks.

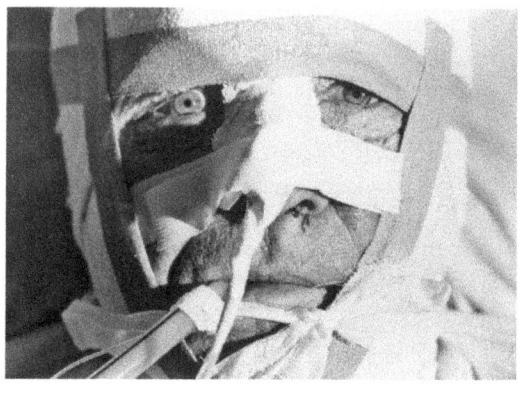

Morlar (Richard Burton) can still project his psi powers from the intensive care unit in *The Medusa Touch* (1973).

Morlar claims that he's a man with a "gift for disaster," who possesses paranormal powers of mind. Throughout his life, Morlar has used his alleged psychic gift to visit vengeance upon his enemies, including his mother and father, a cruel headmaster, a judge, and finally his own unfaithful wife and her lover. Not content merely to settle personal scores, the misanthropic psychic adopts extreme left-wing political views and turns his paranormal wrath on "a besotted establishment," using his telekinesis to cause a string of spectacular disasters while believing he is doing "God's dirty work." Dr. Zonfeld appears to share Brunel's skepticism about Morlar's "Medusa touch," but Brunel's own doubts about the reality of psi begin to crumble as the investigation unfolds. Going through the writer's journals, he finds cryptic entries like, "to build a cenotaph, first choose a million victims," and, "the walls of Jericho fell to the power of thought, so what is the meaning of impossibility?" Brunel watches documentary films of psychics performing dramatic feats of telekinesis in parapsychology labs, and is reluctantly forced to admit that psi might be real after all. There is also the matter of Morlar's miraculous, death-defying recovery, as the psychic seems to be rebuilding his strength in order to launch another round of mega-disasters. Another odd factor is that Brunel's superiors seem to have an intense interest in obtaining the writer's journals, which they believe may hold secrets about British politicians gleaned by Morlar's ESP that could lead to "a dozen Watergates."

Richard Burton as the homicidal psychic John Morlar in *The Medusa Touch* (1973).

Eventually, Zonfeld admits that she became convinced of the truth of Morlar's psi powers when she witnessed him using his psychokinesis to crash an airliner into an office skyscraper, causing hundreds of deaths. She reveals herself as the attempted murderer, and after a second attempt to dispatch Morlar at the hospital fails, she opts to commit suicide. Brunel, now a believer, finds evidence in Morlar's journals that the psychic is going to use his PK to collapse a cathedral on the heads of the Queen and other high dignitaries during a ceremonial visit. No one in the government will take the Frenchman's warning seriously, so Brunel races to the hospital to pull the plug on Morlar's life support as the building collapses during the ceremony. Even this gambit fails, however, as Morlar survives again and indicates that his next feat will be to cause a nuclear explosion at an atomic power plant.

In predictable fashion, Burton overacts shamelessly in some scenes, but fortunately it's not enough to derail this surprisingly effective psychological and parapsychological thriller. The famed British thesp portrays the Morlar character as a combination of Carrie White and Hannibal Lecter. Lead players Lino Ventura and Lee Remick carry most of the film, while Burton remains a remote figure in the background. Director Jack Gold constructs a suspenseful, low-key crime and ESP melodrama around the intriguing screenplay by John Briley in this classy British/French co-production.

The Medusa Touch seems to play upon a particularly British anxiety regarding the notion of witchcraft. For many years the subject was forbidden from being filmed or exhibited in the UK, but these restrictions began to be lifted in the 1970s with films like *The Wicker Man* (1972). *The Medusa Touch* portrays psi as basically demonic, since Morlar's psychic abilities are associated solely with death, destruction and nihilism, and are used only for revenge or other misanthropic purposes. The destruction of the cathedral at the film's climax seems to symbolize the triumph of Morlar's diabolic powers over those of godly righteousness. Note that one of the films on ESP research Inspector Brunel peruses is purportedly real documentary footage of Russian psychic

Nina Kulagina moving small objects via telekinesis, which looks unconvincing and has since been proven an elaborate fraud.

Burton's John Morlar is not the only lay-a-bed psychic plying his telekinetic trade from a hospital room. The Australian production *Patrick* (1978) stars Robert Thompson as the title character, a young man who has been in a coma since he murdered his mother and her lover by electrocuting them in a bathtub with an electric heater. Patrick has been kept on life support for three years at a private hospital run by Dr. Roget (Robert Helpmann), but has shown no change in his condition until newbie nurse Kathy Jacquard (Susan Penhaligon) comes on the scene. Nurse Kathy's tender touch seems to have a positive effect on the comatose young man, who suddenly develops telekinetic powers that enable him to type messages on a typewriter in order to communicate with her. Matters get out of hand, though, when Patrick becomes jealous of Kathy's lovers and uses his PK to lash out at her ex-husband and new boyfriend and to wreak havoc and murder upon the hospital staff. While Kathy and Dr. Roget struggle to pull the plug on their paranormal patient's life support, Patrick defends himself with telekinetic fury.

This minor Aussie effort directed by Richard Franklin is typical of the horror film approach to the subject of psi. As in *Psychic Killer*, an individual acquires telekinetic powers as a result of an incestuous mother-son relationship gone bad, and his psychic abilities have no redeeming social value and are used only for purposes of destruction and revenge. The film's modest budget precludes the depiction of objects moving by themselves, so much of the psychic goings-on occur offscreen. Patrick, with his glassy eyes staring straight ahead while lying prone in his hospital bed, is an unnerving figure described as a "creature of the Id," who would return in a sequel, *Patrick Still Lives* (1980).

High Concept, High Technology Psi

Cinema technology took a quantum leap in the late 1970s, when the emergence of mass-market computer technology began to make its mark on the movie business. Films like *Star Wars* (1977), *Close Encounters* (1977), *Alien* (1979) and *Raiders of the Lost Ark* (1981) were released in the new large-screen, 70mm format with Dolby stereo sound and provided filmgoers with a new level of moviegoing experience. This new technological sophistication was first applied to the world of the paranormal in *wunderkind* director Steven Spielberg's production of *Poltergeist* (1982).

The summer of 1982 would soon become known in the movie biz as the "Spielberg Summer" because of the mega-success of *Poltergeist* and *E.T.: The Extraterrestrial*, which were released within weeks of each other during that season. Due to Spielberg's commitments to *E.T.*, cult fave Toby Hooper, who had lensed the horror sleeper *The Texas Chainsaw Massacre* (1974), was brought in

Five • The Dark Side of ESP 95

The Freeling family, Oliver Robins (left), Craig T. Nelson, JoBeth Williams and Dominique Dunne, watch their property values plummet in *Poltergeist* (1982).

to direct. Spielberg's first effort as a producer was a near disaster, however, due to his micro-management of the production, which included directing many scenes himself and making numerous creative decisions on the film. Due to the contentious nature of the production, the Director's Guild was called upon to decide who had actually directed the movie, and finally awarded directorial credit to Hooper. The result, however, is that *Poltergeist* plays more like a Spielberg film than a Hooper film, and has affinities with the director's other works such as *Close Encounters* and *E.T.*

The action in *Poltergeist* centers on the Freeling family, a suburban clan residing in the newly-minted community of Cuesta Verde Estates in Southern California. Things start to get weird when the youngest child, five-year-old Carol Anne (Heather O'Rourke), starts communicating with mysterious entities inside the family's TV set, announcing, "They're here." Soon other anomalous phenomena begin manifesting in the household, baffling and alarming father Steven (Craig T. Nelson), a real estate salesman, and stay-at-home mom Diane (JoBeth Williams). Silverware bends, objects move by themselves, strange electrical effects plague the household and even more bizarre events threaten the other children, eight-year-old son Robbie (Oliver Robins) and sixteen-year-old Dana (Dominique Dunne). Carol Anne, who has been consorting with the "TV People," is whisked away into another dimension inside

UC Irvine parapsychologists Richard Lawson (left), Beatrice Straight and Martin Casella freak out over the paranormal goings-on in *Poltergeist* (1982).

her closet and disappears into a phantom realm where she can be heard but not seen.

Finally convinced of the preternatural nature of these happenings, Steven consults with UC Irvine parapsychologist Dr. Lesh (Beatrice Straight), who descends upon the Freeling home along with assistant ghostbusters Ryan (Richard Lawson) and Marty (Martin Casella) in tow. Their previous experience in documenting psychokinesis was filming a child's toy that rolled seven feet across a linoleum surface so slowly that the movement was only visible using time-lapse photography. The researchers then witness the dramatic sight of a swarm of objects whirling through the air in Carol Anne's room, including a light bulb that screws itself into a floating lamp and a vinyl record being played by the pointed end of a child's compass. Stunned, Dr. Lesh opines that the disturbances are being caused by a poltergeist rather than a traditional haunting. The parapsychologists set up cameras, audio recorders and other devices to document and measure the psychic events in the Freeling house, but in the end they cannot explain or interact with the paranormal forces at work there, acknowledging only that there are "measurable physical signs in this house."

Realizing she cannot help get Carol Anne back, Dr. Lesh calls upon the services of "extraordinary clairvoyant" Tangina (Zelda Rubinstein), a diminutive middle-aged woman who has reportedly "cleaned many houses." "Y'all mind hangin' back?" she drawls in a Southern accent upon entering, "You're jammin' my frequencies." The pint-sized psychic quickly puts her ESP to work, declaring that Carol Anne is still alive and in the Freeling house, but is threatened both by the spirits of the dead and an entity she calls "The Beast," who is attracted to the innocent child's life force. Tangina formulates a plan to retrieve their daughter by passing Diane through the dimensional portal in the girl's closet after tying a heavy rope around her body. The oddball plan succeeds, and once Carol Anne is rescued the paranormal forces abate and Tangina declares, "This house is clean."

While in the process of moving out of their formerly haunted abode, Steven learns that his real estate developer boss, Mr. Teague (James Karen), had the house built on top of an ancient Indian burial ground, which is the underlying reason for the poltergeist disturbances. Meanwhile, The Beast returns to make another grab at Carol Anne while an earthquake rocks the Freeling house and rotting corpses from the former graveyard emerge from the ground. As the Freelings flee their formerly happy home for the local Holiday Inn, McTeague watches in horror and amazement as the house seems to fold in on itself and vanish into the phantom zone.

Industrial Light & Magic's special effects are the real star of *Poltergeist*, creating a dazzling paranormal environment that frequently overpowers the actors. The film's graphic gore effects (including a hallucinatory scene in which a man's face is torn off), were deemed so distressing to young audiences that a new movie rating category, PG-13, was created after its release. The polished Hooper/Spielberg direction keeps the action moving with little dead space, but the screenplay by Spielberg, Michael Grais and Mark Victor sometimes seems more like a collection of individual episodes than a coherent whole. The writers also borrow liberally from an episode of TV's *The Twilight Zone*, in which a little girl is lost in the fifth dimension. Still, the famous "Spielberg Touch" transformed *Poltergeist* into crowd-pleasing movie gold as the film grossed over $76 million domestically, making it the 8th most popular release of 1982. The cast of mostly unknowns turn in workmanlike performances, but Zelda Rubinstein steals the show as the all-knowing, feisty little medium Tangina. The film was nominated for three Academy Awards, for visual effects, musical score and sound effects, but did not win in any category.

The film occasionally depicts psychic phenomena as reported in real-life poltergeist cases. In one early scene, Diane turns away from the kitchen table for a moment and turns back to find that the kitchen chairs have been neatly stacked on top of the table. Another scene portrays one of the most mind-bending of poltergeist tricks known as an *apport*, in which material objects are made to pass through solid matter. In one recent case, for instance, a number of eggs were apported through a closed refrigerator door without breaking their shells. The film contains a scene in the which a shower of apported jewelry cascades through the home's downstairs ceiling from a room upstairs. Interestingly, director Tobe Hooper claims to have experienced poltergeist activity firsthand. As a teenager, Hooper reportedly witnessed doors breaking in, dishes flying around the residence and other otherworldly phenomena after the death of his father.

Poltergeist also reflects on academic parapsychology in scenes where psychologist Dr. Lesh examines her career choice. "Parapsychology isn't something you master in," she laments. "There are no certificates of graduation. No licenses to practice." She then outlines the limitations of her discipline: "I'm absolutely terrified. It's all the things that we don't understand. I feel like the proto-human coming out of the forest primeval and seeing the moon for

Carla Moran (Barbara Hershey) is subjected to the psychic attacks of *The Entity* (1983).

the first time and throwing rocks at it." Given this sentiment, it's no wonder the film rejects scientific parapsychology in favor of good old-fashioned mediumship. In the end, although it invokes the rational universe of science, *Poltergeist* predictably diverts into the realm of the supernatural with its luminous phantoms, demonic hallucinations and gateways to infinity.

Two sequels would follow, *Poltergeist II: The Other Side* (1986) and *Poltergeist III* (1988), both of which had little or nothing to do with parapsychology. The franchise was thought to be "cursed" in the wake of a series of tragic misfortunes that plagued members of the cast, which was the subject of a *True Hollywood Stories* documentary on cable TV's E! Channel. Dominique Dunne, who played the Freeling's teenage daughter, was murdered by her live-in boyfriend in November of 1982, and Heather O'Rourke, who portrayed little Cathy Anne, died shortly before the release of *Poltergeist III* of complications from a congenital birth defect. The tragic legacy of the "Poltergeist Curse" is attributed to the fact that effects technicians reportedly used real human remains during the scenes of the dead popping out of their coffins in the film's gruesome climax.

The Entity (1983), released in the following year, presented a much more mature and intelligent examination of the poltergeist phenomenon. Inspired by a real-life case investigated by UCLA parapsychologists, the film stars Barbara Hershey as Carla Moran, a hard-working Southern California single mom struggling to raise three children. Carla is suddenly plagued by a ghostly presence that sexually violates her repeatedly, causes objects to fly around the house and sparks weird electrical disturbances. The monstrous entity even violates her in front of her own children and attempts to kill her by making her lose control of her car. Seeking psychiatric help for her afflictions at a local clinic, she is confronted by the ultra-skeptical shrink Dr. Phil Sneiderman (Ron Silver), whose medical expertise leads him to diagnose her as suffering from a hysterical sex disorder.

Seeking to understand her condition, Carla meets two UCLA parapsychologists by chance in a local bookstore. When Gene Kraft (Richard Brestoff) and Joe Mehan (Raymond Singer) experience the strange odors, cold spots and electrical disturbances at the Moran home, the ghostbusters use recording instruments to capture evidence of "classic poltergeist activity." They refer the case to the head of the UCLA parapsychology unit, Dr. Jean Cooley (Jacqueline Brookes), who conceives an elaborate plan to trap the entity and thereby prove its existence. An exact copy of Carla's house is created as a natural environment for the poltergeist, where she will be the bait in the trap. The scientists hope to utilize liquid helium, which is so cold it freezes all molecular motion, to put the entity on ice once it manifests. Dr. Sneiderman gets wind of the experiment and tries to have the university administration shut it down over concern for his patient's safety, but he lacks the political clout to accomplish his aim. Predictably, when the poltergeist shows up the elaborate scheme goes haywire as the entity takes control of the scientists' equipment and tries to kill Carla with bursts of ultra-frigid liquid helium. Even the arch-skeptic Sniederman is convinced of the psychic reality of the entity as it wreaks havoc at the lab before vanishing once more. A postscript informs us that the poltergeist attacks on Carla Moran continue, but have diminished in intensity.

Barbara Hershey's intense performance as the entity's psychologically shattered but still-defiant victim of a force beyond human comprehension is superb. Likewise, Ron Silver's portrayal of the doubting Thomas psychologist Dr. Sniederman is intense and convincing, and the film's principal dramatic *frisson* is the conflict between the well-meaning skeptic and his tormented patient. Unfortunately, veteran Sidney J. Furie's direction is plodding at times, and the screenplay by Frank DeFelitta, adapted from his novel, is overlong at more than two hours. Also, the numerous scenes of Carla being raped by the entity are repetitious and smack of exploitation. *The Entity* received an R-rating due to an explicit nude scene in which Carla's naked body is fondled by unseen hands, and many critics felt the film was overly explicit and even misogynistic. In spite of critical disdain and its R-rating, the film did modestly well at the box office, its mixture of psi and sexuality proving to be a draw.

Despite the film's flaws, *The Entity* is a compelling account of a poltergeist manifestation which, like *The Exorcist*, is a fictionalized version of real events.

In August of 1974 a team of researchers from UCLA's parapsychology lab began documenting a series of poltergeist disturbances at the home of a Culver City woman named Doris Bither. Writer Frank DeFelitta's 1978 novel *The Entity* was based on the facts of the Bither case, but the film's climax, in which parapsychologists utilize millions of dollars' worth of hi-tech equipment to trap the creature in liquid helium, is pure science fiction. The film's tag line, "Based on a true story that isn't over yet," leaves the impression that the more spectacular events depicted in the film also occurred in real life, which serves to muddy up the parapsychological facts of the case. In typical Hollywood fashion, events are exaggerated and overblown for the sake of melodrama. Nonetheless, *The Entity* comes off as a thinking person's version of *Poltergeist*, and is a sincere effort to explore this paranormal enigma in a realistic and informative fashion despite the narrative's frequently lurid subject matter.

The release of *The Entity* on DVD was accompanied by an extra feature entitled "The Entity Files," which contains a fascinating interview with parapsychologist Dr. Barry Taff on the Doris Bither case. Dr. Taff, who served as a technical advisor on the film and became the character "Gene Kraft" in the screenplay, was a research assistant at the UCLA Neuropsychiatric Institute's Parapsychology Lab when he became one of the principal investigators on the case. The documentary follows the UCLA researcher's probe into the reality of the phenomenon and presents still photos and videos of poltergeist activity that make for compelling viewing.

Canadian shockmeister David Cronenberg, creator of horrors such as *They Came from Within* (1975), *Rabid* (1976) and *The Brood* (1979), as well as the psi-oriented sci-fi thriller *Scanners* (1981), directed the screen version of Stephen King's ESP chiller *The Dead Zone* (1983). The protagonist is everyman Johnny Smith (Christopher Walken), an ordinary joe who teaches high school English in a small New England town and is in love with colleague Sarah Bracknell (Brooke Adams), whom he hopes to marry. Driving home from Sarah's place one stormy night, Johnny collides with a truck and winds up in a coma for five years. When he awakens, he finds that Sarah has married, is now a mother, and that he must struggle through a long and painful rehabilitation before he can start to pick up the broken threads of his former life.

During his long recuperation he discovers he has the psychic ability to apprehend hidden things about people just by physically touching them, an ability that might be called bio-psychometry in parapsychological terms. He clairvoyantly envisions that the house of the nurse who is treating him is on fire and her daughter is in danger, all of which turns out to be true. Johnny further amazes the clinic's chief physician, Dr. Sam Weizak (Herbert Lom), by correctly locating Weizak's mother, who he has thought dead since World War II. John's psychic powers make him a minor celebrity and bring him to the attention of Sherriff George Bannerman (Tom Skerritt), who enlists his help in bringing a local serial murderer dubbed, "The Castle Rock Killer" to justice. Working with Bannerman and the police, Johnny nails the killer by handling evidence the murderer has touched, which enables him to project himself inside a vision of past events and ascertain the killer's identity. Afterward, Johnny feels a deep sense of guilt because he was subjectively at the crime site but could not act to avert the murder.

When Johnny shakes the hand of up-and-coming politician Greg Stillson (Martin Sheen) at a political rally, he has a prescient vision of a future in which Stillson, who is secretly a psycho, will become President and start a nuclear war that will presumably destroy the world as we know it. Believing in the dead certainty of this prophecy, Johnny decides to assassinate the candidate at a campaign event. His resolve is further strengthened by the fact that his psychic gift is consuming him physically and will eventually kill him; as his visions get more powerful, his body gets weaker. Johnny is killed by Stillson's bodyguards during the assassination attempt, but in dying knows he has perpetrated a political assassination on Stillson that will prevent the nuclear holocaust he has foreseen.

This was Cronenberg's first movie project that he did not script himself, and the director's lack of intimacy with the material serves to make his treatment somewhat remote. The wintry environment of the film's New England locale (actually filmed in Canada) also has a chilling effect on the film's emotional impact. Casting the quirky Christopher Walken in the lead role serves to make the John Smith character seem eccentric and unappealing. The screenplay by Jeffrey Boam neatly condenses the gist of King's lengthy novel and focuses its dramatic impact more keenly. Cronenberg's signature theme of the horrors of bodily degeneration is realized in the consumption of Johnny Smith by his psychic "gift," but there's little use of the graphic gore and disturbing special effects that grace more quintessentially Cronenbergian productions such as *Scanners* (1981) and *Videodrome* (1983). While it is competently made and reasonably well-acted, *The Dead Zone* is one of the director's less horrific and therefore less effective films.

Unlike some of King's other works, *The Dead Zone* takes a stab at portraying psychic phenomena in a positive light. Johnny Smith is an upright, moral man who uses his psi abilities to warn his fellow citizens about impending disasters, aids in bringing a serial killer to justice, and ultimately saves the entire world from nuclear destruction. But King and Cronenberg also portray the protagonist's abilities with a hint of the demonic, because, after all, it is a horror movie. *The Dead Zone*'s Johnny Smith joins the ranks of comatose psychics in *The Medusa Touch* and *Patrick*, and his ESP is enabled by a debilitating sickness that is consuming him. The film draws inspiration from the real-life bio of Dutch psychic Peter Hurkos, who reputedly acquired ESP after sustaining a head injury and used his powers to help the police solve baffling crimes. Smith's psychometry, which combines aspects of clairvoyance and precognition, has been studied as a genuine psychic ability. The film inspired a Canadian made-for-television series, *The Dead Zone* (2001–2002), starring Anthony Michael Hall as a resurrected Johnny Smith.

King's fellow horror writer Dean R. Koontz conceived his own novel of psychic terror, *Hideaway*, which was filmed under its own title and released in 1995. As the film opens, antiques dealer Hatch Harrison (Jeff Goldblum) is involved in a catastrophic car accident that leaves him hovering on the threshold between life and death. Pulled from the wreckage by his wife, Lindsey (Christine Lahti), and rushed to the emergency room, he is pulled back from the brink by brilliant surgeon Dr. Jonas Nyebern (Alfred Molina), who saves his life using an experimental technique he has developed. After his near-death experience, Hatch finds he is experiencing psychic visions of brutal murders as seen through the killer's eyes. It turns out he has developed a telepathic link with the murderer, who is Dr. Nyebern's son Jeremy (Jeremy Sisto), a Satan worshipper brought back from the brink of death by this same advanced medical procedure used to revive Hatch.

Matters get really dicey when Jeremy becomes aware of Hatch's telepathic presence, makes the mind-to-mind link 2-way, and begins stalking Hatch. Attempting to understand his paranormal condition, Hatch consults Tarot card–reading psychic Rose Orwetto (Rae Dawn Chong), who informs him that he and Jeremy are linked through their near-death experiences, which have transformed them into cosmic agents of good and evil. Rose is later murdered by Jeremy, who has discovered Hatch's identity and kidnaps his daughter, Regina (Alicia Silverstone), in order to sacrifice her to Satan. Using the psychic link, Hatch tracks Jeremy to his hidden lair as the final battle between the forces of light and darkness is joined.

This was director Brett Leonard's second feature, made after *The Lawnmower Man* (1992), another special effects–laden movie involving murder and ESP adapted from a Stephen King short story (see Chapter 8). The screenplay by Neal Jimenez and Andrew Kevin Walker is a clichéd and predictable reworking of plot material from *The Eyes of Laura Mars* (1978). Author Koontz was reportedly so upset with the screen treatment of his novel that he sued (unsuccessfully) to have his name removed from the credits. The psychic angle is conveyed via the usual subjective camerawork showing the killer's POV during the murders, but the special effects sequences at the film's opening and climax, depicting demonic and angelic forces, move the film out of scientific parapsychology and into the realm of the supernatural. As in *Resurrection* and *The Dead Zone*, the film's protagonist acquires psychic powers after having a near-death experience, something sometimes reported in real-life NDE cases.

The Bell Witch Project

In the year 1846 a curious book appeared on what would prove to be the first well-documented poltergeist case in the United States. The author of the book was Richard Bell, who provided details of an infestation that had plagued the Bell family in their home in rural Robertson County, Tennessee, in 1817. The ghostly manifestations were attributed to an unseen entity that came to be called the "Bell Witch," and this famous historical case would become the basis for the film *An American Haunting* (2005), based on the novel *The Bell Witch — An American Haunting* by Brent Monahan.

As the story opens, John Bell (Donald Sutherland) is involved in a dispute over land and debt with his neighbor, Kate Batts (Gaye Brown). When the local church council rules in favor of Bell despite the fact that he has charged usurious rates of interest, Batts is furious, and threatens, "Darkness will fall upon you and your precious daughter, too." Soon afterward, Bell's daughter Betsy (Rachel Hurd-Wood) begins hearing odd sounds in her bedroom, which quickly escalate into a full-blown poltergeist infestation. Doors open and close by themselves, pages are ripped out of the family Bible and fly around the room, and most dramatically of all, an unseen force lifts Betsy off her feet and repeatedly slaps her face as she is suspended in midair. Even the town's skeptical schoolteacher, Richard Powell (James D'Arcy), is forced to admit the reality of the phenomenon after witnessing these dramatic events.

Hatch Harrison (Jeff Goldblum) ponders his telepathic link to a serial killer in *Hideaway* (1995).

When Betsy's mother, Lucy (Sissy Spacek), discovers bloodstains (presumably menstrual blood) on her daughter's nightgown, she begins to suspect there may be hidden motivations influencing the weird events. As the unseen entity acquires a voice and begins to speak to the Bell family, John Bell's behavior becomes more erratic. He pays a visit to Kate Batts and begs her to remove the curse, but she tells him, "I didn't curse you, you cursed yourself." In the wake of this revelation, John attempts to kill himself but fails when his musket does not fire, presumably through the action of the poltergeist. As John begins to succumb to a mysterious illness, Lucy comes to apprehend that Betsy has been sexually molested by her father, and that this is the underlying cause of the Bell family's afflictions. Falling deeper and deeper into a trancelike state, John's desire for suicide is sated when he accepts a spoonful of poison from a feminine hand (that is either his daughter's or that of an apparition) as Lucy looks on approvingly.

Director/scenarist Courtney Solomon crafts a restrained, measured combination of preternatural thriller and costume melodrama that sticks to the basic facts reported about the Bell Witch case. The imputation of incestuous behavior to John Bell is a modern, Freudian interpretation that does not appear in contemporaneous accounts of the case, however. The film also contains a framing story set in the present day that suggests the manifestations will continue in modern times. Solomon shoots in dark, somber tones in the Bell house interiors and misty Tennessee woods to create a drab, claustrophobic environment, but although this approach is appropriate to the film's period setting and subject matter, the muddy-looking colors also suggest the production's modest budget did not allow for more expensive lighting setups. Earnest performances by veteran screen psychics Sutherland (*Don't Look Now*) and Spacek (*Carrie*) fall flat against this dull, uninspiring backdrop. The film is also marred by repetitive sequences of Betsy grappling with unseen forces in her bedroom accompanied by heavy breathing and other spooky noises on the soundtrack.

Despite these deficiencies, *An American Haunting* presents many of the facts of the Bell Witch case accurately. The attacks centered around the teenaged Betsy, who was the typical adolescent "focus" that poltergeists seem to attach themselves to; in reality there was probably no witch's curse involved in the proceedings. The film's presentation of the phenomenon is more measured in comparison with the spectacular treatment of the theme in films like *The Exorcist* or *The Entity*. Unfortunately, the film-makers also muddy the waters by adding the ghostly apparition of a little girl, who seems to have nothing to do with the plot, and later apparitions of Betsy herself. The film was initially released in the UK in 2005 before being re-edited and shown in America, where it was generally panned by the critics and performed poorly at the box-office.

A Paranormal Legacy of Horror

The world of the paranormal has provided film-makers with a wealth of inspiration for some of the most popular and influential horror films of all time. *The Exorcist*, *Carrie* and *Poltergeist* are still frightening viewing audiences decades after their release and are considered classics of the genre, while other excursions into psychic territory such as *Don't Look Now*, *The Last Wave*, *The Dead Zone*, *The Entity* and *The Medusa Touch* provided artistically satisfying and thoughtful insights into the mysteries of the preternatural. The theme has attracted a bevy of world-class directorial talent, including the likes of Robert Wise, Brian De Palma, Peter Weir, Nicolas Roeg, David Cronenberg and Steven Spielberg.

But in the process psi has acquired the trappings of the demonic, as horror films tap into some of our deepest religious and philosophical anxieties. Like the door leading to an alternate dimension in *Poltergeist*, psi-oriented horror exploits humankind's atavistic fear of the unknown that lies beyond the bounds of consensus reality. More than any other genre, horror movies provide a generally negative view of the paranormal, and a number of them blur the distinction between the paranormal and the supernatural. Screen psychics like Carrie White, John Morlar and Johnny Smith are a uniformly unhappy lot of tortured individuals who struggle with mind-bending forces beyond human comprehension and are ultimately consumed in the process.

· SIX ·

Alien ESP

The "forbidden science" of UFOlogy, the study of the UFO phenomenon, has an even lower reputation than parapsychology, which at least has a modicum of scientific respectability. Most scientists, including parapsychologists, avoid UFOlogy like the plague and consider it a mystical New Age quasi-religion that has little, if anything, to do with orthodox science. While there is some truth to this contention, UFOlogy exists on a continuum that extends from a "nuts and bolts" scientific approach on one end to wide-eyed, irrational mysticism on the other. But some of the more thoughtful, scientifically-oriented UFO researchers have delineated areas in which the mysterious realms of ESP and UFOs overlap.

Writing in 1980 on a series of alien abductions in California's Tujunga Canyon, parapsychologist D. Scott Rogo noted: "For years, UFO researchers have been aware of what is popularly called 'paranormal fallout'—often a person who has interacted with a UFO will experience psychic events for years to come, apparently as an indirect outcome of his experience." He goes on to observe, "Some UFO victims also become poltergeist victims,"[1] and cites several examples of this occurrence in UFO literature. More recently, Harvard abduction researcher John Mack wrote in 1999 that abductees experience transformational changes in attitude and lifestyle, including the "apparent expansion of psychic or intuitive abilities ... the collapse of space/time perception, a sense of entering other dimensions of reality or universes."[2] Mind-bending encounters with extraterrestrial forces that confer psychic powers on otherwise ordinary humans is a theme that has featured in a number of science fiction films, including *Forbidden Planet, Five Million Years to Earth, Close Encounters of the Third Kind* and *The Mothman Prophecies*.

Aliens had been portrayed as possessing telepathic abilities, presumably a sub-function of their vastly superior intelligence, for many years in science fiction literature. When the sci-fi film boom of the 1950s came along, mind-melding extraterrestrials naturally transitioned to the silver screen, although this trend was not as prevalent as has been previously supposed. Alien telepaths frequently used their powers to dominate and subdue non-psychic earthlings in thrillers such as *Killers from Space, Not of This Earth* and *Village of the Damned*. On the other hand, benevolent aliens like E.T. and Mr. Spock used their mind reading abilities for positive, human-friendly ends. When alien abduction cases began to surface in the 1960s, abductees reported that the UFOnauts communicated via telepathy — a case of life imitating art, or vice versa?

And if aliens used mind-to-mind communication methods, might it not be possible that human psychics could read the minds of extraterrestrials and tap into their hidden agenda? This scenario actually occurred when U.S. Government remote viewers were reportedly run against extraterrestrial targets at the behest of military intelligence agencies. The "aliens vs. psychics" conflict has also played out on the screen in movies such as *The Crawling Eye, The Dark, Species* and *Starship Troopers*.

Invasion of the Mind Snatchers

The modern science fiction film emerged in the postwar milieu of America in the 1950s, when technological innovations such as television, space rockets, the electric guitar and the hydrogen bomb had profoundly altered the nation's cultural landscape. A parallel development was provided by the emergence of the UFO phenomenon, which began in the late 1940s with a series of sightings of enigmatic craft in the skies over America. The "flying saucers," as they were dubbed by the press, had a profound effect on the national psyche, as they represented an unknown factor during a time of great cultural upheaval.

Another real-world concern that smacked of science fiction was the notion of "brainwashing" that emerged during the Korean War. The Communist bloc was thought to have developed psychological techniques that were capable of re-programming individuals by altering their basic personality and converting them into mind-numbed slaves of the state. National anxiety over the concept of brainwashing was crystallized by Richard Condon's 1959 political thriller *The Manchurian Candidate*, which would be turned into a memorable film during the following decade. Space aliens would become a metaphor for the mind-controlling Commies, who had a similar agenda for world domination. And if Manchurian scientists were capable of tapping into human brains and washing them out, imagine how extraterrestrials could alter hapless human minds with their vastly superior telepathic powers.

Domination of the mind and will by beings with unusual powers of hypnotism and telepathy had long been a staple of horror and sci-fi films as diverse as *Dracula, Svengali* and *Donovan's Brain*. Oddly, the theme of telepathic aliens practicing direct brain-to-brain mind control over people was not especially prevalent in 50s-era sci-fi. It does not appear in any of the major saucer movies of the decade, a list that includes *The Day the Earth Stood Still, The Thing from Another World, It Came from Outer Space, Invaders from Mars, The War of the*

Worlds, This Island Earth, Forbidden Planet, Earth vs. The Flying Saucers and *Invasion of the Body Snatchers*. Aliens in these films relied instead on physical and mechanical devices to bring humans under their domination. In *Invaders from Mars* the Martians rely on an implant inserted in the neck to achieve control, while the ETs in *The Man from Planet X, This Island Earth* and *Earth vs. the Flying Saucers* utilize a lamplike or ray device to brainwash their subjects. Extraterrestrials have to physically enter people's bodies in order to control their minds in *Kronos* and *Enemy from Space*. Aliens are obliged to create full body doubles of human beings in *The Purple Monster Strikes, It Came from Outer Space, Invasion of the Body Snatchers* and *I Married a Monster from Outer Space*. Mind-melding, hypno-telepathic ETs were only featured in a handful of relatively cheesy, low budget 50s sci-fi flicks.

The earliest intimation of telepathy in 50s science fiction films appears in William Cameron Menzies's *Invaders from Mars* (1953), in which a Martian flying saucer buries itself in a sand pit behind the home of a typical American family. The invaders, who are depicted as hulking seven-foot clones with bug eyes, are under the telepathic domination of the Martian "brain," a bodiless, golden-skinned head encased in a crystal globe. As previously mentioned, however, the Martians must resort to utilizing a device implanted in their victims' necks to enable hypno-telepathic mental control.

Killers from Space (1954) represents the first saucer movie of the period to feature ETs who possessed telepathic powers of mind control. Produced and directed by W. Lee Wilder, brother of the acclaimed director Billy Wilder, the film begins in typical 50s sci-fi movie fashion with a flurry of Air Force stock footage showing airplanes taking off during "Operation A-Bomb Test" at Soledad Flats testing ground. Atom scientist Doug Martin (Peter Graves), who is aloft to study radiation fallout from the blast, is flying in the co-pilot's seat of a jet fighter, call sign "Tar Baby 2." After observing an anomalous bright light emanating from the ground, Tar Baby 2 goes into a nosedive and crashes in the desert. The pilot's remains are located in the wreckage, but Dr. Martin's body is nowhere to be found.

Several days later, Dr. Martin limps back to the base, a bit scuffed up but seemingly none the worse for wear except for a weird scar on his chest. In addition, he has total amnesia about what happened during the crash that could have enabled him to survive. His wife Ellen (Barbara Bestar) is delighted to have her husband back, but the scientist is acting awfully funny in the aftermath of the accident. He begins to have nightmares of a pair of bulging, hypnotic eyes peering in his window at night. In light of his erratic behavior, project director Colonel Banks (James Seay) and FBI guy Briggs (Steve Pendleton) decide to pull the savant's security clearance, which puts Dr. Martin into high dudgeon. Pretending to clean out his desk, he conceals himself inside his office, steals classified nuclear data and heads off into the desert. Briggs observes him leaving the pilfered info under a rock, and Dr. Martin is apprehended when he sees the hypnotic eyes once more while driving and cracks up his car.

When Dr. Martin revives in the hospital, he is given an injection of sodium amytol, a "truth serum" that will probe his amnesia. In flashback, he is shown coming to on an operating table inside a cavern surrounded by aliens with bulging eyes that are obviously fashioned from ping-pong balls. Their leader, Denab (John Frederick), explains that Dr. Martin has been given a life-saving heart transplant that enabled him to survive the plane crash because the aliens wish to use him in their plans. Denab explains that they are on a mission of conquest from the dying world of "Astron Delta," and have assembled an army of genetically engineered giant cockroaches, horny toads and assorted larger-than-life creepy-crawlies who "will devour every living thing on the surface of the Earth" and then be disposed of by the Astron Deltans. Martin is then told, "Your thoughts have been recorded," and the aliens subject him to a hypnotic assault from an alien head on a TV screen who tells him, "You will listen and obey, you will remember nothing of what you have seen here." Freed from alien mind domination by the total recall of his amnesiac episode, Dr. Martin blows up the alien base by shutting off the juice at a local power plant.

This earnest but nutty exercise in low-budget sci-fi filmmaking nonetheless contains many motifs that would later emerge in UFO abduction reports, including awakening on an operating table during an alien surgical procedure, missing time amnesia and covert ET mind control of the abductee. Some UFO skeptics cite *Killers from Space* as the fictional source for much of the alien abduction narrative. Although the screenplay penned by Wilder's son Myles Wilder contains many intriguing elements, the execution is plodding and the production values are so poor that all suspension of disbelief is suspended. The Astron Deltans' supposedly hi-tech accoutrements are made out of Army surplus junk, and the aliens' bulging ping-pong eyeballs give modern audiences a good laugh despite the comically deadpan performances of 50s sci-fi icon Peter Graves and the other principals. But despite its lowly pedigree, *Killers from Space* offers the first depiction of hypno-telepathic alien ESP made during the creature-feature cycle.

During the 50s, ace low budget producer/director Roger Corman hit upon the notion of using on-screen telepathy as an economical filmmaking technique. Action could be filmed with a less expensive silent camera and without a sound crew or sound equipment. The actors would then post-dub the dialogue, sometimes with a little added reverb to simulate an inner mind-to-mind dialogue. Another technique involved overdubbing an off-screen voice onto the soundtrack to represent telepathic voices projected into the characters' heads. Thus the mutant creature in Corman's *The Day the World Ended* converses via telepathic voice mail with his former beloved, while the brains of scientists consumed by the monster crustaceans in *Attack of the Crab Monsters* can converse with the living on the telepathic wavelength.

In Corman's *Not of This Earth* (1957), alien vampire "Paul Johnson" (Paul Birch) from the planet Davanna has infiltrated the Earth and taken up residence in a creepy old mansion in Los Angeles. The Davannan dresses in a black business suit and tie and sports dark glasses that hide the hypno-telepathic powers of his eyes. He has come to Earth to determine if human blood is suitable for the aliens' needs, and to help plan the conquest and slaughter of mankind's population should this prove to be the case. Johnson consults with L.A. hematologist Dr. Rochelle (William Roerick), who diagnoses Johnson as dying from a strange degenerative blood disease. The alien then uses his telepathic mind domination to put the doctor into a trance and gives him post-hypnotic commands to devote his time solely to solving the medical problem presented by the alien's diseased blood. He is not to mention his research to anyone, forget about the conversation, and write out a prescription for some take-out pints of blood. Johnson also makes an arrangement to hire the doctor's assistant, nurse Nadine Storey (Beverly Garland), to administer the blood transfusions at his home.

A shrine-like area in Johnson's closet serves as a Davannan matter transmitter and communication device to the home world. Using this technology, the vampiric ET converses telepathically with his talking-head superior on Davanna about the progress of their mission. Thoughts are exchanged in a peculiar Davannan syntax, but their lips do not move while they are speaking. Nurse Nadine begins to suspect foul play as guests to Johnson's home check in but then don't check out. In reality, the alien is using his hypno-telepathic powers to round up human specimens and send them to Davanna in the matter transmitter. In one scene, he mentally dominates a Chinese man and talks to him telepathically in Chinese. Johnson encounters another refugee from the home planet, a Davannan woman (Anne Carroll) who has fled to Earth to escape the carnage on the vampire world. The alien couple conduct a chilling telepathic discourse on the streets of L.A. without any human beings being aware of their silent conversation, before the femalien is killed when Johnson transfuses her with the blood of a rabid dog.

Nadine approaches Dr. Rochelle with her suspicions, but Johnson's hypnotic mental block is still in place preventing the doctor from discussing the case. Worrying that his mental control over Rochelle may be compromised, Johnson dispatches a bat-like creature to murder him and gives Nadine a hypnotic command to place herself inside the matter transmitter and beam herself to Davanna. In the meantime, Nadine's boyfriend Harry (Morgan Jones), an L.A.P.D. cop, is wise to Johnson, pursuing the alien's sedan through the city streets on his motorcycle. The alien gives Harry a hypno-telepathic command to look into his eyes, but the loud wail of the police motorcycle's siren causes Johnson, who has a high sensitivity to loud noises, to lose control of his car and crash. Johnson's death frees Nadine from the ET's mental domination before she can teleport herself to Davanna.

Paul Birch as the sinister alien telepath in Roger Corman's *Not of This Earth* (1957).

Arguably Corman's most chilling and fully realized sci-fi horror flick of the 1950s, *Not of This Earth* neatly updates the classic vampire legend into the UFOlogical world of the 20th century. An intriguing screenplay by Chuck Griffith and Mark Hanna is wonderfully fleshed out by Corman on a low budget and brought to vibrant life by Corman regulars Paul Birch and Beverly Garland. Like the vampires of old, the parasitic space bloodsuckers are able to exert absolute mental domination over their victims. A considerable amount of screen time is devoted to depicting the Davannan's telepathic conversations with each other and with their human prey in Corman's typically economical fashion. *Not of This Earth* was remade in 1988 and 1995 and may have inspired UFOlogical reports of psychic alien emissaries known as the "Men in Black" who are reportedly able to control human minds via hypnotic telepathy.

Psychotronic Alien Brains

By the late 1950s the Hollywood sci-fi cycle had pretty much burned itself out. SF-genre movies continued to be made, but the vast majority were low-

Atom scientist Steve Marsh (John Agar) consults his "nucleometer" to detect the presence of *The Brain from Planet Arous* (1958).

budget, black-and-white drive-in fare. Typical of the late-50s crop of saucer movies was *The Brain from Planet Arous* (1958), a wonderfully silly romp released by the grade-Z production company Howco International. The film stars John Agar as atom scientist Steve Marsh, who gets an anomalous radiation reading on his "nucleometer" emanating from the vicinity of nearby Mystery Mountain. Taking his young protégé Dan Murphy (Robert Fuller) along to investigate, Steve locates a newly excavated cave in the side of the mountain and the two decide to explore its interior. They encounter a giant floating brain with glowing eyes that kills Dan with a burst of energy, renders Steve unconscious and takes possession of his body.

Upon returning home, Steve explains to his fiancée, Sally (Joyce Meadows), that Dan has unexpectedly run off to Las Vegas for some unscheduled R&R. Steve is in an unusually amorous mood as an impromptu make-out session with Sally quickly escalates into an attempted rape. A bit later the brain pops out of Steve's bod for awhile to get a breath of fresh air (literally), and speaks to the scientist using mental telepathy. Its name is Gor, a refugee from the planet Arous who has come to Earth on a mission of conquest. Gor needs Steve's body to gain access to the nuclear test site where he works, but the brain's interests are not entirely cerebral, as the alien has tasted the delight of Sally's flesh after years of disembodied brainhood on Arous. "Even I must have some interest to

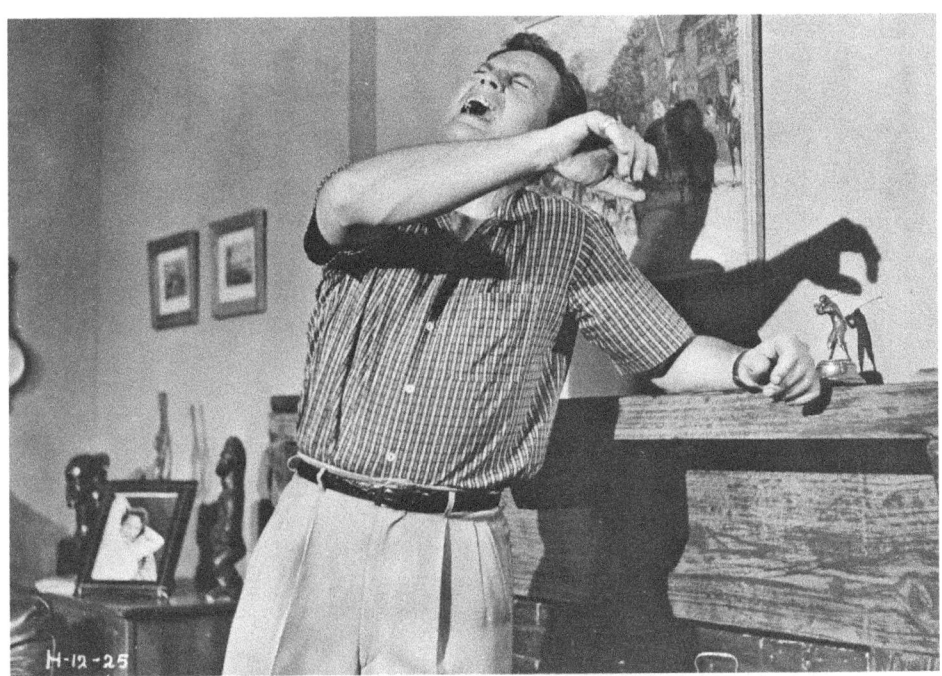

John Agar is possessed by a paranormal alien force in *The Brain from Planet Arous* (1958).

stir me up," Gor explains to the helpless Steve. "She appeals to me. There are some aspects of the life of an Earth savage that are exciting and rewarding." Gloating thus, Gor disappears back inside the scientist's body and continues its nefarious activities.

Weary of fending off the lustful assaults of the alien horndog, Sally enlists the aid of her father, Mr. Fallon (Thomas Browne Henry), to escort her out to Mystery Mountain so they can have a look around. They find Dan's corpse in the cave and encounter a second brain from Arous named Vol. The "good" brain Vol tells them that it has come to destroy the evil Gor, who is a criminal on their home world. Vol then decides to hide its presence inside Sally's dog, George, while giving telepathic advice to the humans. Vol also explains that Gor is invulnerable when ensconced inside Steve and is only vulnerable once a day when it must briefly exit the host body in order to absorb oxygen. Vol also indicates that Gor has a weak spot in the area of the brain called the "Fissure of Rolando."

The Gor-possessed Steve flexes his psychic muscles that night by assuming a glassy-eyed, maniacal expression as he destroys a commercial airliner in flight with a burst of radiation emanating from his eyes. On the following day Steve sits in on an A-bomb test attended by scientists and military brass and demonstrates his psychokinetic abilities by causing an explosion that exceeds the power of the atom bomb with "the power of pure intellect." He also demonstrates that he can't be killed by conventional weapons when he is attacked with a handgun by a military officer and fries the guy in his tracks with a burst of mental energy. Arranging a second conference, this time with dignitaries assembled from the world's major nations, Steve/Gor blows up another airliner as a warning to show he means business. While he is busy conquering the world, Sally and George/Vol are biding their time until the proper moment. When Gor emerges from Steve's body to oxygenate itself, Sally slips Steve the information about Gor's Achilles Heel, and with the alien brain in material form Steve grabs an axe and administers a mind-numbing blow to the Fissure of Rolando. With Gor disposed of and his job well done, the benevolent Vol is free to return to its abode on the planet Arous.

Mere words cannot do justice to this wonderfully hilarious example of 50s-era sci-fi film-making. The screenplay by Ray Buffam, with its unintentionally comedic dialogue, rivals the inanities of Ed Wood Jr. in the infamous *Plan 9 from Outer Space*. The ludicrous-looking brains from Arous, levitating on piano wire while glowering with luminous eyes, are especially laughable. Topping it all off is John Agar's fantastically manic performance as the alien-possessed savant, a portrayal that rivals some of the over-the-top roles later played by Jack Nicholson. Agar shows great enthusiasm for his part, which far exceeds the tenor of his performances in similar genre fare such as *Tarantula* and *The Invisible Invaders*. He seems to glory in the scenes where Gor exults in his destructive, "power of life and death over this civilization," as well as in the love scenes where he is groping Ms. Meadows (as the saying goes, it's great cinema, but it's hell on the actors). Through it all, somehow director Nathan Juran, veteran of 50s sci-fi productions like *The Deadly Mantis* and *Attack of the 50-Foot Woman*, keeps the action flowing smoothly in this lively 74 minutes of sci-fi fun.

Stripped of its loopy storyline, genre clichés and Howco-level production values, *The Brain from Planet Arous* is a serious alien invasion tale that reflects the paranoia engendered by both the atomic bomb and the threat of invasion from outer space early in the nuclear age. In the film's narrative, a single alien invader threatens to conquer the world by means of its telekinetic powers alone. As such, Steve/Gor is one of the most powerful of all screen psychics, and he shares a penchant for aerial destruction with John Morlar, the evil psychic who also destroys an airliner in mid-flight decades later in *The Medusa Touch*. Telepathic conversations between the extraterrestrial brains and human minds are conveyed using reverb-laden voice-over dialogue in the time-honored manner perfected by Roger Corman.

It seemed like alien brains had a thing for hanging out in caves because that same year spawned another tale of a spelunking extraterrestrial cerebrum in *The Space Children* (1958). Directed by genre auteur Jack Arnold, who was

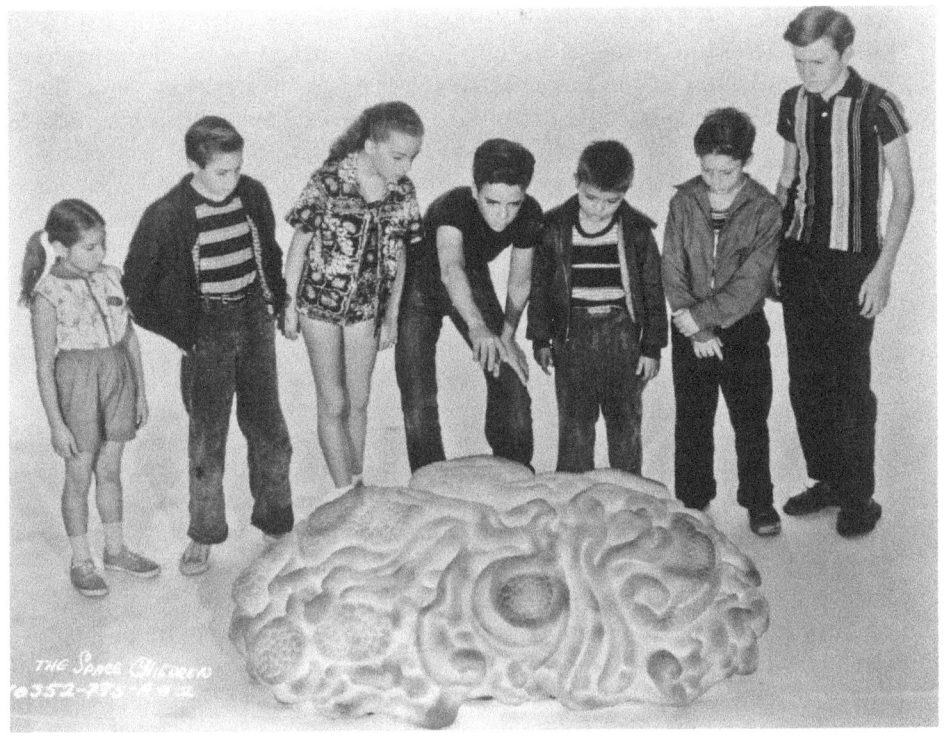

California kids meet a lovable alien brain in Jack Arnold's *The Space Children* (1958).

responsible for some of the most memorable science fiction films of the decade including *It Came from Outer Space*, *The Creature from the Black Lagoon* and *The Incredible Shrinking Man*, the film takes place on a bleak stretch of California beach, where the Brewster family is relocating. Father Dave Brewster (Adam Williams) is a rocket scientist who is travelling to his new job as an engineer for a new type of nuclear missile, dubbed the "Thunderer," at the Eagle Point Missile Range. After settling into their beachfront trailer housing, the two Brewster boys, Bud (Michael Ray) and Ken (John Crawford), link up with five other scientists' kids in exploring a seaside cave, where they find a luminous alien brain that has just arrived on Earth on a beam of light. The glowing brain establishes a telepathic link with the children, and Bud, who appears to have the strongest mind-meld with the ET, becomes the leader of the group.

Under the psychic tutelage of the brain, the children acquire psychokinetic powers, which they use to sabotage the coming launch of the first Thunderer. The children utilize their newfound PK to open locks and infiltrate the base at will and to disable the base's telephone system. Bud uses his mental powers to cause a rocket fuel truck to break down. Even Dave Brewster comes under the hypno-telepathic sway of the brain and is prevented from communicating with his superiors by post-hypnotic suggestion. Other parents who oppose the children's plans are driven to madness or killed outright by the alien intelligence. On the day of the launch the children focus their telekinesis on the Thunderer, which fails to take off, and the children explain that they have telepathically acted in concert with other groups of "space children" around the globe to bring about world peace by trashing their respective nations' weapons programs. Its job completed, the alien brain transports back to its home planet on a beam of light after the world has been "given a second chance."

Compared to the rest of Arnold's rollicking sci-fi output during the 50s, *The Space Children* is pretty thin soup, and it would prove to be his science fiction swan song for the decade. The film's low-budget seaside setting is terribly uninteresting, and the viewer must suffer through a seemingly endless series of shots of the kids and their parents running through the dunes. Worst of all, the screenplay by Bernard Schoenfeld, adapted from a story by Tom Filer, is confusing and fails to engage the audience's sympathies. The motives of the child saboteurs are unclear, as they have been telepathically brainwashed by the space brain, making them appear both angelic and diabolic within the film's Cold War setting. Aimed at a juvenile audience, the film exploits childhood fantasies of control of the adult world by the younger set.

The film is important, however, for being the first treatment of the theme of children acquiring paranormal abilities derived from an extraterrestrial source. Psychic moppets wielding telepathic and/or psychokinetic powers would later become a staple of science fiction cinema, with the most memorable example being displayed in the paranormal antics of Spielberg's *E.T.* (1982). The film's space children acquire telepathy and PK through their contact with the alien intelligence and function together in a communal "hive mind." Either through coincidence or cultural influence, *The Space Children* seems to presage reports of telepathic human/alien hybrid children in alien abduction narratives, and perhaps inspired the notion of so-called "Crystal Children" or "Indigo Children" who are reportedly born with alien-induced ESP.

Village of the Children of the Damned

By 1959 the Hollywood science fiction film boom of the 50s had bottomed out, and as the American film business looked elsewhere for more novel forms of entertainment, a modest resurgence of sci-fi cinema began to bloom in Britain during the following decade. Unlike their American counterparts, British SF films tended to be a bit more literary and thoughtful rather than lowbrow and sensationalistic. The British sci-fi invasion of the 60s was spearheaded by an adaptation of the popular UK author John Wyndham's novel *The Midwich Cuckoos*, released under the title *Village of the Damned* (1960).

As the film opens, the bucolic village of Midwich in rural England expe-

Telepathic alien child Martin Stephens (center) sends out lethal mind waves in this poster for *Village of the Damned* (1960).

riences an anomalistic "Dayout," in which all humans and animals in the little township are mysteriously put to sleep for several hours. Policemen and army troops attempting to enter the zone surrounding Midwich are rendered unconscious by an undetectable force. The denizens of the village awaken without any serious side-effects, but a few weeks later it is discovered that every woman of child-bearing years is inexplicably pregnant. The drama centers on Midwich physicist Gordon Zellaby (George Sanders) and his wife Anthea (Barbara Shelley), who is one of the expectant mothers. Their son, David (Martin Stephens), appears normal, but like the eleven other children conceived during the dayout, is blond-haired and possesses a pair of "arresting eyes." David demonstrates his mind-control powers early on by forcing Anthea to plunge her hand into a pot of scalding water when his bottle of formula is too hot.

Zellaby's scientific curiosity causes him to become fascinated with the Midwich children. Using a puzzle box as part of an experiment, he demonstrates that when one of the children solves the puzzle, all of the kids absorb the solution to the problem via telepathy. The children are apparently linked into a collective "mass mind" in which what one knows, all know. The scientist persuades the military authorities, including his brother-in-law Major Alan Bernard (Michael Gwynne), to allow him to set up a special school for the children where he can study them, believing that their group consciousness represents the intelligence of "one mind to the 12th power," an intellect that might be used to solve all of mankind's ills. Alan, however, points out that other groups of alien children have simultaneously appeared in various locales around the world, with dire results for the local populations, and speculates that the children may be human-alien hybrids conceived during the Dayout. In the end, however, Zellaby is reluctantly granted a year in which to study the Midwich kids while they are under his tutelage.

In the meantime, the village is plagued by a series of baffling, seemingly accidental deaths. In one incident, a man who nearly runs down one of the children is compelled to get back in his car and drive into a wall to his death. Anthea, who witnesses the incident, has a mental block telepathically put on her mind that partially erases her memory of the event. Testifying at a hearing about the death, she is unable to recall that the children were involved, and the killing is ruled an accident. The townsfolk are driven to fury over this miscarriage of justice, but when they attempt to take the law into their own hands, the children dominate them mentally, causing one man to commit suicide with his own shotgun and another to light himself on fire.

Even Zellaby comes to the realization that the children represent a danger to humanity's survival and must be destroyed. The problem is that the children can not only read each other's minds, but can read human thoughts as well. David informs him that they can see "everything that's in the front of your mind," but still have trouble probing deeper into the human thought process.

British officials (including George Sanders, extreme right), are briefed on worldwide outbreaks of alien hybrid births in *Village of the Damned* (1960).

"At least I still have some privacy," Zellaby observes. Deciding to take advantage of the children's incomplete mind-reading abilities, he conceives a plan to blow them up with a bomb concealed in his briefcase, timed to go off a few minutes after he arrives to tutor the children. The scientist knows that he must block out his intentions from the mental probes of the alien kids in order for his plan to succeed. "A brick wall," he muses, "I must think of a brick wall" as a mental barrier to the hybrids' telepathy. In the final confrontation, Zellaby's wall begins to crumble in the face of the children's telepathic onslaught, but holds together long enough for him to sacrifice himself and save humanity from the threat of the extraterrestrial hybrids.

This neat little Brit thriller eschews special effects in favor of acting, screenplay and deft direction to construct a classic alien invasion fable in the manner of Don Siegel's acclaimed *Invasion of the Body Snatchers* (1956). As in Siegel's film, the invasion takes place in an isolated, small-town environment where a tightly knit community struggles to overcome their rationalistic belief system and come to grips with a group of hostile extraterrestrials in their midst with covert plans of world conquest. Wyndham's seminal SF novel was faithfully translated for the screen by scripters Wolf Rilla, Stirling Silliphant and George

Barclay, who improve the dramatic impact of the book by adding the "brick wall" climax, which does not appear in the novel. Director Rilla crafts a tight, well-constructed exercise in sci-fi horror, while the cast of distinguished English actors elevates this modestly budgeted production far beyond the dramatic indifference of much of the genre. Screen veteran George Sanders acquits himself well in the lead role, but young Martin Stephens steals the movie with his chilling portrayal of the precocious star-child David. Stephens would go on to play a similar part as a spirit-possessed boy in Jack Clayton's powerful ghost story *The Innocents* (1961).

This cautionary tale updates the folkloric legend of the *changeling*, which was said to be a fairy child exchanged for a human baby and raised by a human family as their own, into the UFO age. The Midwich "cuckoos" are quiet, intense and otherworldly, their telepathic group mind making vocal speech largely unnecessary. They appear remote, unknowable and unfeeling toward human life and emotions, like alien sociopaths. The film has much in common thematically with Jack Arnold's *The Space Children*, which may have been inspired by Wyndham's novel, published in the preceding year. *Village of the Damned* would provide inspiration for a raft of popular "demonic child" movies that would come down the pike in the years to come, including *Rosemary's Baby*, *The Omen* and *The Exorcist*. All of these films exploited the parent/child relationship in a particularly horrific fashion.

The children's alien psi powers are played for pure horror, their glowing eyes emblematic of their inhuman mind-control abilities. Using optical superimposition (the one special effect utilized in the film), the pupils of the children's eyes light up just before they exert their mental brainwashing, which is always directed as a punishment and usually has fatal results for their hapless human mind-puppets. Their "group mind" connotes loss of individuality and a subservience to a collective central authority that is typical of the Cold War mentality, but also explores the potential nature of a telepathic society. The film's thrilling climax, in which Zellaby's mental shield is depicted as a crumbling brick wall with George Sander's eyes superimposed over the image, is arguably the most compelling visualization of the telepathic process in screen history. *Village* may have inspired accounts of blond-haired human/alien hybrid children who exist within a telepathic hive mind found in contemporary UFO abduction reports.

The popular and critical success of *Village* in the UK and America would produce the inevitable sequel, *Children of the Damned*, released in 1963. After the first film, Wyndham began work on a sequel, a novel entitled *Midwich Main*, which the author eventually abandoned because he felt his ideas from *The Midwich Cuckoos* were merely being recycled. Screenwriter John Briley was therefore obliged to start from scratch for *Children*, and constructed a semi-sequel that is only marginally connected to the first film and does not refer to the events from *Village*. As the film opens, geneticist Dr. David Neville (Alan Badel) and psychologist Dr. Tom Llewellyn (Ian Hendry) are part of a U.N. team working in London on a project to measure children's intelligence worldwide under the auspices of UNESCO. They uncover a child prodigy, Paul Loran (Clive Powell), a young boy whose I.Q. is off the charts. Looking into Paul's background, the scientists are puzzled to learn that his mother is a lower-class prostitute who ironically insists that Paul was conceived before she had ever "known" a man. When Paul attempts to murder his mother for talking to the authorities, she is hospitalized and his aunt Susan (Barbara Ferris) abruptly appears on the scene to take care of him, as if responding to a psychic summons.

Neville and Llewellyn are further unnerved to learn that UNESCO has discovered five more prodigal children in China, India, Russia, Nigeria and the United States. The superkids, three boys and three girls, all have the same personal history as Paul in that they have been conceived without a father through the biological process of parthenogenesis. Brought to London to be studied by the U.N. and restricted to their respective embassies, they slip out of confinement, link up telepathically into a group mind, and seek sanctuary in a ruined church. When pursued by the authorities, the children assemble an ultrasound weapon out of the church's dilapidated pipe organ which forces a standoff. The discovery of the children leads to an international crisis, as the various governments involved fret over the implications posed by their powers of mind. Some fear that the childrens' telepathic abilities will be used for espionage and precipitate a psychic arms race, others that their superior intelligence will enable the construction of new and exotic weaponry.

Predictably, British troops surround the church as Neville and Llewellyn square off against each other on how to resolve the situation. Llewellyn, believing the children to be a potential boon to mankind, wants to save them, while Neville believes their superior intellect and powers of mind constitute a threat to the survival of the human species. Susan, who appears to have latent psychic powers of her own, establishes a telepathic link with the superkids but is ultimately unable to come up with any answers as to their origin or motivations. The children themselves seem oddly resigned to their fate and are destroyed when a soldier accidentally drops a screwdriver onto a circuit board and activates the electronic signal to fire, causing the church and the children to be blown to kingdom come.

Some critics consider *Children* to be superior to the original *Village*, and while this might be a matter of taste, Briley's screenplay does contain one major flaw. Unlike the earlier film, in which the alien kids are clearly evil and bent on world domination, the sequel portrays the children as being both sympathetic and malevolent. In an early scene Paul coldly and cruelly utilizes his telepathic domination to compel his mother to attempt suicide, but by the end of the film the children are clearly victims of human frailty in the face of the unknown, and are mercilessly slaughtered by the power structure. Briley's script may also have been influenced by Olaf Stapledon's science fiction novel *Odd*

Psychic kids Yoke-Moon Lee (left), Mahdu Mathen, Frank Summerscale, Gerald Delsol, Roberta Rex and Clive Powell and their mentor, Barbara Ferris, defy humankind in *Children of the Damned* (1963).

John (see Chapter One), in which a colony of mutant supergeniuses is destroyed by the world's military forces. One intriguing subplot concerns Neville and Llewellyn, who live together in what appears to be a same-sex marriage that mirrors the children's "otherness" and constitutes a plea for tolerance for those in society who are different from the norm. The screenplay also de-emphasizes the children's alien identity, and though their origin remains obscure they appear to be human mutations rather than human/alien hybrids. Director Anton M. Leader coaxes earnest performances from a fine British cast, while the crisp black-and-white cinematography of Davis Boulton, who would also provide the spooky visuals for Robert Wise's *The Haunting*, imbues the film with the proper atmosphere of dread.

As in *Village*, the demonic attributes of the children's psychic powers are exploited, but here are combined with the notion that the children have the potential to become a boon to humankind. The film's open-ended ambiguity, however, never actually resolves this question. The superkids are practically mute in the sequel, emphasizing the non-verbal nature of their telepathic hive mind but at the same time making them more distant and less sympathetic to the audience. *Children of the Damned* is one of the first films to express concerns about the potentially destabilizing effects of psychic espionage during the dangerous days of the Cold War and anticipates the development of paranormal spies for the U.S. Government's remote viewing projects decades later.

Cult director John Carpenter, who penned the psychic thriller *The Eyes of Laura Mars*, lensed an updated remake of *Village of the Damned* in 1995. The village has been relocated from England to Marin County in Northern California, and the basic plotline of Wyndham's novel is preserved intact, but the characters have been altered. The role of protagonist has been switched to the person of Dr. Alan Chaffee (Christopher Reeve), Midwich's general practitioner, and the leader of the platinum-haired children is his "daughter," Mara (Lindsey Haun). Kirstie Alley portrays an entirely new character, Dr. Susan Verner, a chain-smoking epidemiologist from the National Science Foundation who spearheads the government's investigation of the children, and *Star Wars'* Mark Hamill appears in a throwaway role as the town minister who goes gunning for the children with a rifle. Unfortunately, Carpenter's retread lacks verve and merely adds a gloss of gore and horror to the proceedings. In one scene Dr. Verner is forced to cut herself open with a surgical scalpel by the evil space kids. The children's eyes do not merely glow, but emit bursts of light energy; however, their psychic world and mental gestalt are hardly explored in the banal screenplay by David Himmelstein.

More Alien Psychics

Alien-themed movies went into a general decline beginning in the early 1960s as the Cold War paranoia that characterized the 50s slowly abated and mind-controlling extraterrestrials were replaced by more benign notions of visitors from outer space. These updated ETs did not lose their paranormal faculties, however. Typical of this new breed was Jerry Lewis' Kreton, the alien space traveler in *Visit to a Small Planet* (1960), a comic treatment of the theme based on a hit Broadway play by satirist Gore Vidal. Descending from the skies in his flying saucer, Kreton takes up residence with the Speldings, a typical suburban American family, and wreaks havoc on their regimented lifestyle with his paranormal antics. The goofy alien can read (and broadcast) human thoughts, and is even able to read the minds of the family cat and dog. He also has psychokinetic powers that threaten to precipitate World War III. Kreton takes a shine to the Spelding's teenage daughter, Ellen (Joan Blackman), and shows her how to do telepathic and telekinetic mind tricks, but this proves to be his undoing when she broadcasts a telepathic distress signal to Kreton's superior, Delton (John Williams), who soon arrives to collect the extraterrestrial delinquent.

Visit to a Small Planet was a welcome antidote to the grim ET invaders of the previous decade, although Gore Vidal's satire becomes subsumed in Mr. Lewis's manic style of comedy. Director Norman Taurog drops the ball, with an assist from scripters Edmund Beloin and Henry Garson in this sci-fi comedy misfire. In one semi-amusing scene, Kreton demonstrates his powers during a visit to a beatnik coffee house by playing a percussion solo on a pair of onstage bongos from the audience while mugging shamelessly. Kreton's paranormal talents are played for laughs, although in theory the alien's psychic abilities are sufficient to enable him to destroy the entire world singlehandedly.

Mormon feminist writer Zenna Henderson's science fiction stories about the "People," a group of extraterrestrials with psi powers who live in secret in a small California community after fleeing to Earth in the 19th century, was adapted as an ABC-TV movie-of-the-week entitled *The People* (1972). Henderson's concept of The People was *Village of the Damned* turned inside-out; a colony of benevolent, psychic aliens has been established on Earth, but instead of being on a mission of conquest, they are motivated by a desire to remain hidden and obscure their superhuman abilities.

The story unfolds from the viewpoint of schoolmarm Melodye Arniston (Kim Darby), who has been assigned to a school district in a remote rural area (actually Nicasio, California). She soon begins to suspect her young charges are not what they seem, and confesses her misgivings to local medico Dr. Curtis (William Shatner). The two manage to learn the truth about the gentle extraterrestrial children, who possess telekinetic and healing talents, from Valancy Carmody (Diane Varsi) and Sol Diemus (Dan O'Herlihy), the nominal leaders of the alien colony. The People wish only to conceal themselves from the prejudice and hostility of their neighbors, and do not use their powers to subjugate or control humankind. When one of the children suffers a broken neck and is in danger of dying, the People focus their healing powers in a ritual called "the Gathering" that cures him using alien telekinesis. After finding out the truth about the colony, Valancy and Dr. Curtis decide to allow the People to remain unknown to the world in their hidden community. In return, Sol Diemus allows Dr. Curtis to covertly seed curative technology developed by the People into human society.

The telefilm's most memorable sequence occurs when Melodye follows two of the children into the woods and observes the extraterrestrial kids levitating into the air and gliding through the trees while playing the harmonica. Directed by John Korty and executive-produced by Francis Ford Coppola, acclaimed director of *The Godfather*, it's a cut above the usual made-for-TV fare. Many of the film's ideas, including harmonica-playing, telekinetic alien children, were cribbed for Disney's juvenile saucer movie *Escape to Witch Mountain*. This is one of the few films to depict psychic aliens in a positive light, as the paranormal powers of the People are associated primarily with healing rather than the destructive motivations evidenced in most science fiction fare.

Argentine director Eliseo Subiela's *Man Facing Southeast* (1986) takes place in a Buenos Aires mental hospital, where cynical psychiatrist Dr. Julio Denis (Lorenzo Quinteros) is confronted by the case of an enigmatic mental patient named Rantes (Hugo Soto). The charismatic Rantes has a genius I.Q. and claims to be a hologram projected from an alien planet. Delusions of being an extraterrestrial represent a fairly common psychotic disorder, but Denis's patient seems to have an uncanny empathy with the other patients in the institution, which appears to have a beneficial, curative effect. During a visit to a restaurant, Rantes demonstrates psychokinetic abilities when he uses PK to slide plates of steaks ordered by another customer to a poor woman and her family who cannot afford them, then causes a pile of glasses to break in order to distract the proprietor so he will not notice. Rantes spends a lot of time just standing motionless in the hospital's courtyard facing southeast, presumably picking up signals from the home planet. Although the issue of Rantes's extraterrestrial origin remains unresolved at the end of the film, he does possess telekinetic abilities which are used for the benefit of others.

Two other famous cinema aliens were gifted with psychic talents: *Star Trek*'s Mr. Spock and Steven Spielberg's *E.T.: The Extraterrestrial*. Actor Leonard Nimoy originated the role of the pointy-eared Spock on the late-60s TV series *Star Trek*, in which he portrayed the half-human, half-Vulcan science officer on the starship *Enterprise*. While Mr. Spock could not exercise telepathy spontaneously, he was able to tap into the thoughts of others by utilizing a maneuver called the "Vulcan Mind Meld," a ritual that involved placing his hand on the side of the subject's head and going into a telepathic trance in order to receive their thoughts. When *Trek* hit the big screen in a series of space opera adventures beginning in 1979, Spock continued using his telepathic skills to communicate with a variety of life forms. Who can forget the spectacle of Spock putting the mind meld on a humpback whale in its aquarium enclosure in *Star Trek IV: The Voyage Home* (1986)?

In Spielberg's *E.T.* a gnomelike, beneficent alien on a scientific mission to Earth is accidentally left behind by the rest of the crew and is forced to fend for himself in our world. The extraterrestrial takes refuge in a suburban California home, where he forges a deep emotional bond with ten-year-old Elliott (Henry Thomas) and his family. Gentle little E.T. possesses telekinetic and telepathic powers, but only uses them in a defensive manner. In one scene the alien levitates a group of objects in order to indicate his point of origin in space. Elliott and E.T. establish a telepathic link that leads to Elliott getting drunk at school when the UFOnaut quaffs beer for the first time back at home, and when Earth's polluted environment makes E.T. mortally ill, Elliott also gets sick until cured by E.T.'s healing powers. In the most iconic scene in the film, Elliott's bicycle, with his alien friend riding in the bike's basket, is levitated into the night sky until they are silhouetted by the moon. Similarly, at the movie's climax Elliott's bicycle and those of his friends take to the air via E.T.'s psychoki-

Top: E.T. takes refuge among a group of suburban children in Steven Spielberg's *E.T.: The Extraterrestrial* (1982). *Bottom:* E.T. and Elliott (Henry Thomas) are propelled aloft by the creature's psychokinetic powers in *E.T.: The Extraterrestrial* (1982).

nesis to elude their government pursuers. Unlike the spooky paranormal antics of extraterrestrials in most UFO–themed science fiction, E.T.'s psychic powers are just for fun and become part of a child's wish-fulfillment fantasy about using psi to confound the adult world. Spielberg's juvenile sci-fi romp proved to be an international mega-blockbuster. It remains one of the most popular movies (in terms of box-office receipts) of all time, and is arguably the most widely-seen film featuring psychic content.

Can Aliens Make You Psychic?

As previously mentioned, researchers claim that individuals coming into contact with a UFO have obtained psychic powers as a result, and there are a number of films that reflect this phenomenon. In *Forbidden Planet* (1956), a group of space explorers land on the planet Altair IV, where a previous expedition has mysteriously vanished without a trace. Commander J.J. Adams (Leslie Nielsen) heads up the investigation, and discovers the only survivor of the first expedition, Dr. Morbius (Walter Pidgeon), living in hi-tech luxury with his young adult daughter, Altaira (Anne Francis), who was born on Altair IV, and cybernetic butler/valet Robby the Robot. Morbius explains that the other members of the expedition all died of a strange, wasting illness, leaving only the scientist and his infant daughter alive. He wishes only to be left alone to continue his research in this isolated location, and urges Adams to depart immediately lest the dread plague return. The commander figures that Morbius' story doesn't pass the smell test, and decides to await further orders from his superiors on Earth.

On their first night on Altair IV an invisible creature invades their starship and disables the communications equipment. When confronted, Morbius clues Adams and his crew in on his research into the original inhabitants of the planet, the alien Krell race, who also mysteriously vanished eons ago but have left their ancient technology intact. A Krell intelligence-enhancement device has enabled the scientist to bring his I.Q. to the level where he can comprehend the workings of their ultimate achievement, a gigantic machine that can transform an individual's thought into material reality. After another attack on the ship by the invisible monster, Adams eventually discovers that the big machine is tapping into Morbius's subconscious thoughts and converting the murderous impulses of his Freudian Id, the mindless primitive "reptile brain" from which all intelligent creatures evolve into material form. These "monsters from the Id" destroyed the Krell, and in the film's climactic scene focus Morbuis's incestuous rage at Altaira, who has fallen in love with the commander, into a rampaging sci-fi beast that threatens to destroy everyone until Morbius sacrifices himself to stop it.

Although the aliens in *Forbidden Planet* have been dead for centuries, con-

The black-clad renegade scientist Dr. Morbius (Walter Pidgeon, in black) and his daughter Altaira (Anne Francis) confront Commander J. J. Adams (Leslie Nielsen) as cyber-chauffeur Robby the Robot awaits driving instructions in *Forbidden Planet* (1956).

tact with the technology they have left behind confers psychokinetic powers with destructive potential on humans. Parapsychologists have pointed out similarities between the Krell machine in the movie and the theoretical machinations of the poltergeist. Like a poltergeist, the machine amplifies the subconscious sexual tensions of an individual to create an invisible force with anti-social tendencies that seems to operate independently of the person who is its focus. One of the true gems of 50s science fiction cinema, *Forbidden Planet* is still fondly remembered by sci-fi buffs today for the deft direction of Fred Wilcox, the intriguing pulp-fiction screenplay by Cyril Hume, and the brilliant "Tonalities" electronic musical score composed by avant-garde musicians Louis and Bebe Barron.

The British sci-fi thriller *Five Million Years to Earth* (1967) continued in a similar vein. One of a series of films revolving around alien-busting scientist Dr. Bernard Quatermass (here played by Andrew Keir), the film begins with the excavation of a London subway tunnel in the vicinity of an ancient street known as "Hobb's Lane," which translates as "the Devil's Lane" from Old English. The workmen dig up an alien spaceship from Mars that has been buried for five million years, and Dr. Quatermass is called in to investigate, along with his assistants Dr. Roney (James Donald) and Barbara Judd (Barbara Shelley). While the ship's locust-like ETs have been dead for millennia, a strange psi force is potentiated when a worker at the site accidentally zaps the ship with a burst of high-voltage current. This activates a mechanism within the spaceship that amplifies and focuses human psychic energy, producing waves of severe poltergeist-like activity throughout the city. When a giant horned apparition of an insectoid alien "thought form" appears, generated by the collective psi force of the populace, Dr. Roney sacrifices himself by plunging a giant crane into the phantom being, grounding its electrical force in a burst of energy.

Directed by Roy Ward Baker from a script by Nigel Kneale, who also penned the other two entries in the Quatermass series, the film is a prime example of thought-provoking British sci-fi cinema. Well acted and tautly directed, the film originated as a BBC-TV teleplay entitled *Quatermass and the Pit*, which was first broadcast in 1958. Due to censorship laws in England banning the depiction of witchcraft on the big screen, Kneale's script took almost ten years to be filmed, and was only lensed when the laws were relaxed in the 1960s. As in *Forbidden Planet*, an alien machine built by a vanished race serves to focus and intensify human psychic energy in a distinctly negative and even homicidal fashion. The film associates psi forces with medieval devil worship and inhuman extraterrestrials that try to dominate humankind even after the ghost-like aliens have ceased to exist.

Steven Spielberg's *Close Encounters of the Third Kind* (1977) was the director's magnum opus on the UFO subject. The film's protagonist, electrical

Scientists Dr. Bernard Quatermass (Andrew Kier, left) and Dr. Roney (James Donald) examine the corpse of a diabolical insectoid Martian in *Five Million Years to Earth* (1967).

worker Roy Neary (Richard Dreyfuss), has a telepathic contact with a UFO that imprints an image of the alien's landing site, Devils Tower, Wyoming, into his mind. Unaware of its meaning, Neary becomes obsessed with the unusual image, sculpting it in various media before accidentally learning its location during a news broadcast. Nor is he alone in his obsession, for others have also received telepathic pictures of the striking geological formation, including local single mom Gillian (Melinda Dillon). Later in the film a small number of people show up at the contact site, all having been summoned by an identical vision of Devils Tower beamed into their minds by the aliens. "They were invited," muses project scientist Lacombe (François Truffaut), further noting, "They belong here more than we." The film does not, however, provide a reason why these particular individuals have been psychically summoned to partake in mankind's first contact with extraterrestrials.

While telepathic aliens are a dime a dozen at the movies, precognitive ETs are another matter. *The Mothman Prophecies* (2002), based on UFO researcher John Keel's 1975 non-fiction book of the same name, is a highly fictionalized account of Keel's investigations into sightings of the "Mothman," a bat-winged, humanoid apparition that reportedly plagued the denizens of the small town of Point Pleasant, West Virginia, in 1966. In the film, Keel has been replaced by the character of John Klien (Richard Gere), a veteran journalist for the *Washington Post*, who suffers an amnesiac episode while driving and mysteriously finds himself in Point Pleasant with no notion of why he has traveled there. Klein's journalistic instincts are aroused by strange goings-on in the town, and he decides to stay on awhile to sort things out. Teaming up with pretty local sheriff Connie Parker (Laura Linney), he encounters more reports of the winged anomaly from the local townsfolk, and begins to receive spooky phone calls in his motel room in the middle of the night from an individual calling himself "Indrid Cold." Mr. Cold's eerie voice foretells coming disasters, culminating in his prophecy of the collapse of the nearby Silver Bridge, a real event in which 46 people lost their lives, which provides the climactic ending sequence of the film.

This confused mish-mosh of science fiction and demonology transforms Keel's book into something akin to an episode of TV's *The X-Files*, although it does capture some of the breathless hysteria of the author's account. High strangeness abounds as apparitions of the moth-creature unreel in flashback (although the alien is never seen because of the film's low budget, reportedly cut an additional $2 mil during production), while weird prophetic voices emanate from the telephone. Absent, however, are the mysterious Men in Black who play such a large part in Keel's book. Shot in drab environments in Pittsburgh and Kittanning, Pennsylvania, by director Mark Pellington, the film has a depressive, confining quality that is exacerbated by a profusion of night-for-night scenes. Aliens spouting prophetic utterances are rare in UFO literature, and the allegedly predicted collapse of the Silver Bridge was found to be the result of the failure of an eye-bar on a suspension chain rather than remaining unexplained as stated at the conclusion of the movie.

Hollywood Psychics vs. the Aliens

In his 1990 book on the UFO phenomenon *Out There*, Pulitzer Prize–nominated author Howard Blum described a remote viewing demonstration conducted inside the Old Executive Office Building of the White House in 1985. Blum relates how a. U.S. Government viewer (most probably ace psychic Ingo Swann) was tasked with locating American and Soviet submarines in front of an audience that included high-ranking officials and military brass. Swann's demonstration of RV was abruptly interrupted when he described the intrusion of a UFO in the sky above the submarine he was viewing.

Richard Gere gets a prophetic phone from the mysterious Indrid Cold in *The Mothman Prophecies* (2002).

This confluence of ESP and UFO was not an isolated occurrence. Blum described how remote viewers were run against an anomalous object that had invaded U.S. airspace and baffled the NORAD defense system in December of 1986. After details of the RV program were revealed to public scrutiny during the 1990s, other viewers came forward to reveal that they had been tasked with viewing extraterrestrial targets on behalf of various defense agencies. Investigative author Jim Marrs notes, "If alien visitors are using mental or psychic powers to communicate with humans, perhaps humans could use those same powers to penetrate the alien agenda. In fact, many people familiar with remote viewing believe this process may be the best method yet available to penetrate the UFO enigma."[3] Interestingly, this theme appears in a number of films that seem to anticipate the use of RV to confront an alien presence on Earth.

The first instance of this motif occurs in the low-budget British sci-fi thriller *The Crawling Eye* (1958). As the film opens, U.N. science investigator Alan Brooks (Forrest Tucker) is en route to the Swiss village of Trollenberg to examine reports of a series of strange events taking place on Trollenberg Mountain. Seated across from him are the Pilgrim sisters, Sarah (Jennifer Jayne) and

Anne (Janet Munro), who are traveling to Geneva on vacation. When the train arrives in Trollenberg, however, Anne goes into a trance while staring at the mountain and announces they are not continuing on to their destination, but are debarking at Trollenberg. It turns out the Pilgrim sisters have a successful mind-reading nightclub act, and Anne has genuine psychic powers. She also knows about a series of strange disappearances and mysterious deaths that have plagued the mountain village.

Alan continues on to a fortress-like scientific observatory situated high on the mountainside, where he confers with his old friend and colleague Professor Crevett (Warren Mitchell) about the anomalous events. The professor informs Alan that mountain climbers on the Trollenberg have been vanishing into thin air, and that some of the climbers' bodies have been found decapitated. Furthermore, there is a mysterious radioactive cloud that remains motionless on the summit of the mountain. Crevett suspects the weird cloud is actually the atmosphere of a group of alien invaders. That night, as Susan and Anne perform their mind reading act at the village hotel, Anne spontaneously remote-views the murder of mountaineer Dewhurst (Stuart Saunders) at the hands of his companion Brett (Andrew Faulds) in a hut high on the Trollenberg. When Brett later reappears he has been transformed into a zombie slave of an alien intelligence residing inside the cloud, and he attempts to murder Anne. In the aftermath, Alan and Crevett discuss an identical case that occurred several years earlier in the Andes, in which an elderly clairvoyant woman began to probe the aliens' agenda and was murdered by a local villager who had been dead for 24 hours.

When the cloud begins to move down the mountain toward the village, the townsfolk are evacuated to the observatory, where another attempt is made on Anne's life by one of the zombie villagers. In the wake of the assault the psychic goes into shock and cannot provide further information about the ETs' motives. As the frigid cloud surrounds the scientific outpost, the aliens are revealed as monstrosities that resemble tentacled venous brains sporting a single cyclopean eye. After causing some mayhem at the observatory, the crawling eyes are summarily dispatched when Alan calls in a U.N. airstrike using thermite heat bombs that incinerate the monstrous extraterrestrials.

Long a favorite of bad film buffs and lampooned on cable-TV's *Mystery Science Theater*, *The Crawling Eye* (known in the UK under its more sedate British title *The Trollenberg Terror*) is a surprisingly lively little sci-fi chiller. Scripted by cult fave Jimmy Sangster, who would turn out a string of horror hits for England's Hammer Studios beginning with *Curse of Frankenstein* (1957) and *Horror of Dracula* (1958), the film might have proven to be a sci-fi classic if it had a larger budget and more robust production values. The last film produced by Britain's venerable Southall Studios, *The Crawling Eye* is competently directed by Quentin Lawrence and earnestly acted by a predominately British cast. Janet Munro steals every scene she's in with her wide-eyed portrayal of the agitated psychic girl, Anne Pilgrim. Ultimately, though, it's the silly-looking crawling eye creatures and dismal special effects that compromise the movie and remove it from serious critical consideration.

The psychic theme is front and center in *The Crawling Eye*, and is essential to the plot. For the first time in movie history, ESP is employed by a human psychic to probe the agenda of alien invaders and gather intelligence about them. Although it is not emphasized in the script, the crawling eyes appear to have telepathic powers as well, as Alan and Crevett theorize that the aliens have drawn Anne to Trollenberg in order to eliminate her because they fear her psychic abilities will uncover their plans. Anne is depicted as a nervous, withdrawn individual, and her older sibling, Sarah, reveals that the sisters have taken a vacation because Anne has incurred severe stress reading others' thoughts while performing their nightclub act.

The Dark (1979), another low-budget sci-fi monster mash, stars William Devane as long-haired, ex-con crime novelist Steve Dupree, whose daughter (Kathy Richards) is the first victim of a homicidal alien stalking Santa Monica. During an exclusive party held aboard a yacht on the night of the murder, gypsy fortune-teller De Renzy (Jacquelyn Hyde) has a vision of the killing of young actor Randy Morse (Jeffrey Reese) by the ET while reading his cards. The creature, who kills with laser blasts emitted from its eyes, is soon dubbed "the Mangler" by the press, and Detective Dave Mooney (Richard Jaeckel) is assigned to the case. Crusading newslady Zoe Owens (Cathy Lee Crosby) also takes a personal interest in the controversial serial killings under the patronage of eccentric station owner Sherman "Sherm" Moss (Keenan Wynn).

Zoe joins forces with Dupree to track the elusive Mangler, while psychic dowager De Renzy pays a visit to Detective Mooney and relates her visionary episode with the actor at the party (whose name she does not know) but is rebuffed by the police. De Rezny then approaches Zoe wearing a mysterioso black Druid outfit and informs her that there has been another murder, but the newswoman similarly takes her for a kook. Undaunted by the intensive police manhunt, the Mangler continues its murder spree, while forensics experts are baffled to find physical evidence that the killer is a dead/alive "zombie." Knowing that the actor is fated to be stalked by the creature, Dupree and Zoe race to discover Randy Morse's identity in order to prevent his murder. In the meantime, the alien invades De Renzy's consciousness, and during the resulting telepathic exchange she learns that the Mangler is an alien who gets stronger with every killing. Discovered after the encounter by Zoe and Dupree, the psychic imparts her knowledge of the Mangler to them before being hospitalized with a stroke. The couple track down the elusive murderer while being followed by Mooney, leading to the final showdown between the cops and the laser-eyed alien killer.

This slow-moving horror thriller was reportedly thrust upon director John "Bud" Cardos when *Poltergeist*'s Tobe Hooper, the original director, bailed to

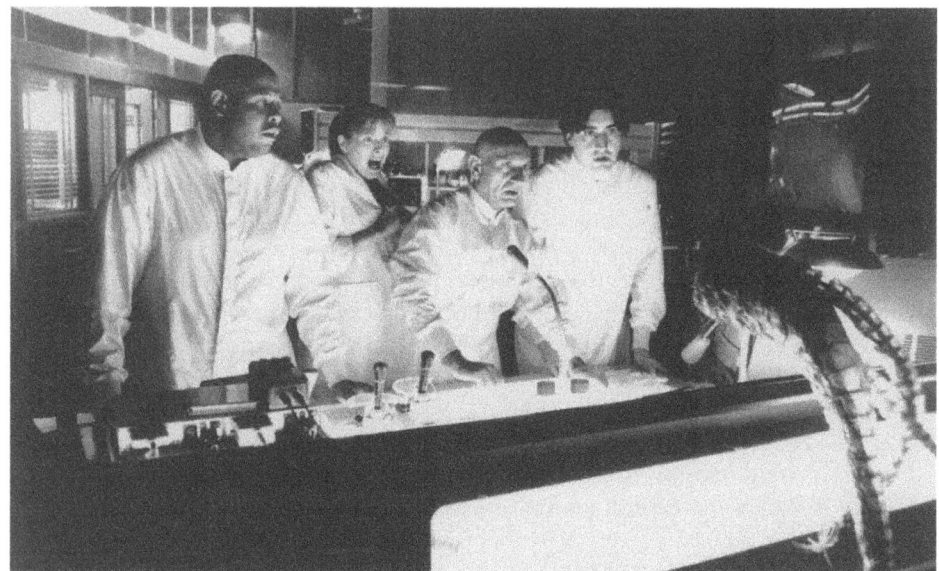

Empath Forest Whitaker (left) confronts the alien creature in *Species* (1995), along with team members Susan Bartkowiak, Ben Kingsley and Alfred Molina.

go work with Spielberg when *The Dark* was only days into production. The film's original zombie-killer plot was jettisoned in favor of making the creature into an extraterrestrial due to the success of Ridley Scott's *Alien* (1979). Shot largely on the nighted streets of Los Angeles, *The Dark* has visual elements of *film noir*, and its mix of horror/sci-fi and police procedural recall the similarly-themed *Psychic Killer* (1975). In addition to its sluggish pacing, the film also suffers from lackluster performances by an interesting cast. William Devane, a competent actor who had recently appeared in Hitchcock's psychic crime comedy *Family Plot* (1976), is especially loopy in his portrayal of the long-haired hippie writer Dupree. Of key interest here is Jacquelyn Hyde's portrait of gypsy psychic De Renzy, who cuts a flamboyant, witchy figure that recalls Gloria Swanson's famous performance as Norma Desmond in Billy Wilder's *Sunset Boulevard* (1950). As a character, De Renzy seems rather flip about the murder and mayhem she is privy to by virtue of her ESP until the alien invades her mind. As in *The Crawling Eye*, the ET intelligence targets a psychic individual as a threat due to her capacity to tap into the alien's intentions.

Monstrous creatures from outer space never seem to go out of style. In *Species* (1995), a group of SETI (an acronym for the Search for Extraterrestrial Intelligence) scientists intercept a radio message from outer space that contains instructions on how to create a human/alien hybrid being. Using this information, a viable female embryo has been manufactured and allowed to mature to adolescence. In the movie's opening scenes, project head Xavier Fitch (Ben Kingsley) is presiding over the experimental creature's termination at a secure government facility located in Dugway, Utah. Named "Sil" by the scientists, the hybrid resembles an innocent 12-year-old girl (Michelle Williams) who is kept imprisoned inside a transparent cage. When Fitch attempts to gas the creature to death, Sil uses her alien powers to escape from the facility. Pursued by troops and helicopters, the alien girl manages to give Fitch and his men the slip and boards a train bound for Los Angeles.

Fitch assembles a special team to locate and dispatch the creature, consisting of anthropologist Steve Arden (Alfred Molina), biologist Laura Baker (Marg Helgenberger) and government assassin Preston Lennox (Michael Madsen). The most unusual member of the team, however, is Dan Smithson (Forest Whitaker), a self-described "empath" who "feels things deeply" and works for the police as a psychic profiler (à la *Manhunter*). "Sometimes they show me awful things that people have done," he explains, "and I try to tell them why they did it."

By the time Sil's train reaches L.A. she has metamorphosed into her mature form as a twentysomething blonde woman with supermodel good looks (Natasha Hentsridge) who effortlessly blends into the general populace. Sil's prime directive is to become pregnant and spawn the new hybrid race that will eventually supplant mankind. The clever, homicidal femalien leaves the corpses of her lovers/victims in her wake as she cuts a wide swath through the L.A. dating scene in search of a viable mate. Clued by Sil's use of a stolen credit card, Fitch's team track the creature to the Club Id, an L.A. singles' spot. As the team tours the homicide scenes, Dan offers his psychic impressions of their quarry. "She's a predator," he elucidates. "She kills because she feels threatened."

Fitch's team plays a deadly game of cat-and-mouse with the alien, but Sil has telepathic powers of her own. She is able to invade Fitch's mind and give him mental commands that enable her to set up an elaborate scheme to fake her death. Using the body of a kidnapped woman along with a specimen of her own DNA, the wily Sil cleverly stages her apparent demise. Their mission apparently accomplished, the team return to their L.A. hotel for some much needed downtime, but with their guard down Sil returns to their hotel and stalks Steve Arden as a prospective father. As she aggressively seduces the unwitting Steve, Dan's psi sensitivities tell him that his friend is in danger while the couple are engaged in the act of love. Dan alerts the other team members, but they are too late to prevent the creature from murdering Steve after her successful mating with the scientist. Now pregnant, Sil flees into the rat-infested L.A. sewer system pursued by Fitch and his team, where Dan's psychic powers enable them to locate the hybrid monstrosity in the final confrontation between the two species.

This superior sci-fi thriller is smoothly realized by director Roger Donaldson from an intriguing original screenplay by Dennis Feldman. On the minus

Lt. Colonel Carl Jenkins (Neil Patrick Harris) puts the mind-meld on a captured alien "brain bug" in Paul Verhoeven's *Starship Troopers* (1997).

side, the fine cast, including Oscar–winners Kingsley and Whitaker, deliver performances that are surprisingly flat, leaving the movie to be carried by newcomers Natasha Henstridge and Michelle Williams in the role of Sil. The creature's non-human form, shown mostly at the end of the movie, was devised by Swiss artist H.R. Giger, the designer of the extraterrestrial beastie in Ridley Scott's sci-fi megahit *Alien* (1979). Forest Whitaker portrays empath Dan Smithson as a kind of psychic *zaftig*, a big, amiable guy who projects a certain softness of personality that is in accord with his mental hypersensitivity. Almost nothing in the way of backstory is presented about the character, and the ESP angle doesn't receive sufficient attention. Similarly, the psychic powers of the alien are downplayed and are only shown in a single scene in the film.

Perhaps the first instance of psychics being utilized to combat extraterrestrials with their paranormal powers in science fiction literature occurs in Robert A. Heinlein's classic space opera *Starship Troopers* (1959). In the novel, mankind is locked in an all-out battle that rages throughout the galaxy with an insectoid alien race. Psychics known as "special talents" are utilized to combat the murderous Arachnids, known commonly as the "Bugs." The novel's protagonist, mobile infantryman Johnnie Rico, observes one of the talents, a "spatial sensor," at work on the battlefield mapping out the underground location of the aliens. "He was dressed in a fatigue uniform without insignia and he seemed terribly bored by everything. I was not introduced to him. He looked like a sixteen-year-old boy ... until I got close and saw a network of wrinkles around his weary eyes."[4] As Johnny watches, the sensor performs a dowsing operation to locate the Bugs' underground lair from the surface.

The psychic angle in Heinlein's novel was greatly amplified in Paul Verhoeven's screen version of *Starship Troopers* (1997). The film follows the exploits of Johnny Rico (Casper Van Dien) and his friends Carl Jenkins (Neil Patrick Harris) and Carmen Ibanez (Denise Richards) as they enlist in Earth's futuristic armed forces to fight the Bugs. Prior to their enlistment, Carl tests Johnny's ESP on an elaborate rig with multiple large-format TV screens and other equipment that would be the envy of any present-day parapsychologist. Carl, who possesses psychic talent, is testing Johnny as part of a Federal project to identify individuals with psi powers. When Johnny's responses are incorrect more than chance allows (a well-known phenomenon in psychic research that may indicate the hidden presence of psi), he grouses, "So my psychic abilities are zero and I'm unlucky." Carl replies, "No, luck's not a factor. No one really knows why some people are sensitive and some aren't. Who knows? Maybe it's a new stage of human evolution. That's why they do these kinds of federal studies." Carl then demonstrates his own psychic acumen by giving his pet ferret a mental impression that a grub is crawling up his mother's leg, and when Johnny protests, Carl tells him, "Don't worry. Can't do human. Yet."

After enlisting in federal service, Johnny is drafted into the mobile infantry, Carmen becomes a star pilot and Carl's psi talents are utilized in military intelligence. During a "Fednet" TV broadcast a commercial announcer asks, "Are you psychic?" while showing a man growing a third eye in the middle of his forehead. "If you think you're psychic, maybe you are," the announcer continues. "Federal studies are being conducted in your community. Would you like to know more?" The three friends join in a series of spectacular battles against the Arachnids, culminating with an assault on the alien base on Planet P, where the Bugs are conducting their own brand of psychic warfare. "They get inside your mind, they make you do things," explains one officer who survives an Arachnid assault. The Bugs accomplish this by literally sucking the brains out of their hapless human victims and absorbing the information. When Carmen is taken hostage by the Bugs, Johnny manages to locate her in an underground tunnel using his latent ESP. After the battle is won by the humans, Johnny questions Carl about the event. "You told me how to find Carmen," he asks, to which Carl replies, "That's classified." Carl then puts the mind-meld on a captured "Brain Bug" and reads its thoughts. "It's afraid," he announces to the assembled troopers, "It's afraid!"

Although it's only a sub-plot to the film's space-opera action and CGI-generated star warfare, the psychic motif in Heinlein's book has been expanded and made into an important plot element by screenwriter Ed Neumeier. As the interstellar war rages throughout the galaxy, a beleaguered humankind must employ all of its talents in an inter-species conflict that is being fought partly on a psychic level. Years in production and sporting cutting-edge computer-generated special effects, Verhoeven's space war extravaganza failed to resonate with movie audiences. The film was assigned an R-rating due to graphic scenes of violence culled from Verhoeven's memories of World War II, which eliminated a core sci-fi audience of under 17-year-olds; the film's excessive gore turned off many hardened adult viewers as well. Nonetheless, in retrospect *Starship Troopers* remains an impressive achievement in the annals of science fiction cinema. It also reflects the military aspects of real-world psychic remote viewing as indicated in the title of ex–Army viewer Paul H. Smith's 2005 book on the subject, *Reading the Enemy's Mind*. As originally envisioned by military planners, remote viewers were supposed to be used on the battlefield to ascertain an enemy's location and tactics in a manner similar to that depicted in the film.

Mindscan

Before we leave the subject of aliens and ESP, the confluence between paranormal motifs found both in films and reported during purported alien abduction events must be examined. Although reports of human/alien communications via mental telepathy are commonplace in abduction literature, the UFOnauts do not exhibit psychic talents in the fields of precognition, clairvoyance or psychokinesis. The abductors are apparently able to float or hover in the air in defiance of gravity and can even pass through solid matter, but it is unclear whether these abilities are enabled by their advanced technology or induced by paranormal telekinesis.

From the first American abduction narrative, the famous case of Betty and Barney Hill in New Hampshire in 1961, alien telepathy has played a prominent role. Driving from Canada to their home in Massachusetts during the wee hours of the morning, the Hills' car was followed by a disc-shaped UFO with a row of windows. Stopping the car for a better look, Barney observed several figures through the windows of the disc, including a "leader" who sent Barney a mental command to remain stationary. Barney fled back to his car and attempted to drive away, but instead was compelled to swerve from the highway and onto a secluded turnoff where the abduction took place. The aliens then placed the couple in a somnolent, semi-conscious mental state so that they would not resist capture. Although Barney remained semi-comatose during most of the abduction, Betty was more mentally aware and held conversations with some of the crew members. She later explained she was somehow able to comprehend the aliens' verbal communications as English speech. During one examination procedure when a long needle was placed in Betty's navel during a "pregnancy test," the alien "Leader" passed its hand in front of her eyes and made the pain vanish. When the abduction concluded, the Hills were compelled to forget the entire episode, a process that was only partly successful as they were later able to recover their memories of the event via hypnotic therapy administered by a physician. In the aftermath of the abduction, the couple was plagued by a series of enigmatic poltergeist-like happenings that continued for years before gradually fading away. Some of these paranormal aspects of the Hills' close encounter would become commonplace features of subsequent abduction reports.

The Hills' abduction experience would be popularized in John Fuller's 1966 book *The Interrupted Journey*, which was the basis for the 1975 NBC-TV movie *The UFO Incident*. James Earl Jones and Estelle Parsons turn in riveting portrayals of the Hills, deriving their performances from the tapes of their actual hypnosis sessions. A suspenseful teleplay by S. Lee Pogostin and Hesper Anderson unfurls the narrative in flashbacks as the couple undergoes hypnosis to uncover the truth about their missing-time episode. The telefilm depicts many of the paranormal events the Hills experienced during the abduction with great fidelity, but the movie's modest budget does not allow for the use of special effects to show the UFO or the aliens clearly. Contrary to popular belief, big-brained, big-eyed, telepathic humanoid ETs did not appear in any film produced prior to *The UFO Incident*, which established the visual image of what have come to be known as "Gray Aliens" in a feature film. Skeptics point out, though, that episodes of sci-fi TV shows like *The Twilight Zone* and *The Outer Limits* that were broadcast prior to the Hill abduction do exhibit some of this ET iconography. Like the UFOnauts in the saucer movies of the 1950s, the aliens in the Hill case are skilled in mental manipulation, being able to manipulate human consciousness, immobilize their victims, communicate telepathically and cause amnesia solely through the psychic powers of the alien mind.

Subsequent abduction narratives unearthed by prominent UFO researchers like Budd Hopkins, David Jacobs, Ray Fowler and John Mack have presented further details about the Gray's telepathic abilities. Jacobs, a history professor at Temple University, has conducted numerous hypnotic sessions with abductees and uncovered a wealth of information on this topic. "During the entire abduction experience," he writes in his 1992 book *Secret Life*, "communication between aliens and abductees is telepathic.... Usually the abductee receives only an 'impression' of what the Beings are communicating and has difficulty repeating specific words or sentences, although some people 'hear' sentences in their minds and can recall not only the sense of the communication but the words as well. So far no cases have emerged whereby Beings and abductees communicate mainly through sound waves."[5]

According to Jacobs, the Grays are said to employ a process he refers to as "mindscan," wherein they utilize their enormous black eyes to enter into the furthest reaches of the abductees' minds, possibly by accessing the brain directly through the optic nerve. The aliens may induce "envisioning" procedures, in which illusions are telepathically projected into the mind of the human subject, possibly as a test of their emotional responses. Like their science fiction counterparts in films like *Village of the Damned*, the extraterrestrials and their genetically-engineered human/alien hybrid beings exist within a telepathic "hive mind" in a regimented society in which separate, individual thought is impermissible and perhaps impossible. During multiple kidnappings, abductees report the use of a "telepathic public address system" to communicate with more than one human mind simultaneously. These telepathic interactions between aliens and abductees are reportedly more profound than corresponding human-to-human mind-melds. While the veracity of these narratives cannot be verified, abduction stories might offer a glimpse of how an organic society of telepaths could function.

Regarding the notion of pitting human psychics against alien minds, there is the curious matter of a 1998 book written by remote viewer Ingo Swann entitled *Penetration: The Question of Extraterrestrial and Human Telepathy*. The book reads like a science fiction novel, but Swann insists it is a true record of events that transpired when he was working on developing remote-viewing protocols at the Stanford Research Institute during the 1970s. He relates how he was approached by an enigmatic individual named "Mr. Axelrod" who contracted Swann to do some private remote viewing of anomalous objects on the moon, and later showed him the apparent materialization of a UFO in a remote location in Alaska. Another incident involved a seemingly chance meeting with a highly telepathic woman in Los Angeles. Swann eventually came to believe that his own psychic powers were being tested against those of the aliens in a confrontation between "earthside telepathy and spaceside telepathy." He believes the ETs have a definite advantage over us in this area, which he describes as "a type of telepathy plus, as one might suppose, a type which beyond being a channel for information exchange might also achieve something along the lines of mind bending and fried brains."[6]

Swann's obscure book, privately printed in a small press run, is currently selling for between $400 and $1500 on the internet book site amazon.com, making it the most expensive book on the UFO subject to date. While the scientific establishment marches in ideological lockstep to deny the reality of ESP, it is possible that some day earthlings may be contending with mentally superior beings who can not only read our minds but are in possession of "telepathy plus."

• SEVEN •

Psi-Fi: Psychic Science Fiction Blockbusters

The portrayal of psi on film is not always conducted in an obscure, low-budget venue. While in the real world the paranormal is shunted aside into fringe areas of science and lurid supermarket tabloid headlines, in the universe of entertainment psychic themes have vast currency with film audiences. In the movie theater the disturbing, otherworldly associations of psi are burnished and converted into box-office gold, and the powers of the paranormal are utilized in the service of fantasy and just plain fun. Of course, the primary example of this is George Lucas's enormously successful *Star Wars* series.

As writer/director/producer triple-threat, Lucas was single-handedly responsible for creating the hi-tech concepts of the epic science fiction series over more than two decades. While the dazzling, sometimes overwhelming technology of this alternate universe set "a long time ago in a galaxy far, far away" is breath-taking, Lucas injects an element of the paranormal that moves the series into the magical realm of heroic fantasy. It is precisely this element of mysticism that elevates the *Star Wars* films from being mere space opera into a quasi-religious exercise. The technologically advanced world of futuristic machines may appear to dominate the star-flung landscape, but behind the scenes the universe is ruled by an elite of psychic sorcerers who wield the fantastic powers of "The Force." Speaking of the world-destroying potential of the evil Empire's humongous Death Star satellite, Sith lord Darth Vader reminds his fellow villains that "the ability to destroy a planet is insignificant next to the power of the Force."

Much ink has been spilled over Lucas's inspiration for some of the most popular films in the history of cinema. The most prominent analysis of Lucas's themes was conducted by mythographer Joseph Campbell in conversations with journalist Bill Moyers on the popular PBS television series *The Power of Myth*. Campbell astutely pointed out many points of similarity between motifs found in *Star Wars* and myths from Classical antiquity and world mythology, but many analyses of the film tend to gloss over a number of more contemporaneous literary influences, all of which revolve around the paranormal.

Arguably the most obvious of these is Frank Herbert's seminal science fiction novel *Dune* (1967), which posited a space-faring future civilization in which all computers have been outlawed after a horrendous galactic war between humankind and rebellious cybernetic intelligences. In order to compensate for this handicap, human potential has been developed to an astonishing degree; human computers called "Mentats" perform lightning mathematical calculations that rival their silicon counterparts, for instance. Psi powers have also evolved into an essential element of this futureworld. The Bene Gesserit, an order of paranormal nuns, have honed their powers of telepathy, clairvoyance and mental manipulation while playing a centuries-old Machiavellian game to breed a female messiah. The Spacing Guild relies on the psychotropic drug mélange, more commonly called "spice," to augment a psychic prescience that enables travel between star systems. As in *Star Wars*, individuals with psi powers covertly dominate the workings of an interstellar civilization. The protagonist of *Dune*, Paul Atreides, matures into a psychic superman against the backdrop of a remote desert planet and a war against the far superior military forces of a galactic empire. There are even mentions of the "Dune Sea," the "spice mines of Kessel" and a "spice freighter" in *Star Wars* that self-consciously reference *Dune*, and after the film's release author Herbert sued 20th Century–Fox over similarities to his novel and settled the case out of court. In the wake of the success of the of *Star Wars* movies, a highly eccentric version of *Dune* was lensed by cult director David Lynch and released in 1984.

The works of British fantasy writer J.R.R. Tolkein, author of *The Hobbit* and the heroic epic *The Lord of the Rings*, provide another obvious influence on *Star Wars*. As in *The Lord of the Rings*, a diverse group of human and non-human adventurers led by a powerful wizard go on a quest to infiltrate their enemy's hidden fortress in order to destroy the basis of his power. Tolkein's epic is set in the mythical realm of "Middle Earth," a time in Earth's antiquity when magic and sorcery constitute a kind of alternative technology. The narrative centers around the Luke Skywalker–like person of hobbit Frodo Baggins, a gentle country lad who acquires supernatural powers and deep wisdom under the tutelage of the wizard Galdalf, who bears a resemblance to Luke's mentor Obi-Wan Kenobi. Like their counterparts in *Star Wars*, the characters in *The Lord of the Rings* possess preternatural powers of telepathy, precognition and clairvoyance.

A third influence was a series of purportedly non-fiction books penned by UCLA anthropologist Carlos Castaneda that became popular in the late 1960s. Beginning with *The Teachings of Don Juan* in 1968, Castaneda's books detail his apprenticeship to a Yaqui Indian shaman named Don Juan Matus, a "man of power" who initiated Castaneda into the fantastic realm of indigenous Indian magic and sorcery. Unlike the works of Herbert or Tolkein, however, Cas-

Former Jedi Knight Obi-Wan Kenobi (Sir Alec Guinness) convinces Luke Skywalker (Mark Hamill) to follow him on the path to Jedi-hood in George Lucas's *Star Wars* (1977).

taneda's journeys into the unknown were allegedly fact, not fiction. The Yaqui sorcerer Don Juan utilized hallucinogenic "power plants" such as peyote and magic mushrooms to propel his pupil into "a separate reality" of spirit entities and paranormal mysteries. This shamanic path to psychic power is called "the Way of the Warrior" in Don Juan's parlance, recalling the psi-equipped warriors of Lucas's space epic. Castaneda's books were eventually decried as bogus anthropology by the academic establishment, and the accounts of his encounters with the elusive Don Juan were considered to be novels, not non-fiction. Whatever the nature of Castaneda's works, they had a profound influence on *Star Wars*, and Don Juan seems to have been the template for Luke's ancient mentor, the all-wise, all-powerful being Master Yoda.

The Coming of the Force

In the series opener, *Star Wars* (now known as *Star Wars Episode IV: A New Hope*, 1977), a group of rebels against the tyranny of an evil galactic Empire steal the plans for the Empire's new super-weapon, an enormous space station called the "Death Star." They conceal the plans inside the robot R2-D2 (Kenny

Baker), who together with his robotic pal C-3PO (Anthony Daniels) transport them to a remote world where the plans remain hidden. Farm boy Luke Skywalker (Mark Hamill), living on the backwater planet of Tatooine, joins the battle against the Empire and becomes apprenticed to aged desert rat Obi-Wan Kenobi (Sir Alec Guinness). Obi-Wan is in reality the last of the "Jedi Knights," a group of paranormal warriors who have been hunted down and destroyed by the minions of the Empire. "For over a thousand generations the Jedi Knights were the guardians of peace and justice in the old Republic," Obi-Wan laments. The ancient Jedi informs Luke that he is in reality the son of a Jedi himself, and is destined to claim his father's psi powers as his birthright. Kenobi begins instructing Luke in the use of "the Force," a mystical power that gives the Jedi their paranormal abilities. Obi-Wan explains, "The Force is what gives a Jedi his power. It's an energy field created by all living things. It surrounds us and penetrates us. It binds the galaxy together."

Obi-Wan's opposite number is Darth Vader (David Prowse, voiced by James Earl Jones), a mysterious figure completely swathed in black body armor who sports an operatic cape and oversized Nazi helmet to emphasize the Wagnerian depths of his evil persona. Vader, Kenobi explains, was "seduced by the dark side of the force," and was responsible for betraying and murdering Luke's father, Anakin Skywalker. The menacing Vader displays his paranormal powers in an early scene inside the Death Star, when his judgment is challenged during a war conference by technocrat General Dodonna (Alex McCrindle), who insists that the battle station is the ultimate power in the universe. "The ability to destroy a planet is insignificant," Vader explains, "next to the power of the Force." "Don't try to frighten us with your sorcerer's ways, Lord Vader," the general snarls back. "Your sad devotion to that ancient religion has not helped you conjure up the stolen data tapes, or given you clairvoyance enough to find the Rebel's hidden fort…" The general's speech is abruptly cut off as Vader psychokinetically begins to strangle him using only the Force. "I find your lack of faith disturbing," he quips before releasing Dodonna from the psychic assault.

After intercepting a holographic message from Princess Leia Organa (Carrie Fisher), who has been taken prisoner by Vader, Obi-Wan is urged to take the robots to the planet Alderaan where the Death Star data can be analyzed for weaknesses. Luke and Obi-Wan travel to Mos Eisley spaceport to book passage off the planet, and Luke is amazed when Obi-Wan uses his Jedi skills to flummox Empire stormtroopers into not recognizing them. "The force can have a strong influence on the weak-minded," the wizard explains. At the spaceport, they contract smuggler Han Solo (Harrison Ford) and his alien pal Chewbacca (Peter Mayhew) to provide off-world passage for themselves and the two robots to Alderaan. Pursued by Vader and the Empire's troops, they escape into hyperspace in Solo's starship *The Millennium Falcon*. In the meantime, Alderaan is destroyed by the power of the Death Star in an unsuccessful effort to get

Princess Leia to reveal the location of the Rebels' secret base. Obi-Wan, on board the *Falcon*, psychically perceives a "great disturbance in the Force" at the moment that the planet is obliterated.

While they are en route to Alderaan, Obi-Wan begins Luke's paranormal training in earnest, explaining the workings of the Force while Han Solo cynically scoffs that it's all a bunch of "simple tricks and nonsense." When Luke

The dark Jedi knight Darth Vader (David Prowse) in *Star Wars* (1977).

finds he can anticipate the moves of a combat training droid by using the Force, Obi-Wan approvingly tells him, "You've taken your first step into a larger world." Arriving at Alderaan's location, they find the planet destroyed and are taken captive inside the Death Star. The ragtag team of adventurers manage to elude their captors and rescue the Princess from the innards of the labyrinthine battle station while Obi-Wan falls in single combat against his erstwhile Jedi pupil, Vader. The rest travel in the newly-liberated *Falcon* to the Rebel stronghold where Rebel military commanders plan to attack the enormous Death Star with a fleet of tiny, one-man fighter craft. The Rebel forces must penetrate the battle station's formidable defenses in order to drop photon torpedoes into a small vent, hitting the Death Star's main reactor and destroying it. After most of the Rebel X–wing fighters are shot down during the final battle, Luke hears Obi-Wan's voice telepathically urging him to "use the Force." Shutting off his targeting computer, Luke relies instead on his newly-acquired Jedi ESP to hit the target and destroy the Death Star.

One of the major themes in *Star Wars* is the conflict between the intuitive, preternatural realm of the Force and the futuristic universe of technology and machines. Vader's seemingly counter-intuitive contention that the "technological terror" and overwhelming military might represented by the Death Star is vulnerable to the mystical workings of the Force proves to be correct. Within the dazzling techno-world of *Star Wars* the Jedi way represents an anachronism, an atavistic return to the ancient shamanic traditions of centuries past. Obi-Wan trains his apprentice, Luke, to apprehend a shadow world of paranormal power that has become obscured by high technology. Vader represents the co-opting of these shamanic traditions by the machine world, his human identity having been subsumed by mechanical life-support systems that have transformed him into a quasi-human cyborg. Like many mystical warriors throughout history from Norse berserkers to Zen samurai, the Jedi Knights utilize their psychic skills to give themselves a paranormal edge in combat. It is only through the development of Luke's nascent ESP talents that the ultimate machine, the Death Star, is defeated. As Vader insisted, the Force is superior to even the most dire technology.

Lucas's mystical space opera struck a chord with audiences in America and around the world as *Star Wars* became a mega-blockbuster and pre-eminent cultural phenomenon. No science fiction film since Stanley Kubrick's equally mystical *2001: A Space Odyssey* (1968) had captured the public imagination and been embraced by such a wide popular audience. Art direction, costume, sound and special effects all came together under Lucas's direction to create a new science fiction movie *gestalt*. The film was released in the brand-new 70mm format with enhanced stereo sound, which gave movie audiences a novel, hi-tech viewing experience. The fine cast, headed by the distinguished Sir Alec Guinness, became American cultural icons and made the Force entirely believable. Extensive marketing of children's toys based on the film ensured a success far beyond the box office.

The enormous success of *Star Wars* cried out for a sequel, and Lucas was soon hard at work fashioning a series of films that would continue the saga. While the paranormal powers of Obi-Wan, Vader and Luke Skywalker were relatively modest in the original movie, Lucas would up the psychic ante considerably as the franchise continued. Unbelievably, *Star Wars* was made on a minuscule budget of $9 million, and as budgets for Lucas's epics increased exponentially, so did the psychic powers of the Jedi.

Psychic Sequelae

Lucas farmed out the first sequel, *The Empire Strikes Back* (a.k.a. *Star Wars Episode V*, 1980), to screenwriters Leigh Brackett and Lawrence Kasdan and director Irvin Kershner, while he continued in the executive producer role. The story picks up Luke Skywalker on the Rebel base located on the ice planet of Hoth. While investigating the landing of an Empire probe droid out in the frigid wastes, Luke is attacked by a wampa, an abominable snow-creature that knocks him unconscious and brings him back to his lair for a snack. Hung upside down with his feet encased in ice, Luke spies his discarded lightsaber lying just out of reach, and uses Jedi telekinesis to make the weapon fly into his hand. Armed and dangerous, Luke quickly deals with the wampa and staggers out into the wintry waste, where he experiences a vision of Obi-Wan, who is now a ghostly presence existing in a kind of phantom zone. Obi-Wan tells Luke to go to the Dagobah System, where he is to be instructed in the Jedi arts by psychic instructor Master Yoda. Immediately after this communication,

Jedi master Yoda (voiced by Frank Oz) instructs Luke Skywalker (Mark Hamill) in the ways of "the Force" in *The Empire Strikes Back* (1980).

Luke is rescued from a cold night's death by the sudden appearance of Han Solo, who has been out searching for him.

One of the Empire probe droids surveying Hoth has transmitted an image of the Rebel's power generator to Darth Vader's command ship. Upon viewing the picture, Vader clairvoyantly knows it indicates the location of the Rebel base, and that Luke is there. In the ensuing assault on Hoth by Empire forces, the Rebels are routed and flee into outer space, but instead of heading to the rendezvous point with the other Rebel forces, Luke zooms off to Dagobah to find Yoda. Vader punishes one of the starfleet admirals for his failure to capture Skywalker by psychokinetically strangling him while watching his death on a viewscreen. The black Jedi also communicates Luke's escape to his superior, the Emperor (played here by Clive Revill), a robed, hooded, Druid-like figure who speaks of a "great disturbance in the Force" caused by this turn of events.

While Vader and the Empire fleet pursue Solo and Princess Leia through space, Luke lands on the jungle world of Dagobah, where he meets Yoda, a diminutive, gnome-like alien creature who trained Jedi for 800 years before secluding himself on the obscure planet. Yoda, sizing up Luke with his psychic intuition, is hesitant to train the youth, to whom he emphasizes that becoming a Jedi requires "the deepest commitment, the most serious mind." Yoda is eventually persuaded by the disembodied voice of Obi-Wan. Luke trains hard

Darth Vader (David Prowse, left) reveals he is the father of Luke Skywalker (Mark Hamill) in *The Empire Strikes Back* (1980).

mentally and physically under Yoda's strict tutelage, while the Jedi instills him with Jedi wisdom. "A Jedi uses the Force for knowledge and defense," he tells Luke, "never for attack." However, the rambunctious Luke can't seem to get the hang of pumping up his psi powers. When challenged by Yoda to free his X-wing space fighter using psychokinesis from the swampy muck in which it has sunk, Luke moves it slightly but fails to dislodge it, adding, "You want the impossible." Yoda then demonstrates his industrial-strength PK by mentally lifting the ship and depositing it on dry land. "I don't believe it," Luke marvels, to which Yoda replies, "That is why you fail."

During one of Yoda's telekinetic exercises, the Jedi master explains that Luke will experience psychic visions as his powers develop. "Through the Force, things you will see," he says. "Other places, the future, the past, old friends long gone." Immediately Luke sees a vision of a city in the clouds where Han and Leia are being tortured. "It is the future you see," Yoda explains. He urges Luke to remain on Dagobah to complete his training rather than dash off to his friends' rescue, but the brash youngster will not be dissuaded. As Luke blasts off on his way to the cloud city, Obi-Wan laments, "That boy is our last hope," to which Yoda replies enigmatically, "No, there is another."

In the meantime, Han and Leia have temporarily escaped the clutches of the Empire and have taken refuge with Solo's one-time gambling buddy Lando Calrissian (Billy Dee Williams), who now administers a mining-colony operation from a city suspended in the sky on the distant planet of Bespin — the "city in the clouds" Luke has already remote-viewed. Unfortunately, Solo and the Princess are betrayed by Lando and handed over to Vader. Oddly, they are tortured without being questioned about anything, their torment being used instead as a psychic lure to draw Skywalker into a trap. Arriving in Bespin, Luke attempts to come to the aid of his friends, but Han Solo is placed in carbonite-freeze suspended animation by Vader and handed over to a bounty hunter to settle a regional feud. Meanwhile Lando flips back once more and rescues the Princess, the Wookie and the robots, who escape in the *Millennium Falcon*.

Luke steps into the trap set by Vader, and as the mystic warriors do battle the youngling displays impressive mind-over-matter skills that enable him to retrieve his lightsaber from a distance and even levitate. It soon becomes apparent, however, that despite his swordsmanship and newfound paranormal skills the wannabe Jedi is outclassed by Vader's command of the Force as the evil one assaults Luke with a barrage of heavy objects propelled by his PK. Then Darth Vader drops the ultimate bomb, revealing that, contrary to Obi-Wan's story, Vader is in reality Anakin Skywalker, Luke's father. Luke's ESP intuition tells him that Vader speaks the truth, and the dark lord reveals his plan for the two of them to combine their powers to overthrow the Emperor and rule the galaxy as father and son. Devastated by this dire news and by his betrayal by Obi-Wan, Luke throws himself down one of the city's ventilation ducts and winds up hanging onto a protrubance far above the clouds. In desperation, he calls Leia's name aloud, and at that moment she has an intuitive flash while flying away from the city in the *Falcon*. "I know where Luke is," she tells Lando, and guides the ship to his location, where he is rescued. As the *Falcon* departs, Luke can feel Vader's presence inside his mind before the Rebels escape into hyperspace.

Many *Star Wars* fans consider *The Empire Strikes Back* the best film in the series, and part of the reason for the movie's success was the augmentation of the psychic theme in the sequel. In the first film the paranormal element is restricted to Obi-Wan's occasional bouts of ESP and a single scene in which Darth Vader demonstrates his psychokinesis, while in *Empire* Luke's attempts to acquire the Force becomes a major plotline and Yoda and Vader demonstrate major-league PK by moving large, heavy objects using their powers of mind. Even Luke has acquired the ability to move small objects and levitate his body, and has become a formidable psychic warrior in the process. As the series evolves, the Jedi's telekinetic powers tend to be emphasized at the expense of their extrasensory perception. This is because the depiction of PK is more dramatic on-screen than mere ESP, which is an internal mental process. Dramatic license also dictates that the Jedi's psychic talents be limited because, if their inner vision reveals too much, there will be no suspense.

Luke (Mark Hamill) has attained full Jedi-hood in *Return of the Jedi* (1983).

The Yoda character is obviously modeled after Carlos Castaneda's Yaqui Indian sorcerer, Don Juan Matus, in Castaneda's series of popular "non-fiction" books on Native American magic and sorcery. Like Don Juan, Yoda is an aged figure possessing great wisdom who upbraids his young apprentice unmercifully at every turn while subjecting him to a series of harrowing supernatural ordeals. Luke, like the hapless Castaneda, seems to fail most of his mentor's psychic tests. Although the overwhelming majority of Jedi are human beings, Yoda, who is strongest on the right side of the Force, is an alien creature. The Jedi master's philosophy combines elements of pacifistic, Eastern religious mysticism with Don Juan's more combative "way of the warrior" in an uneasy mixture of shamanic thought and Buddhism. Yoda would eventually become one of the central characters in Lucas' series of *Star Wars* prequels beginning with *The Phantom Menace* (1999).

The Empire Strikes Back arguably contains more paranormal material than any of the other *Star Wars* films. Luke's apprenticeship, along with Yoda's ruminations on the nature of the Force, take up a good chunk of screen time. One of the more intriguing plot elements is Vader's setting the psychic trap for Luke by torturing Han and Leia, an act which transmits a clairvoyant vision of their suffering to the reckless youth and induces him to abandon his Jedi training. This implies that Jedi ESP can function over interstellar distances, an ability that is also implied in Obi-Wan's remote perception of the destruction of Alder-

The Emperor (Ian McDiarmid, center) confronts Luke (Mark Hamill) while Vader (David Prowse) looks on in *Return of the Jedi* (1983).

aan in the first movie. The emergence of Leia's psychic talents during the film's final scenes is another interesting subplot that is, unfortunately, left dangling. The sequel's most stunning revelation, however, is the fact that the entire galaxy is ruled by a single individual, the Emperor, by virtue of his superhuman psychic powers. Thus the destiny of this vast interstellar civilization is decided not by technology, but by a small elite's command of the paranormal.

In the third installment in the series, *Return of the Jedi* (*Star Wars Episode VI*, 1983), Luke Skywalker has assumed the mantle of a full-blown Jedi Knight. Returning to the desert world of Tatooine to rescue Han Solo from the sluglike alien outlaw Jabba the Hutt, Luke sports an austere black outfit complete with Druidic hood and black cape. The self-proclaimed Jedi infiltrates Jabba's underground lair using a "Jedi mind trick" to mentally dominate Jabba's henchmen, but Jabba himself proves to be immune to Luke's hypno-telepathy. Luke's Jedi credentials are called into question as he is taken prisoner and subjected to trials and ordeals by Jabba, but in the climactic battle he destroys the outlaw's gang and rescues Han, while Jabba himself winds up getting strangled to death by Leia.

His mission accomplished, Luke returns to Dagobah in order to complete his training, but after living for hundreds of years Yoda has suddenly taken ill, and is in fact dying. On his deathbed, the Jedi master warns his pupil against the dangers of the Dark Side of the Force, and further not to underestimate the powers of the Emperor. After Yoda dies, Luke continues the conversation with the ghost of Obi-Wan, who explains his reasons for dissembling about Luke's true ancestry, and also makes a stunning revelation: Leia is Luke's twin sister, and since the Force runs strong in the Skywalker family, she has paranormal powers of her own that remain latent. Obi-Wan also knows that the Emperor has foreseen that Luke's powers will surpass those of his father, Darth Vader, and that the Emperor will pit father against son in his quest for ultimate power.

In the meantime, the Emperor (Ian McDiarmid) visits Vader at a second, partially completed Death Star battle station, where the evil ones plan their next moves in the space war. The new Death Star is in orbit around the forest world of Endor, where a power generator on Endor's surface generates a force field that makes the battle station impregnable. The Emperor hopes to lure the Rebel forces into attacking what they think is an uncompleted Death Star, which despite its rough appearance is actually fully operational. Then he will destroy the Rebel fleet with the battle station's massive firepower.

The Rebels take the bait, and organize a coordinated attack on their enemy's space fortress. Luke, Han and Leia volunteer to land on Endor and disable the power generator that protects the Death Star. While they try to sneak by Vader's command ship in a stolen shuttlecraft, however, Luke and Vader become aware of each other's presence through their father-son telepathic link. Knowing that Luke is on Endor, Vader pursues his son; for his part, Luke knows he is endangering the mission due to the father/son mind-meld. Once on Endor, Han, Luke and Leia manage to elude the Empire's forces but are instead captured by a band of Ewoks—fuzzy, teddy bear–like primitives who plan to have them for dinner until Luke levitates C-3P0 using his Jedi PK. This display of "magic" convinces the Ewoks that the robot is some kind of deity, which makes the little fuzzies decide to join the Rebels in fighting against the Empire. Luke decides he must face Vader alone, and before leaving he reveals to Leia that they are brother and sister. Because the Force is strong in their family, she is also heir to the Jedi's paranormal abilities. "You have that power too," he tells her. "In time you'll learn to use it as I have."

Realizing that his presence with the Rebel forces on Endor will compromise their mission because Vader "can feel when I'm near," Luke chooses to give himself over to Vader's forces. Luke suspects Vader may harbor sentiments against the Emperor, and believes he can be turned away from the Dark Side through the power of their familial bond. Vader is indeed conflicted, but hands his son over to the Emperor on the Death Star anyway. For his part, the Emperor hopes to inflame Luke's hatred of Vader into a murderous rage that will compel him to kill his father, turning the young Jedi irrevocably to the Dark Side.

During the heat of their final combat, Vader telepathically plucks the knowledge that Leia is his daughter from Luke's mind, enraging the young Jedi into defeating his father. When Luke will not take the ultimate step into evil and kill his vanquished enemy, the Emperor unleashes bursts of lightning-like psi energy at Luke. Watching his son being slowly electrocuted by the Emperor, Vader turns on his master and hurls him into the depths of the Death Star. The effort, however, has mortally wounded Vader, who dies redeemed in the arms of his son. Luke escapes in a shuttlecraft while the Rebel forces blow up the Death Star and the Empire is finally defeated.

After the Wagnerian high tragedy of *Empire*, *The Return of the Jedi* adopted a lighter tone, but the third installment in the series was something of a letdown for some *Star Wars* fans, who felt it was too juvenile in its approach and featured too much of Frank Oz's puppetry. Director Richard Marquand and scenarist Lawrence Kasdan craft a superior sci-fi programmer with an able assist from the technicians at Industrial Light & Magic, but *Jedi* represents a flawed ending to the series and did not (and perhaps could not) exceed the hype of the first two films. Nonetheless, the culmination of Lucas's space opera cycle was still a critical and popular success that tied up all the loose ends of the Skywalker family saga.

Luke, the central character of all three films, achieves full Jedi-hood as a star warrior and even defeats the dread Darth Vader in single combat, but his paranormal powers cannot equal the Emperor's, whose command of the Force is such that he can hurl electrical bolts at Luke. In contrast to the cyborg-like Vader, the Emperor appears to be an atavistic throwback to ancient Druidic sorcery. Attired in a black robe and a cowl that partly conceals his withered features, he represents the primal fear of humankind toward the unknown forces of the preternatural. As the emissary of the Dark Side of the Force, he wields powers greater than any of the Jedi, powers that enable him to tyrannize the entire galaxy. His abilities of precognition and clairvoyance allow him to penetrate his enemies' secrets and weave his nefarious webs of evil far into the future.

In addition to his martial skills, Luke's wisdom also comes to fruition in the series closer. It is this newfound maturity that enables him to triumph over those who command a greater control over the Force. His telepathic insights into his father's psychology make it possible for Luke to predict correctly that Vader will betray the Emperor. *Jedi* develops the notion of the ESP mind-link between Luke and Vader, a plot device that reflects real-world psi functioning between family members as documented by parapsychologists. The *Star Wars* films posit a genetic basis for psychic abilities passed down over generations, or as Luke tells Leia, "the Force is strong in our family." Disappointingly, the matter of Leia's psi talents is hardly explored, even after her spontaneous burst of prescience that enables her to locate Luke near the end of *Empire*. Psychic powers are almost exclusively the province of male characters in Lucas's tril-

Left: Ewan McGregor as a youthful Obi-Wan Kenobi in George Lucas's *Star Wars Episode I: The Phantom Menace* (2000). *Right:* Liam Neeson as Obi-Wan's Jedi mentor Qui-Gon Jinn in *Star Wars Episode I: The Phantom Menace* (2000).

ogy, a trend that would continue in the *Star Wars* prequels. Similarly, psi is associated primarily with interplanetary warfare and high levels of testosterone throughout the series. There is no correspondingly feminine aspect of psi to balance the violent hypermasculinity of the Jedi. In many respects, the *Star Wars* films present a negative vision of how psychically gifted individuals might utilize their powers for warfare in a future society.

Psychic Prequels

After their initial release, the *Star Wars* series had a profound effect on the American cultural landscape. They revitalized the science fiction genre and led to a revival of the form in big-budget blockbusters such as *Superman: The Movie* (1978), *Star Trek: The Motion Picture* (1979), *Alien* (1979), *The Black Hole* (1979), *The Final Countdown* (1980), *Outland* (1981), *Blade Runner* (1982), *E.T.: The Extraterrestrial* (1982), *The Thing* (1982) and *Tron* (1982). Like *Star Wars*, the *Superman* and *Star Trek* films created popular franchises that extended the sci-fi movie wave into the 1980s.

During this time Lucas was developing his ideas for a second series of *Star Wars* films, which would be prequels based on backstory elements from the original movies. The new films would take place thirty years before the events depicted in *Star Wars*, at a time when the Jedi Knights existed as an established institution of galactic society, and would chronicle the coming of dark knight Anakin Skywalker and the eventual downfall of the Jedi. Work on the new trilogy would begin in earnest in 1994 as Lucas went to work on the screenplay for what would come to be known as "Episode I" of the series. In order to prepare the public for the next generation of *Star Wars* films, the original movies were re-released in 1997 in "Special Editions," with updated special effects and new scenes added. *Star Wars Episode I: The Phantom Menace* was released in 1999, to kick off the new series amid great hype and fanfare.

As the film opens, two Jedi, Qui-Gon Jinn (Liam Neeson) and his apprentice, the youthful Obi-Wan Kenobi (Ewan McGregor) have been dispatched as ambassadors of the Republic to the backwater world of Naboo to negotiate with the perfidious and avaricious Trade Federation. The Federation has placed a blockade of space cruisers around the planet with the intent of invading and occupying Naboo, and Queen Amidala (Natalie Portman) has refused to acquiesce to their economic demands. Before the negotiations can even begin, the Jedi diplomats are betrayed by the devious Federation, who attempt to murder them as part of a deeper conspiracy directed by the shadowy Darth Sidious, who is the "Phantom Menace" of the title. Qui-Gon and Obi-Wan display their psychic martial skills in battle with killer robots, and at one point Qui-Gon focuses the Force through his lightsaber with sufficient energy to melt through a heavy blast door on the Federation command ship. The two Jedi are outclassed by the sheer numbers of the droids, however, and escape to the planet's surface in landing craft during the invasion of Naboo.

The two Jedi convince Queen Amidala to accompany them back to the Republic's capitol of Coruscant to plead her case, and she agrees, as the Trade Federation armies now occupy Naboo. They depart with the Queen and a retinue of her followers, but their ship's hyperdrive is damaged while running the Federation blockade, forcing them to put in for repairs on the outlaw desert planet of Tatooine (familiar to audiences as Luke Skywalker's home world in the original movie). Lacking the funds to purchase parts for their starship, they are forced to haggle with alien junk dealer Watto (voice of Andrew Secombe), who is impervious to Qui-Gon's Jedi mind tricks. In the process they encounter a strange little 12-year-old boy, Anakin Skywalker (Jake Lloyd), who is Watto's slave.

Qui-Gon immediately senses a peculiarity of the Force surrounding young Anakin, who otherwise seems like a normal child except for a certain feistiness, and has Obi-Wan run a test for "midi-chlorians" on a sample of the boy's blood. These midi-chlorians are sub-microscopic living organisms that abide inside of human body cells in a symbiotic relationship. Their specific function is to enable humans to interface with the Force, and a high midi-chlorian count is an indicator of Jedi talent. Obi-wan reports that Anakin's count is off the charts, and at over 20,000 is higher than even Jedi Master Yoda's. Questioning Anakin's mother, Shmi (Pernilla August), Qui-Gon learns that Anakin was a virgin birth, conceived without a father through the action of the midi-chlorians. These anomalies of origin and physiology lead Qui-Gon to suspect that Anakin may be fated with an unusual destiny. He explains to Shmi that if the child had been born on a planet ruled by the Republic, his abilities would have been detected and he would have been selected for training as a Jedi, but because Tatooine lies outside the Republic's jurisdiction, Anakin's psychic potential will not be realized.

Employing his hyper-quick Jedi reflexes, little Anakin wins a dangerous pod-race on Tatooine, earning enough money to fix the hyperdrive on Amidala's spaceship. In addition, Qui-Gon uses his PK to influence a "chance cube" in a wager with Watto for the boy's freedom. A slave no longer, Anakin is free to travel to Coruscant to be trained in the Jedi arts, although he must leave his mother in slavery on Tatooine. As they depart, Qui-Gon is attacked by Darth Sidious's dread apprentice Darth Maul (Ray Park), who has trailed the Jedi to the desert planet. Qui-Gon fends off the attack as the spaceship takes off for Coruscant with Anakin on board, and they arrive without further incident.

Amidala is greeted by Senator Palpatine (Ian McDiarmid), who is supporting her cause in the Senate, while Qui-Gon takes Anakin before the Jedi council for examination. Master Yoda, Mace Windu (Samuel L. Jackson) and the other Council members are dubious about training the lad. Anakin is subjected to a telepathy test by the Council, which consists of remote viewing images on a small TV-like screen and receiving emotional impressions from Yoda. Even though the boy acquits himself well on the tests, the Council rejects Qui-Gon's bid to have him trained as a Jedi, citing his age (he's too old) and prescient mixed signals regarding the boy's fate. Yoda detects a "divergence in the Force" surrounding Anakin, but Qui-Gon believes that he may be "The One," a super-powerful Jedi who will bring balance to the Force according to an ancient prophecy. In spite of the Council's decision, the willful Qui-Gon announces that he will train Anakin with or without the Council's consent.

When the Senate refuses to aid Naboo, Amidala decides to return home with Qui-Gon, Obi-wan and Anakin to combat the Federation forces and free her people. As battles in space and on the planet's surface ensue, Qui-Gon and Obi-Wan are drawn into mortal combat with the formidable Darth Maul. Qui-Gon is killed during the lightsaber duel, and Darth Maul is in turn dispatched by Obi-Wan while the Trade Federation forces are defeated and Naboo is liberated. With his dying breath, Qui-Gon makes Obi-Wan promise he will train Anakin as a Jedi. Yoda ruminates about the resurgence of the Sith, evil psychics who have given themselves over to the Dark Side of the Force and oppose the benevolence of the Jedi. The Jedi Master further notes that the Sith always operate in pairs consisting of a master and an apprentice.

Once again Lucas struck box-office gold with *The Phantom Menace*, as the updated, upgraded *Star Wars* installment broke movie attendance records. While the film had the benefit of dazzling, ultra-sophisticated, computer-generated special effects, some critics pointed to weaknesses in Lucas's screenplay and even complained of racial insensitivity in the portrayal of various characters. Much of the film is carried on the broad shoulders of Irish actor Liam Neeson, whose performance as the Jedi Knight Qui-Gon Jinn brings a quiet dignity and a detached lack of bellicosity to his role as master warrior. Sitting in the director's chair for the first time since the original *Star Wars* in 1977, Lucas delivered a slick piece of entertainment that would turn out to be an international crowd-pleaser.

In *The Phantom Menace* the audience is shown the Jedi organization just before its destruction during the wars that ended the old Republic. The Jedi temple on Coruscant is a large, imposing structure housing the psychic outfit's administrative offices, records systems and training facilities for the "Padawan Learners" or "younglings" being instructed in the paranormal arts. A semi-autonomous organization, the Jedi function as a diplomatic and/or law enforcement arm of the Republic's Senate, dispatched to hot spots around the galaxy to ensure the stability of the Republic against various factions that tear at its fabric. Their psychic talents are thus employed in the service of a state governed by democratic principles, and their psi talents are a glue that binds the disparate elements of their multiracial society together. The Sith, who wish to use their powers to dominate this futuristic society, represent a paranormal counterforce to the Jedi. Either way, the entire universe is destined to be ruled by the psychic abilities of a few despite the technological sophistication of this mega-civilization.

The profound cultural influence of Lucas's paranormal mythology on society at large was illustrated in a quirky news item reported after the release of *The Phantom Menace*. During the 2001 census in the United Kingdom, nearly 400,000 Britons indicated their religion on census forms as "Jedi Knight," a statistic that could theoretically elevate Jedi-ism to the level of a fully recognized and legal religion. Shortly thereafter the situation was repeated in the Australian census, in which more than 70,000 Aussies also noted their Jedi faith on population forms. These figures speak to the compelling nature of a mythic religion based on psychic principles.

In the next series installment, *Star Wars Episode II: Attack of the Clones* (2002), the saga continues ten years after the events of *The Phantom Menace*. Anakin Skywalker (Hayden Christensen) has grown to young adulthood on Coruscant as Obi-Wan Kenobi's Jedi apprentice. It is a time of unrest in the galactic Republic, where a separatist movement led by rogue Jedi Count Dooku (Christopher Lee) in alliance with the Trade Federation and Banking Clan is attempting to secede from the Republic. Amidala (a.k.a. Padmé) is no longer queen of her home planet, but instead represents Naboo in the Senate. In the wake of an assassination attempt on the life of Senator Padmé, Anakin and Obi-Wan are assigned to protect her. Romantic sparks start to fly between Anakin and Padmé after they renew their acquaintance, a situation that may compromise Anakin's Jedi vows.

Investigating the assassination plot, Obi-Wan travels to the hidden planet of Kamino in search of the guilty party, bounty hunter Jango Fett (Temuera Morrison). Instead he discovers that a Jedi Knight has contracted for the manufacture of a clone army for the Republic ten years ago, an army that is now ready to be deployed. (All of the soldiers have been cloned from Fett's DNA.) After Obi-Wan speaks to the bounty hunter, Fett flees to the factory planet of Geonosis, with Obi-Wan in hot pursuit. In the meantime, the Jedi Council assigns Anakin to protect Padmé as she returns to Naboo to report on the situation to the new queen. Predictably, love blossoms between the senator and the Jedi during their close acquaintance, but Anakin is troubled by vivid dreams of his mother's suffering, and the couple decide to travel to Tatooine in order to discover clues to her fate. Anakin finds that Shmi Skywalker has been kidnapped and enslaved by Tusken Raiders (a.k.a. the "Sand People"), a group of primitive, nomadic desert dwellers. He locates Shmi, who has been mistreated so badly she is nearly dead, at a Tusken desert camp, and has one moment with his mother before she dies in his arms. In a fit of rage, Anakin exacts vengeance upon the Sand People by slaughtering every man, woman and child in the camp, while back in Coruscant Yoda feels Anakin's pain via interstellar telepathy.

With the prospect of a galactic war looming, the Senate confers emergency dictatorial powers upon Senator Palpatine, while Yoda decides to visit Kamino to inspect the clone army. In the meantime, Obi-Wan discovers that Count Dooku is building an army of droids on the factory world of Geonosis, which will be used to attack the Republic and overwhelm the Jedi. Obi-Wan winds up being taken prisoner by Dooku, who informs him that a Sith lord is secretly trying to dominate the Republic. Intercepting a message to the Jedi Council from Obi-Wan, Anakin and Padmé learn of Obi-Wan's distress and travel to Geonosis to rescue him, but instead are taken prisoner by Dooku and forced to fight for their lives in a giant arena. A contingent of Jedi led by Mace Windu arrive but are overwhelmed by Dooku's army. Fortunately Yoda shows up in a timely fashion with the entire clone army in tow, and a full-scale battle erupts.

Dooku flees into his stronghold on Geonosis, with Anakin, Obi-Wan and Yoda in hot pursuit. When cornered by the two young Jedi, Dooku defeats both of them with his augmented Sith powers, for like the Emperor, Dooku can shoot lightning bolts from his fingertips. After Dooku overwhelms Anakin and Obi-Wan, Yoda arrives and the Sith and the Jedi Master square off. Yoda deflects Dooku's electrical streams and displays equally impressive powers of telekinesis as the two hurl heavy objects at each other, but since their duel cannot be settled by their mastery of the Force, they continue with lightsabers. With the clone army closing in, Dooku suddenly breaks off the fight and escapes from Geonosis, but despite their early victory Yoda fears that "the shroud of the Dark Side has fallen," and that the Jedi's ability to use the Force has been diminished. In the film's final scene, Anakin and Padmé are secretly wed on Naboo.

As audiences were well aware, *Clones* was the set-up for the final installment of the saga, in which Anakin Skywalker is transformed into the gothic Darth Vader. Like *Empire*, the middle film of the first trilogy, *Clones* serves as an intermediary second act in which loose ends are deliberately left dangling, giving the end product a lack of a sense of resolution. As a result, the film seems more like a series of unconnected episodes than a coherent whole. There is an undercurrent of impending doom surrounding the proceedings, as the Jedi suffer a major setback in their mastery of the Force that will ultimately lead to their destruction in the series finale. The film suffers from Lucas's confusing screenplay, a dearth of interesting characters (Christopher Lee's Count Dooku is introduced late in the film), too many silly love scenes, and Hayden Christensen's leaden performance in the lead role of Anakin.

While tantalizingly little was shown of the Jedi Temple on Coruscant in *The Phantom Menace*, *Clones* took audiences deep inside this sanctum sanctorum, which is revealed as a palatial affair housing vast archives and databanks, training facilities and meeting rooms in this high-tech headquarters devoted to the development of individual psychic potential. In one scene, Yoda is shown instructing a group of Jedi children or "younglings" on the use of the Force with tot-sized laser swords. A couple of female Jedi finally make a brief appearance in the *Star Wars* series in the battle scenes near the film's conclusion. The Jedi organization is depicted as an integral cog in the functioning of the democratic Republic, their paranormal skills utilized for the benefit of the galactic megastate. In many ways the Jedi represent the glue that holds the political structure of the state together, for with their passing the Republic cannot function and descends into chaos. The Sith represent a totalitarian alternative to the pluralistic Jedi, their psi powers concentrated into the hands of only the Sith Lord and his apprentice. *The Phantom Menace*'s intriguing subplot regarding Anakin being "The One," a super-being who will restore balance to the Force, is hardly mentioned in *Clones*.

In the saga's final installment, *Star Wars Episode III: Revenge of the Sith* (2005), the cycle comes full circle as the final downfall of the Jedi is chronicled. Just a few years after the events in *Clones*, the Republic is crumbling under the assault of Separatist forces led by Dooku and his lieutenant, the cyborg warrior General Grievous. As the film opens Grievous has launched a daring attack on Coruscant and has taken former Senator (now Chancellor) Palpatine hostage on his command ship. Obi-Wan and Anakin infiltrate the ship to rescue the Senator, but instead are trapped into fighting Dooku, who quickly puts Obi-Wan out of action. Anakin's powers have grown in the interim, however, and he defeats the Sith Lord and kills his helpless adversary at Palpatine's request, contrary to Jedi custom.

A bond between the Chancellor and the young Jedi deepens after the resolution of the hostage crisis as Anakin comes more and more under the sway of Palpatine. Anakin is haunted by recurring precognitive dreams about the pregnant Padmé dying in childbirth that are similar to the prophetic dreams he had about his mother before she died. Learning of this obsession, Palpatine exploits Anakin's fears by hinting that there are aspects of the Force that the Jedi consider unnatural, involving the manipulation of the midi-chlorians to defeat death itself. "Let me help you to know the subtleties of the Force," the Chancellor suggests, to "study all aspects of the great mystery." Yoda, however, counsels Anakin to be detached, telling him, "The fear of loss is a path to the dark side." Anakin ignores Yoda's advice and continues to fall under the influence of the Sith Lord.

As battles rage on various worlds throughout the galaxy, Obi-Wan locates and dispatches General Grievous, while back on Coruscant Palpatine decrees that Anakin will be the Chancellor's representative on the Jedi Council. This move causes mistrust between the Council and Anakin, who fear (rightly) that he has become the Chancellor's puppet. The Jedi, in turn, want Anakin to spy on Palpatine, as the young Jedi's loyalties are conflicted. Things get even dicier when Anakin learns for certain that Palpatine is the Sith Lord, the phantom menace who has been preparing to destroy the Republic and assume power. When Mace Windu attempts to take Palpatine into custody, the Chancellor reveals his Sith powers as he duels with the Jedi Master. As he hurls bolts of electricity at Windu, Palpatine's features age dramatically and he assumes the wizened visage of an old man. Windu is at the point of defeating the Sith Lord when Anakin arrives and is tipped over into the Dark Side with his decision to help Palpatine kill the Jedi Master. His transition to the Dark Side complete, Palpatine confers a new identity on Anakin and gives him the Sith name "Darth Vader." Anakin/Vader is then dispatched to the Jedi Temple to slaughter the unsuspecting Knights, including the younglings.

Yoda and Obi-Wan, returning to Coruscant from far-flung fronts in the war, become aware of Anakin's treachery, but it is too late. The Jedi have been decimated and Palpatine has dissolved the Republic and assumed the role of Galactic Emperor. While Obi-Wan departs with the pregnant Padmé in tow to confront Anakin, Yoda goes one-on-one with the Emperor in a psychic duel inside the Senate building, where democracy is symbolically destroyed as the Jedi Master and the Sith Lord tear up the chamber with feats of industrial-strength telekinesis. Yoda and the Emperor fight to a draw as Yoda escapes from Coruscant, while Obi-Wan soundly defeats Anakin and leaves his charred body for dead. In all the excitement Padmé has gone into labor, and she is rushed to a medical facility where she gives birth to twins but dies in childbirth as predicted by Anakin. Feeling his new disciple's suffering via telepathy, the Emperor locates Anakin and surgically transforms him into the black-suited, Nazi-helmeted Darth Vader familiar from the original trilogy, while Padmé's children, destined to become Luke Skywalker and Princess Leia, are concealed from the Emperor on Alderaan and Tatooine. Yoda and Obi-Wan, the last of the Jedi, go into hiding and the stage is set for the events of the 1977 *Star Wars* as the epic begins anew.

In *Episode III*, glimpses of the Sith philosophy are provided for the first time. Unlike the detached, monastic Jedi, the Sith draw their power from exploiting their baser passions. They have explored aspects of the Force that are forbidden to the Jedi, and seemingly have even more power. Only the Sith Lords like Count Dooku and the Emperor can shoot lightning bolts from their fingers, a feat that none of the Jedi can duplicate (although Yoda is able to deflect the bolts back). The Sith stand for totalitarian dominance of the galaxy by only two persons in contrast to the democratic Jedi, who are solely an instrument of majority rule. Anakin is corrupted by the Dark Side when he is willing to overthrow the Republic and betray his friends in his selfish desire to preserve Padmé's life.

It seems ironic that the series that began with the light-hearted *Star Wars*, a film that avoided taking itself too seriously, should conclude with the heavy-handed *Sturm und Drang* of *Revenge of the Sith*. The Wagnerian high tragedy of the final installment removes much of the fun factor from *Sith* that had enlivened the other films in the saga. Thus the *Star Wars* epic concludes with death, disfigurement, the killing of children and a primal evil triumphant throughout the galaxy, a situation that is not ameliorated by the knowledge that the series actually ends with the cartoon antics of *Return of the Jedi* in Lucas's confusing chronology. As in *The Phantom Menace* and *Attack of the Clones*, the audience is granted a glimpse into the Jedi Temple, a cathedral-like edifice of vaulted halls, columns and polished marble floors that somewhat resembles the Vatican. Continuing the trend in *Clones*, a couple of female Jedi Knights are briefly glimpsed in this male-dominated psychic society.

With the notion of the Jedi Knights, Lucas conjured a vision of psychically gifted individuals who are fully integrated into their high-tech society and use their talents for the betterment of humankind. In this sense he presents a positive picture of psi, but at the same time the paranormal is associated with warfare and shown to have an evil, anti-human potential as well. For the most part, Lucas's star warriors emphasize telekinetic martial skills at the expense of more inter-personal psychic talents such as telepathy, empathy or clairvoyance. Curiously, the Jedi's hyper-masculinity also partakes of what are traditionally thought of as aspects of feminine mysticism and magic. The Jedi are trained to rely on their feelings and intuitions rather than their rational minds— in other words, to abandon their logical, masculine, materialist ways of thinking that are externalized by the super-science of their high-tech environment, and embrace a deeper wisdom, which is usually associated with the feminine, within themselves. Thus, the *Star Wars* series transforms the witchy, intuitive powers of the paranormal traditionally associated with women into a male virtue. There is no overt female influence on Jedi culture, however. The Jedi Temple, symbolic of the Order, sports five prominently displayed phallic towers that advertise the organization's masculine orientation, and although it is not specifically stated, the Jedi are obliged to take a vow of celibacy in order to preserve their lifestyle as warrior-monks. The female Jedi briefly depicted in *Clones* and *Sith* seem to have been added as an afterthought in order to avoid charges of sexism on Lucas's part.

Dune

Ironically, the success of the first *Star Wars* trilogy served to revive interest in bringing Frank Herbert's epic novel *Dune*, which had provided much of the inspiration for Lucas's space opera, to the screen. Like the original *Star Wars*, *Dune* also featured a young hero with psychic powers coming of age on a desert planet and defying the overwhelming military superiority of a totalitarian galactic empire. After a couple of false starts by directors Alejandro Jodorowsky and Ridley Scott, producer Dino De Laurentiis obtained the rights to Herbert's novel and greenlighted the project with quirky cult director David Lynch at the helm. No expense would reportedly be spared by Dino in striving to bring Herbert's beloved science fiction classic to an adoring multitude of fans. An international cast of illustrious thespians was assembled for the task, including Max von Sydow, José Ferrer, Siân Phillips, Sylvana Mangano, Jürgen Prochnow, Patrick Stewart, Kenneth McMillan, Sean Young and the pop singer Sting. First-time screen actor Kyle MacLachlan was cast in the lead role as the film's protagonist, psychic superman Paul Atreides.

In the year 10,191, interstellar space travel has enabled humankind to populate the galaxy. These far-flung worlds are ruled by "noble houses," familial clans that have jurisdiction over individual star systems, with the houses in turn organized into a vast galactic Empire and ruled by an emperor. As in the *Star Wars* movies, however, much of the real power in the universe is concentrated in the hands of a few psychically gifted individuals and organizations. The Bene Gesserit, a sisterhood of black-robed, nun-like women with paranormal talents, permeate every institution of the Empire and covertly influence much of what goes on behind the scenes with their psi abilities. Like Jedi Knights, Bene Gesserit sisters are trained from early childhood to develop their ESP, mind-control powers and feminine human potential in general. They are employed throughout the Empire as "truthsayers," individuals who utilize their telepathy to probe human minds and ascertain their motives. The Bene Gesserit have a grand strategy to manipulate various bloodlines in order to produce the "Kwisatz Haderach," the universe's super-being who will possess unimaginable psychic powers.

Another critically important group with ESP abilities is the Spacing Guild, who "fold space" between the stars by "traveling without moving" over interstellar distances. In order to accomplish this, Guild star pilots utilize a drug called mélange, a spice-like substance that makes space travel possible. The spice is found on only one world in the entire galaxy, the desert planet of Arrakis, more commonly called Dune, where it is produced by the excretions of gigantic sandworms in the deep desert. Arrakis, and the spice, are therefore of primary importance to the cohesion of the Empire, and the spice must flow in order to keep the Guild happy.

As *Dune* opens, a third-stage Guild navigator pays an unscheduled visit to Emperor Shaddam IV (Jose Ferrer) to quiz him about his plans concerning the future of Arrakis. The Emperor tells his Bene Gesserit truthsayer, the Reverend Mother Helen Mohiam (Siân Phillips), "I shall want telepathy during his visit and a report when we're finished." The spacers, however, insist "the Bene Gesserit witch must leave" before the meeting can start. Wheeled into the throne room in an imposing, tank-like structure, the Navigator, who has been mutated into an inhuman, slug-like form by the spice, wastes no time in focusing his own telepathic powers on the Emperor's mind. "You are transparent," he informs Shaddam, "I see many things. I see plans within plans. I see you behind it."

Realizing that deception is impossible, the Emperor explains that he intends to transfer ownership of Arrakis from its current administrators, the Harkonnen clan, to the House Atreides. This is really only a ploy to destroy the Atreides, whose growing popularity he fears, for once they have taken possession of Dune he is plotting to secretly back the Harkonnens with imperial military forces in order to help them depose the Atreides in what will be perceived as merely a clan war between the two great Houses. The Navigator, however, informs him that the Guild has foreseen a glitch in his plan in the person of the Atreides heir, Paul Atreides (Kyle MacLachlan). For reasons they do not reveal, the Guild wants him killed. Unknown to both parties, Reverend Mother Mohiam has monitored the entire conversation from an adjacent room via telepathy, and she makes plans to examine Paul Atreides on the clan's current home world of Caladan.

Paul's mother Jessica (Francesca Annis) is a Bene Gesserit adept who is the bound concubine of Duke Leto Atreides (Jürgen Prochnow) and has used her abilities to conceive a son for the Duke instead of a daughter as mandated by the Bene Gesserit breeding program. Fearing Jessica may have inadvertently produced a Kwisatz Haderach, once on Caladan the Reverend Mother tests Paul by placing his hand inside a metal box and telepathically producing "pain by nerve induction," but Paul, who has received psychic training from Jessica, resists the pain to prove his awareness is powerful enough to control his instincts. "No woman-child ever withstood so much," the Reverend Mother marvels, but goes on to warn Paul against drinking the "Water of Life," a toxic

Telepathic Bene Gesserit "truthsayer" Gaius Helen Moiham (Siân Phillips) and Emperor Shaddam IV (José Ferrer) await the coming of a Spacing Guild navigator in *Dune* (1984).

drug derived from the bile of newborn worms on Arrakis. Only women may imbibe the ESP-inducing fluid, as all men who have tried have died.

The transition of power from House Harkonnen to House Atriedes on Dune goes smoothly as clan leader Baron Harkonnen (Kenneth MacMillan) plots the covert takeover of Arrakis. The Baron, an obese pervert who is so fat he needs an antigravity device to move his vast bulk around, is relying on a traitor in the House Atriedes to disable the clan's protective energy shield during the invasion. On Arrakis, Paul is exposed to the prescient effects of the spice mélange for the first time, and begins to experience precognitive visions of his future wife, Chani (Sean Young), and an impending life-threatening duel with his opposite number, the Harkonnen nobleman Feyd-Rautha (Sting).

When invasion time comes, the Atreides traitor, House physician Dr. Yueh (Dean Stockwell), betrays his Duke and takes out the shield device, leaving Dune's defenses wide open to Harkonnen and Imperial forces. Duke Leto is killed during the battle, but Paul and Jessica, who are being escorted to the deep desert to die of exposure, use the mind-control technique of "the Voice" to kill their Harkonnen captors and escape. They take refuge with the Fremen, the indigenous nomadic warrior people of Dune's deserts, who are duly impressed with Paul's and Jessica's psychic powers. The Fremen have a prophecy—"One will come, a voice from the outer world," who will restore the Fremen to their rightful place as rulers of Arrakis—and they suspect Paul may be the One. Under the tutelage of the Fremen, Paul learns the way of the desert and he and

The Lady Jessica (Francesca Annis) and Paul Atreides (Kyle MacLachlan) in David Lynch's *Dune* (1984).

Jessica become accepted as members of their nomadic society. As he has long foreseen, Paul marries the Fremen woman, Chani (Sean Young). Working with his new allies, the young Atreides wages a guerrilla desert war against the Harkonnens that brings spice production to a standstill.

In order to become a Fremen Reverend Mother, Jessica must undergo the ordeal of drinking the Water of Life. If her body transmutes the poison she will gain additional powers. Jessica survives the ordeal, but the female child she is carrying (she had been impregnated by Duke Leto just prior to the invasion) is born prematurely during the ceremony. Paul's sister, named Alia by the Fremen, is born with all the psychic abilities of a Reverend Mother. Realizing that he must take the Water of Life himself, Paul also survives and becomes, in essence, the Kwisatz Haderach. During the experience, Paul remote-views the Emperor plotting with the Guild to wrest Arrakis from the Harkonnens using his legions of Sardaukar terror troops. In the final battle, Paul routs the Imperial forces and the Baron is killed, but Paul must fight Feyd-Rautha Harkonnen one-on-one to become the heir of the Empire. Paul kills Feyd-Rautha during a knife duel and demonstrates his newly-acquired psychic powers by using telekinesis to split the stone floor underneath his opponent and control the weather to produce the first-ever rainfall on Arrakis.

While Lynch and De Laurentiis were obliged to follow the general outlines of the novel's plot, in its execution *Dune* was transformed into a work barely recognizable to fans of Herbert's novel. Director Lynch's mordant sensibilities crafted a failed science fiction epic that was unnecessarily grotesque and frequently descended into unintentional humor. Sci-fi fans who were expecting a more literary, sophisticated version of *Star Wars* were doomed to grave disappointment, and movie audiences stayed away in droves. Even the film's much-touted special effects looked pitiful in comparison with the dazzling technology that enlivened Lucas's space opera. The stellar cast of international thespians and the camerawork of ace British cinematographer Freddie Francis were unable to rescue the production from the general silliness of Lynch's screenplay and warped directorial sensibilities.

Despite its profound shortcomings, *Dune* contains some interesting ideas (culled from Herbert's book) concerning the role of psychic individuals in a technologically advanced society. Even more than the galactic society depicted in *Star Wars*, the interstellar empire in *Dune* is dependent on the paranormal abilities of a small group of elites. The star navigators of the Spacing Guild require the spice mélange to provide them with the precognitive abilities needed to journey between the many planets that make up the Empire. Without their psychic talents, their far-flung spacefaring civilization would immediately collapse.

The psi-enabled Bene Gesserit sisterhood present an interesting contrast with *Star Wars'* Jedi Knights. Unlike the Jedi, the Bene Gesserit wield their paranormal powers in secret. They use their talents to realize their own selfish ends, rather than for the good of society at large. Their ultimate aim is to breed a genetic superwoman, the Kwisatz Haderach, who will dominate the universe under the auspices of the sisterhood, for like *Star Wars*, *Dune* posits a genetic basis for the possession of psychic abilities. If the Jedi represent the appropriation of psi powers of clairvoyance and intuition usually associated with the feminine, *Dune* reverses this equation by having Paul Atreides penetrate the female realm of the Bene Gesserit in order to acquire their paranormal talents. By drinking the Water of Life and metabolizing the poison in an ordeal that no man has ever survived, Paul appropriates the psi powers of the sisterhood and is able to dominate them mentally.

Perhaps the most controversial aspect of the paranormal universe of *Dune* is the role of drugs in acquiring psychic abilities. Psychedelic drugs such as peyote and magic mushrooms were used by shamans and priests in Pre-Columbian Mexico and South America to induce visions and potentiate psi powers. Although author Herbert reportedly had minimal exposure to hallucinogenic substances, *Dune* was published during the psychedelic revival of the 1960s, when experimentation with these drugs was rampant and thought to increase one's psychic potential. The South American psychedelic plant known as yage or ayahuasca was initially called "telepathine" for its alleged telepathic properties, for instance. By the time *Dune* was made, however, these drugs had acquired a bad rep and the drug angle had to be downplayed, though it still constitutes an integral part of the plot. Paul is shown chowing down on a spice stick (which resembles an orange-colored Tootsie Roll) in only one sequence in the film, after which he spontaneously experiences a vision. Similarly, the sequences in which Jessica and Paul quaff the hallucinogenic Water of Life are central to the film's narrative. It is only through taking this powerful toxic substance that Paul finally acquires his true powers.

"Is It Now?"

Acclaimed director Steven Spielberg, veteran of big-budget, crowd-pleasing excursions into the realm of science fiction that included *Close Encounters of the Third Kind* (1977), *E.T.: The Extraterrestrial* (1982) and *Jurassic Park* (1993), returned to the genre with the sci-fi action thriller *Minority Report* (2002). One of a number of films based on the works of cult SF writer Philip K. Dick that includes *Blade Runner* (1982) and *Total Recall* (1990), the screenplay was adapted from Dick's short story "The Minority Report."

In the futureopolis of Washington D.C. circa 2054, murder has become non-existent as a result of a novel law-enforcement technique labeled "Pre-Crime" that employs the psychic talents of three mutants who possess precognitive powers. These "Pre-Cogs," as they are called, consist of one female, Agatha, and a pair of male twins, Dashiell and Arthur, who are ensconced in a high-tech facility known as the "Temple" in D.C. The three techno-prophets float in a water tank in a drug-induced, semi-comatose state that enables their prescience, their brains hooked up to a machine that displays and records their visions like movie films via "optical tomography." They are able to foresee premeditated murders up to four days before they are going to occur, although spontaneous crimes of passion may occur with much less lead time. The names of the murderers and victims are laser-inscribed onto wooden balls so that they may not be altered. Pre-crime has been so successful in preventing murders before they happen that a national referendum on whether to expand the program to the rest of the USA is soon to be voted on by the national electorate.

The Pre-Crime unit is headed up by John Anderton (Tom Cruise), who is still recovering from the trauma of the abduction of his son at a public swimming pool and the breakup of his marriage in the aftermath. In anticipation of the national referendum on Pre-Crime, the Justice Department is obliged to conduct an oversight investigation of the process, and they dispatch official Danny Witwer (Colin Farrell) to examine this revolutionary technology for possible flaws. After observing Anderton and his Pre-Cops in action as they prevent a "future murder," Witwer remains skeptical, and wants to know if the Pre-Cogs ever come up with false positives. He is assured they never have, and that it is impossible for them to provide fake cerebral output. He also has misgivings about the way the Pre-Cogs are maintained in a semi-comatose state, but is told by Anderton, "It's better if you don't think of them as human." "No, they're much more than that," counters Witwer, who was formerly a seminary student and has a religious streak. "Science has stolen most of our miracles. In a way they give us hope of the existence of the divine," he muses. He also notes that, historically, the real power of exploiting precognition has been with the priests, not with the oracle, and wonders if the process could be corrupted by human error.

After Witwer's inspection concludes, Anderton lingers by the edge of the Pre-Cog pool when Agatha (Samantha Morton) suddenly breaks into full consciousness and grabs him by the arm. "Can you see?" she asks him, as the data screen displays her visionary images of a murder that occurred several years earlier. Intrigued, Anderton does a little research and finds that Agatha's "pre-vision" was of the murder of an individual named Ann Lively, who has disappeared. He also learns that Agatha's pre-vision of the crime has mysteriously been erased. Soon afterward, the Pre-Cogs proclaim another future murder, that of a person named Leo Crow (Mike Binder), who is destined to be killed by Chief Anderton himself. Believing he might have been set up to murder a man he doesn't even know, Anderton finds himself on the run from his own Pre-Cops, who attempt to hunt him down using rocket packs, heat sensors and a squad of robotic "spiders," but the former Chief manages to stay one step ahead of the law.

Visiting the reclusive, middle-aged scientist Dr. Iris Hineman (Lois Smith), one of the architects of Pre-Crime, Anderton learns that the three Pre-Cogs are not always in perfect agreement about their prescient visions of the future. The pre-visions of the twin male psychics, Arthur and Dashiell, are often allowed to overrule those of Agatha in order to preserve consensus, even though Agatha is the most gifted seer of the three. Agatha's pre-visions are routinely purged from the Unit's database, but her dissenting opinions, or "minority reports," are still stored inside her head. Dr. Hineman also reveals that the Pre-Cogs were the result of a mutation caused by neorin, a highly addictive street drug. Most children of neorin addicts were born with severe brain damage, but three of them survived to "dream only of murder" before being placed in the Temple to serve the Pre-Crime unit.

Armed with this knowledge, Anderton kidnaps Agatha, whose mind is still unstuck in time. "Is it now?" she inquires, being existentially unable to distinguish the present from the future. He transports her to a shopping mall where hardware hacker Rufus Riley (Jason Antoon) uses a homemade rig to download her minority reports of both the impending murder of Leo Crow and the past murder of Ann Lively. While the Crow murder download shows that Anderton will indeed commit the homicide, the record of the Lively murder shows an odd anomaly that implicates his superior in the Pre-Crime program, the elderly Lamar Burgess (Max Von Sydow). Agatha utilizes her precise knowledge of the future to help Anderton escape from the police, but tries to dissuade him from committing the murder. "You have a choice," she pleads, "the others never saw their future."

Managing to locate Crow in a high-rise apartment building, Anderton discovers a photograph of his missing son, while Crow informs him that he has killed the boy. Anderton is driven into a murderous rage by this revelation, and levels his handgun at Crow to fulfill the prophecy, but at the last moment resists the impulse and decides to arrest Crow instead. Crow has other ideas. Claiming that his family will be paid off only if he is killed, Crow manages to commit suicide using Anderton's gun. In the meantime, Witwer also suspects that Burgess has set up Anderton in order to conceal his involvement in the murder of Ann Lively. When he confronts Burgess about the issue, Burgess murders Witwer, knowing that the Pre-Crime unit is inoperable in Agatha's absence because the three Pre-Cogs must function together as a "hive mind."

Tom Cruise escorts "Pre-Cog" Samantha Morton through a futuristic shopping mall in Steven Spielberg's *Minority Report* (2002).

It turns out the deceased Ann Lively was in reality Agatha's mother, who was murdered by Burgess when she sought to terminate her daughter's involvement in the Pre-Crime program. Burgess cleverly covered up the homicide by using his knowledge of the precognitive process to create a falsified pre-vision. In the wake of revelations about how the allegedly perfect system was compromised, the Pre-Crime unit is shut down permanently and the future-gazing technique abandoned. Anderton is exonerated and Agatha, Arthur and Dashiell are granted "relief from their gifts," and are shown living normal lives.

Dick's modest short story was expanded to epic length by scripters Scott Frank and Jon Cohen, who imbue the plot with numerous twists and turns in this tech-noir melodrama. The screenplay emphasizes the intrusive, crypto-fascist nature of a future society dominated by the exploitation of psychic powers in the context of concerns over misuse of police authority associated with the contemporaneous "war on terror." Spielberg's directorial touch is sure, and his affinity for sci-fi serves him in good stead in this fast-paced techno-thriller, which is further enlivened by the special effects of Industrial Light & Magic and the music of John Williams. Action hero Tom Cruise carries the film, but Samantha Morton's intense portrayal of the tortured Pre-Cog Agatha provides the movie's true dramatic grit.

The complex plot of *Minority Report* raises serious questions about the utilization of paranormal talents for the general welfare of society. During his investigation, Witwer notes that in antiquity the power of prophecy was always with the priests who interpreted the utterances of the oracle and not with the oracle itself, implying that the Pre-Cops can game the system. The three alien-like Pre-Cogs, who inhabit a neo-pagan, high-tech "temple," stand in for the three Fates who declared the destinies of men and gods in ancient Greek and Roman mythology, their frail dreaming forms suspended in the grotto's sacred waters in timeless contemplation. Their miraculous prophetic abilities earn the adulation of society, as one Pre-Cop reveals that they receive more letters than Santa Claus. Public relations for the Pre-Crime unit broadcasts the lie that the Pre-Cogs live a sequestered but otherwise normal existence in luxurious surroundings. In reality, they are exploited to the max, maintained like patients in a coma care facility, drugged into insensibility and forced to endure recurrent visions of horrifying murders. While the film's backstory provides no clues to the Pre-Cog's motivations for joining the unit, it is difficult to imagine individuals agreeing to live this kind of nightmarish existence voluntarily, even for the most selfless of motives.

Minority Report's psychics seem to have surrendered part of their humanity as a function of their ESP. "It's better if you don't think of them as human," Anderton expounds, and at another point refers to the Pre-Cogs as merely being "pattern recognition filters." The psychics are treated like fortune-telling machines, as if they are disembodied brains or software programs. Isolated from humankind at large, the bald-headed Pre-Cogs resemble space aliens, their outward appearance providing a visual metaphor for their inhuman powers. Ultimately, the film presents a highly negative portrayal of the integration of paranormal abilities into society for positive ends. Despite its lofty goals, Pre-Crime emerges as a path to psychic fascism, which, despite its obvious successes, is ultimately rejected. Like the *Star Wars* films and *Dune*, *Minority Report* also addresses gender issues in regard to ESP. The sole female, Agatha, who is in reality the most psychically gifted of the trio, is routinely overruled by the judgments of the two male psychics, which serves to make their predictions less accurate and skewed toward a predominately male perspective.

Psychic X-Men

Stan Lee and Jack Kirby's 1960s-era comic book superhero team known as the "X-Men," which featured a group of mutants with superhuman powers, was adapted for a series of sci-fi actioners beginning with Bryan Singer's *X-Men* in 2000. The concept of biological mutation was used as the explanation for the group's super powers, which are genetic in nature rather than being

The X-Men (2000): rear, left to right: Hugh Jackman (Wolverine), James Marsden (Cyclops), Halle Berry (Storm), Famke Janssen (Dr. Jean Grey) and (center front) Patrick Stewart (Professor Xavier).

acquired from the environment as is the case with most comic-book heroes. Scott Summers, a.k.a. Cyclops (James Marsden) can shoot bolts of energy from his eyes, while Ororo Munroe, or Storm (Halle Berry), is able to control the weather. The most powerful mutants of all, however, are those who wield psychic powers.

X-Men begins with a brief but powerful prologue set in Nazi-occupied Poland in 1944, where Jewish youth Erik Lensherr (Brett Morris) is separated from his parents at a concentration camp. The boy's distress at being separated from his parents is such that some mysterious force bends the camp's metal barrier fence and pops the front gate open. This display of PK is abruptly terminated when a quick-thinking German guard renders the telekinetic boy unconscious by applying a rifle butt to the child's head.

Cut to the opening years of the 21st century, where mutant advocate Dr. Jean Grey (Famke Janssen) is testifying before a Senate committee in D.C. regarding the "Mutant Registration Act," a McCarthyite piece of legislation designed to identify and register every mutant in the United States. Disregarding Dr. Grey's pleas for tolerance, anti-mutant senator Robert Kelly (Bruce Davison) dema-

Professor Xavier (Patrick Stewart) plugs into the Cerebro machine that enhances his telepathic powers in *X-Men* (2000).

gogues the issue while expressing the public's misgivings about powerful mutants living secretly in our midst. "There are even rumors, Ms. Grey," he orates in the Senate chamber, "of mutants so powerful they can enter our minds and control our thoughts, taking away our free will." It soon becomes clear that the senator is exploiting the fear of mutants to advance his own political career. In the aftermath of the hearings, metal master Erik Lenserr (Ian McKellen), who is now middle-aged and has assumed the persona of "Magneto," is confronted by Professor Charles Xavier (Patrick Stewart), a wheelchair-bound paraplegic with powerful telepathic powers, over the intertwined fate of humans and mutants. The professor wishes to live alongside humankind in peace, while Holocaust-survivor Magneto believes that the two species cannot coexist.

Most of the action centers on the characters of Logan, alias Wolverine (Hugh Jackman)—an amnesiac mutant with regenerative powers, metal claw implants and a bad attitude—and Marie/Rogue (Anna Paquin), whose touch is death. The pair are rescued from Magneto's henchmen, the Brotherhood of Evil Mutants, and brought to the Xavier School for Gifted Youngsters, a mutant training facility located in a sprawling mansion in Westchester, New York. Xavier's school is dedicated to helping mutants develop their powers and to integrating them into human society. "When I was a boy I discovered I had the power to control people's minds, to make them think or do whatever I wanted," the professor explains to a doubting Logan. Xavier has chosen to use his telepathic and mind control abilities for more constructive purposes, noting that if mutants went to war with homo sapiens, "Humanity's days will be over." Logan also discovers that Dr. Jean Grey has telekinetic powers and rudimentary telepathic abilities, and is Xavier's most trusted lieutenant.

Magneto, who wears a special helmet that foils Xavier's mind control powers, hatches a scheme to destroy humanity by amplifying Rogue's destructive powers in a machine he has invented. During a showdown with the X-Men and the police while abducting Rogue, Magneto displays his psychokinetic talents by levitating police cars and turning the cops' guns against them. Installing his machine on Liberty Island in New York harbor, Magneto hopes to activate the machine during an upcoming United Nations summit and destroy much of the world's political elite in one fell swoop. The final battle between Xavier's X-Men and Magneto's Brotherhood takes place in the shadow of the Statue of Liberty, an edifice that symbolizes America's inclusiveness. The Brotherhood is soundly defeated, and Magneto is taken into custody and placed in a special holding cell constructed completely from plastic materials.

X-Men would turn out to be the eighth highest–grossing Hollywood movie of 2000, and would go on to gross approximately $296 million worldwide. It would inspire a raft of popular movie adaptations of Marvel comic-book characters that would continue unabated during the first decade of the 21st century. Blending science fiction with comic-book action and character-driven dramatics in a crowd-pleasing meld, director Singer concocts a sleek piece of fast-flowing action entertainment that creates the formula for the entire superhero subgenre. The film's screenplay, which reportedly went through several extensive revisions by a number of scriptwriters before finally being credited to David Hayter, clocks in at a svelte 90-plus minutes and is a model of narrative economy. Sizzling performances by Hugh Jackman as the feral Wolverine, Halle Berry as the ethereal Storm, and Shakespearean-trained British actors Patrick Stewart and Ian McKellen as Professor Xavier and Magneto, add a much-needed human depth to the Marvel comic-book characters.

In the sequel, *X2: X-Men United* (2003), after a mutant attack on the president in the Oval Office a wave of anti-mutant sentiment sweeps America, allowing rogue U.S. Army colonel William Stryker (Brian Cox) to devise a plan to destroy all mutants by building a copy of Professor Xavier's "Cerebro" machine, a chunk of hardware that enhances mutant telepathy. In order to accomplish this, Stryker organizes a military raid on the professor's mansion and captures Xavier and Cyclops, who are transported to Stryker's Cerebro site near Alkali Lake in the north country. Many of Xavier's mutant students are sedated and captured during the raid, but a small group including Storm, Wolverine, Rogue and Jean Grey remain at large.

At Alkali Lake, Professor Xavier is introduced to Stryker's son Jason (Michael Reid MacKay), a.k.a. "Mutant 143," who is also confined to a wheelchair and has mind-control powers similar to the professor's. Jason is able to dominate the professor's mind, creating the illusion that he is a little girl in the process, and attempts to compel Xavier to use the Cerebro machine to locate and destroy every mutant on earth. In the meantime, Magneto's shapeshifting henchwoman Mystique (Rebecca Romijn) has sprung Magneto from his plastic jail cell, and the Brotherhood of Mutants join with the remaining X-Men to foil Stryker's plot to eliminate mutantkind. The mutants manage to infiltrate Stryker's Cerebro facility and rescue Xavier, but afterward the Brotherhood and the X-Men go their separate ways once more. As the super-team's jet plane is attempting to take off, however, a nearby dam bursts, flooding the area, and Jean Grey sacrifices herself by using her psychokinesis to hold back the flood waters while simultaneously levitating the jet. As the professor and the other X-Men fly to safety, Jean is apparently killed when her powers can no longer hold back the flood.

The third and final film in the series, Brett Ratner's *X3: The Last Stand* (2006), begins with a flashback that takes place twenty years in the past, in which Xavier and Magneto (who at this point are still working together) pay a visit ten-year-old Jean Grey (Haley Ramm). The feisty youngster displays plenty of attitude in confronting the two powerful mutants. "It's very rude, you know," Xavier tells her, "to read my thoughts or Mr. Lenserr's without our permission." In reply the psychic girl levitates every automobile (and even a powered lawnmower) on the block, and then drops them down again. As the audience knows, Jean is somehow persuaded to join Xavier at his school for mutants and learns to control her psi powers. This sequence is meant to illustrate the extent of Jean's formidable psychokinetic powers.

Back in the not-too-distant future, relations between humans and mutants have improved to the extent that a government bureau called the Department of Mutant Affairs has been established and is headed by Dr. Henry "Hank" McCoy, alias Beast (Kelsey Grammer), a bestial, blue-furred intellectual mutant. Secretary McCoy is chagrined to learn that a pharmaceutical firm called Worthington Labs has developed a "mutant antibody" that can change mutants into ordinary humans, thereby "curing" them of their "affliction." The mutant community becomes sharply divided on the pros and cons of this issue, but Magneto uses the controversy to recruit a new generation of anti-human mutants.

In the meantime, Scott Summers (Cyclops) has been experiencing a series of telepathic dreams about the supposedly dead Jean Grey, and feels compelled to leave the X-Mansion and journey back to the scene of her demise, Alkali Lake. Cyclops feels Jean's presence emanating from the lake, and soon she emerges from a whirlpool to embrace him as the scene fades into ambiguity. Back in Westchester, Professor Xavier receives a telepathic flash that something has happened to Scott, and dispatches Wolverine and Storm to investigate. They find that the lakeshore area has become a zone of anomaly in which small objects whirl in the air in a poltergeist-like display. Jean is discovered in an unconscious state, while there is no trace of Scott except for his sunglasses.

The comatose Jean is brought back to the Mansion, where the professor is forced to make a startling admission. It seems that the psychic powers of Jean's unconscious mind were so awesome and unpredictable that he "created a series of psychic barriers to isolate her powers from her conscious mind." Xavier has used his telepathic abilities to turn Jean into a split personality, and he fears that in the aftermath of her calling upon her reserves of psychic energy to survive the flood, she may have tapped into her more powerful unconscious persona, that of "Phoenix." When Jean appears to awaken in Wolverine's presence, it soon becomes apparent that the Phoenix personality is in charge, as she immediately attempts to seduce him, going so far as to use her psi powers to telekinetically pop Logan's belt buckle open. Sensing something is not right, Logan resists Phoenix/Jean's advances, causing her to fling him across the room like a rag doll and effortlessly hurl the heavy vault door open with her enhanced paranormal powers. Bolting from the X-Mansion, she flees to the suburban home of her parents, as seen in the film's opening sequence.

Both Xavier and Magneto quickly beat a path to her door, each hoping to recruit Jean to his side. When Phoenix surfaces once more, her Id-driven personality is more in tune with the ethos of Magneto and his evil Brotherhood. Furious at Xavier for having imposed mental blocks against her, she turns her full fury on the professor. In the psychic duel that follows, the entire house is levitated off its foundations, and Xavier is vaporized by Jean's paranormal energies. While the X-Men strive to overcome the loss of their leader, Magneto rallies his followers and cultivates Jean, who he realizes has become the most powerful mutant of all.

The Brotherhood attacks the Worthington laboratory, located on Alcatraz Island in San Francisco Bay. In a feat of mega-PK, Magneto diverts the Golden Gate Bridge to Alcatraz to facilitate the invasion. Learning of Magneto's plans, the X-Men join with the humans in repelling the mutants' assault. In the ensuing battle Magneto is robbed of his powers by an injection of the mutant antigen, while Jean/Phoenix becomes a Carrie White–type diabolic psychic who turns Alcatraz into an inferno before being killed by a disconsolate Logan.

Although in the *X-Men* series the psi angle is subordinated by the concept of super powers in general, it should be noted that the most powerful mutants, namely Xavier, Magneto and Jean Grey, are those who possess the conventional psychic abilities of telepathy and psychokinesis. All three of the X-films contain the theme of imprisonment: Magneto is confined inside his special plastic jail; Xavier's mutant schoolchildren are hidden inside the X-Mansion; the Phoenix personality is imprisoned inside Jean Grey; the Worthington Labs facility is located on Alcatraz, formerly a federal prison. This theme is possibly a metaphor for the hidden, literally "occult" nature of the mutants' powers, which must be geographically confined and concealed from common view. The series deals with issues of tolerance for those in our society who are exotic, mysterious or subtly "different," including psychics and those who partake of the paranormal. There are distant echoes of Olaf Stapledon's classic SF novel *Odd John* (see Chapter One) which also dealt with a deadly conflict between mutant supermen and homo sapiens.

Psychic talents present a mixed bag of negative and positive virtues in the *X-Men* movies. On the one hand, Professor Xavier and the X-Men represent the positive utilization of psi for the good of human and mutant alike. On the other, Magneto and his Brotherhood of Mutants stand for the threat of those with uncanny powers who would destroy humankind. The pivotal character of Jean Grey stands at the crossroads between these two poles. The plot of *X3* seems to suggest that psychic powers are linked to the negative aspects of the unconscious mind, as Jean is transformed from an emotionally controlled, selfless individual into a paranormal psychopath with libidinous and homicidal tendencies. As in *Forbidden Planet*, psi is linked to the Freudian concept of the Id, the purely emotional, irrational aspect of the mind.

Like the Jedi in the *Star Wars* films or the Pre-Cogs of *Minority Report*, the X-Men represent an elite with special powers who exist apart from the mainstream of society. Those who have been smitten with paranormal talents are fundamentally different, genetic mutations who are forced to confront or challenge the status quo. In these sci-fi blockbusters psi is fraught with great danger as villainous Sith Lords and evil mutants vie for control of worlds or galaxies with their superhuman powers. The psychic landscape is littered with evil oligarchs, corrupt religions, wars and broken institutions in these big-budget science fiction excursions into the realm of the paranormal.

• EIGHT •

Remote Viewing, Black PSI-OPS and Paranoia

It all started with a magazine article.

The French publication *Science and Life* ran an unusual story about ESP in its February 1960 issue entitled "The Secret of the Nautilus," which claimed that the U.S. government had conducted a successful experiment in telepathic communication with the crew of the nuclear submarine *Nautilus* while the craft was submerged beneath the Arctic ice cap. This experiment was reportedly given very high priority by the president, the Navy and the Air Force, as well as by private companies like Westinghouse, General Electric and the Rand Corporation. The *Nautilus* experiment had important defense implications because communication with submarines is problematic due to the fact that radio waves cannot penetrate seawater.

While the facts alleged in the *Nautilus* article were later proven to be bogus, someone in the Kremlin took notice. Although the Soviets' materialist ideology had prevented them from studying psi for many years, the notion that the Americans were on to something provided the impetus for a resurgence of paranormal research in Russia, Czechoslovakia and Bulgaria during the 1960s. Soviet researchers such as Lenin Prize–winner Leonid Vasiliev and I.M. Kogan began receiving funding for their parapsychology projects, which were soon in full swing. In 1970 Sheila Ostrander and Lynn Schroeder's book *Psychic Discoveries Behind the Iron Curtain* was published, causing some consternation in the American defense community. According to the authors, the Soviet bloc countries were hard at work researching psi with an emphasis on mind-control techniques, which they referred to as "psycho-energetics" or "psychotronics." American officials became concerned that the Soviets could use ESP to read the contents of top secret documents, pinpoint the location of our military forces, dominate the minds of top military or civilian leaders or even cause their deaths, and to remotely disable U.S. military equipment. A new arms race based on psychic technology had emerged into the fabric of the Cold War.

Remote Viewing

By a fortuitous circumstance, physicist Hal Puthoff would begin a series of psi experiments in his laboratory at the Stanford Research Institute (SRI) in Palo Alto, California in 1972. Puthoff conducted an experiment in which psychic Ingo Swann was able to affect the output of a specially sealed magnetometer at an SRI lab in a display of what is called "micro-PK" or psychokinesis that affects equipment on the electron level. The Puthoff-Swann magnetometer experiment drew the attention of the CIA, and after a test in which Swann clairvoyantly viewed a live moth concealed inside a box, decided to fund Puthoff's psi research at SRI. Puthoff was soon joined in his paranormal endeavors by fellow physicist Russell Targ as the scientists worked with Swann and other psychics (including the flamboyant Israeli magician Uri Geller) to explore the mysterious realm of extrasensory perception.

Ingo Swann would soon go beyond his role as a seer to become one of the primary theorists of psychic functioning. Drawing upon the earlier work of Upton Sinclair and Rene Warcollier as well as his background as an artist, Swann conjectured that ESP takes place in the right hemisphere of the brain, the area associated with artistic, non-verbal functioning, rather than in the left hemisphere that governs language. This meant psi information was transmitted and received primarily as pictures or images rather than words, and the SRI team adopted the term "remote viewing" to describe this process of visual information exchange. Swann is credited with the formulation of the protocols for "coordinate remote viewing," or CRV, a system in which the viewer was given the latitude and longitude co-ordinates of a target site and psychically saw what was located at the coordinates. The viewer would then draw a series of pictures of what hw saw at the selected site, and in the final stage would even build a three-dimensional model of the site. Swann's CRV technique was sometimes referred to as "SCANNATE," a contraction of the term "scanning by coordinate."

Targ and Puthoff presented the results of their early remote viewing experiments in their 1977 book *Mind-Reach: Scientists Look at Psychic Ability*. That same year saw the release of Steven Spielberg's UFO opus *Close Encounters of the Third Kind*, a film which incorporated coordinate remote viewing techniques into its script (written by Spielberg). In *Close Encounters*, electrical worker Roy Neary (Richard Dreyfuss) telepathically receives the image of Devils Tower, an unusual geological formation in Wyoming, during an encounter with a UFO. Soon afterward, the aliens broadcast the latitude and longitude coordinates of Devils Tower to a secret government UFO research group indicating where the aliens will land and make contact. In the meantime, Neary has become obsessed with the image in his mind, and attempts to sculpt the form out of shaving cream and mashed potatoes before building an enormous, highly detailed model of the mountain in his basement. When he happens to see a news spot about Devils Tower on TV, he intuitively knows this is where the extraterrestrials are going to land. Why or how these details of remote viewing techniques found their way into *Close Encounters* has never been explained.

Remote viewing differed from previous parapsychological experimentation in two significant ways. First, very stringent scientific protocols were always used to eliminate the possibility of fakery or accidental information contamination that might invalidate the results. Second, after initial research had been completed the RV program went beyond the laboratory to tackle real-world military intelligence targets, and somehow this practical, task-oriented approach seemed to potentiate psi functioning. In 1978, for instance, remote viewers located a downed Soviet TU-22 bomber in the African nation of Zaire, an event that was later corroborated by former president Jimmy Carter. Beginning in that same year, a U.S. Army remote viewing unit was established at Ft. Meade, Maryland to train and deploy a cadre of psychic spies for military intelligence missions. The psi-spy program, initially called "Gondola Wish," would continue under code names such as "Sun Streak," "Grill Flame," and finally, "Star Gate" until finally being disbanded in 1994.

Throughout its existence the RV program had been run on a miniscule budget and afforded a very low priority, which ensured it existed on the fringes of the American intelligence community. The remote viewing unit required very little in the way of materiel, and was run out of a couple of ramshackle buildings at Ft. Meade. All that was needed were some quiet, windowless rooms equipped with couches, video cameras and tape recorders. The viewer would recline on the couch while a monitor gave him the geographical coordinates of the site to be viewed, after which the viewer would enter an altered state of consciousness and begin to record his sensory impressions of the target.

By the 1980s the workings of the psychic espionage unit had become clouded in secrecy. Those in the parapsychological community knew that the SRI research had become classified in response to Soviet psi research efforts, but could only conjecture about the nature of the program. In 1985 nationally syndicated Washington columnist Jack Anderson published a column about "Project SCANNATE" techniques covertly being employed for psychic espionage by the CIA. All the general public knew was that the U.S. Government was secretly exploiting the paranormal for spying and for military purposes, a notion that made many people uneasy. After all, didn't the psychic warriors of the *Star Wars* movies wield unimaginable psi powers in the service of warfare and empire building?

In the wake of the Watergate scandal, Americans were feeling especially paranoid and Congress had assumed more of an oversight role in running the government. One target was the CIA, which had reportedly aided President Nixon during the Watergate affair and was perceived to be an out-of-control "rogue" agency. In 1975, a Senate committee chaired by Sen. Frank Church began to investigate the CIA and uncovered evidence that the Agency's MK-

ULTRA psychological warfare program had experimented with the mind-bending hallucinogen LSD on unwitting American citizens. It was revealed that LSD had even been given to CIA employee Frank Olson, who subsequently committed suicide by jumping from a high window in a New York hotel. Clandestine CIA experiments with LSD and secret government psychic spying programs were thus linked in the public mind, and the stage was set for a series of novels and films about secret CIA experiments into the paranormal gone horribly wrong.

The Power *and* The Fury

The first film to portray government projects linked to psi, however, had been made several years prior to the inception of remote viewing experiments at SRI: *The Power* (1968), produced by George Pal and directed by long time collaborator Byron Haskin. Known primarily as the producer of big-budget sci-fi extravaganzas during the SF wave of the 1950s such as *Destination Moon, When Worlds Collide* and *The War of the Worlds*, Pal tackled Frank Robinson's acclaimed novel of psychic intrigue.

The Power begins "Tomorrow," at a futuristic research facility in San Marino, California, where Dr. Arthur Nordlund (Michael Rennie), a scientific liaison officer from Washington, has been sent to investigate cost overruns on a government project called the "Committee on Human Endurance." The group is studying aspects of human potential that might enable astronauts to survive in the harsh environment of outer space, and Nordlund is given a tour of the facility by project scientist Dr. Jim Tanner (George Hamilton).

Dr. Nordlund is to be briefed about the project's work at a committee meeting attended by the project's head administrator, N.E. Van Zandt (Richard Carlson), physicist Dr. Melnicker (Nehemiah Persoff), biologist Professor Scott (Earl Holliman), anthropologist Dr. Hallson (Arthur O'Connell) and geneticist Dr. Margery Lansing (Suzanne Pleshette). As the meeting gets under way, Dr. Hallson makes the startling announcement that he has given all of the committee members an intelligence test that indicates one of them is a super genius whose I.Q. is "beyond the known limits of measurability," but since the tests were submitted anonymously, no one knows the prodigy's identity. Hallson theorizes that this superbrain "could take control of all the minds in this room." Dr. Melnicker proposes that the committee conduct a spontaneous ESP experiment to determine who is the psychic superman in their midst. He props up a pencil in the middle of the table and spears a sheet of writing paper into it and proposes that they all concentrate on moving the paper using psychokinesis. The paper soon begins to whirl around, proving that someone in the room is the psychic mutant.

Soon after the conference Hallson is found dead inside the project's centrifuge as Tanner and Margery discover the name of his killer, "Adam Hart," inscribed on a note. Hallson's I.Q. test results have also mysteriously vanished, leading the couple to suspect that he has been murdered by the psychic in order to conceal his identity. The mystery deepens when all of Tanner's academic records are erased and he is summarily dismissed from the project for defrauding the committee about his background. Then Adam Hart launches a psychic assault on Tanner's mind. While he is walking down a city street, Tanner observes a group of toy soldiers marching around in a store window that are animated by telekinesis. (Or is it an hallucination?) Fleeing into a funhouse arcade, Tanner is nearly killed when a merry-go-round breaks down and spins wildly out of control.

Trying to fight back against the murderous psychic, Tanner attempts to ascertain Hart's true identity. Finding out that Hallson and Hart knew each other as children, Tanner visits the small desert town of Joshua Flats looking for clues. The townsfolk are curiously reticent about Hart, giving conflicting descriptions of his appearance and concealing information about his character and background. One of the townies, who is apparently under Hart's mental domination, abducts Tanner and dumps him on a nearby Air Force firing range, where he is nearly killed by fighter planes on a gunnery exercise before alerting the pilots to his presence by lighting a fire.

The attractions and perils of the psychic realm are detailed in this poster from George Pal's *The Power* (1968).

Returning to Marge's house in San Marino, Tanner is assaulted by the usually peaceable Dr. Melnicker, who has also fallen under Hart's psychic control. The fight brings Melnicker to his senses, and he agrees to help his two colleagues in the battle against Hart. European émigré Melnicker compares Adam Hart to Hitler because he has seen through bitter experience that one man can have the capability to destroy the entire world. Believing in the safety of numbers, the trio take refuge inside a large hotel and crash a wild, all-night party. When one of the female partygoers begins performing a striptease and attempts to kiss a sleeping Melnicker, she cries out in horror when she realizes that he is dead, another victim of Adam Hart's murderous psychokinesis. Tanner is nearly killed by a malfunctioning elevator and a car without a driver, and Marge muses that they are "like dogs trying to catch a dogcatcher."

Receiving a mysterious note directing him to return to the research facility at San Marino, Tanner enters the building at night and encounters Dr. Nordlund within the darkened halls. Nordlund reveals himself to be Hart when he telekinetically forces Tanner's heart rate to accelerate wildly in order to produce a fatal heart attack. As the scientist comes under the psychic's direct attack, Tanner begins to resist using his own mental powers. A torrent of special effects depict the paranormal struggle between the two men as Tanner begins to prevail over Nordlund/Hart and finally triumphs by stopping Nordlund's heart with a burst of his newly-found psi energy. In the aftermath of the psychic struggle, Tanner muses to Margery, "They say that power corrupts, and absolute power ... I wonder?" His voice trails off as he leaves the notion of the possibility of his own corruption unresolved.

Considered one of Pal's and Haskin's lesser efforts, *The Power* is nonetheless a well-crafted mystery/science fiction thriller built around an intriguing premise. Pal departs from his usual effects-oriented approach in favor of a real-world setting and character-driven melodrama. John Gay's screenplay contains many plot twists and interesting situations, and the film has an erotic edge that is absent from Pal's other productions. Haskin's brisk direction crafts a well-paced psychic chiller as the B-list cast turn in workmanlike performances (Pleshette in particular seems a bit too laid back in light of the film's homicidal preoccupations), but veteran thesps Michael Rennie (who portrayed alien emissary Klaatu in the SF classic *The Day the Earth Stood Still*) and Nehemiah Persoff (who would go on to play a parapsychologist in *Psychic Killer*), deliver a little something extra.

Released a few years before the inception of U.S. Government funded psi research at SRI, *The Power* anticipates governmental involvement in the psychic realm, although it should be noted that the film's "Committee on Human Endurance" is studying aspects of human potential that have nothing to do with psi. The heart-stopping psychic antics of Adam Hart were reportedly duplicated in the laboratory by Siberian shamans in the course of Soviet paranor-

Eight • Remote Viewing, Black Psi-Ops and Paranoia

Suzanne Pleshette and George Hamilton escape from the clutches of the evil psychic Adam Hart in *The Power* (1968).

mal research. In one anecdotal story, the shaman's cardio-busting spell was reflected back on him and stopped the shaman's heart instead.

Like many of the government paranoia-themed psychic films to follow, *The Power* paints psi in a decidedly negative light. The Adam Hart character bears a resemblance to Fritz Lang's silent-era psychic criminal Dr. Mabuse, a phantom menace who wields vast paranormal powers in secret. Interestingly, the Dr. Mabuse character was thought to presage the coming of Adolf Hitler (who some think had occult or paranormal powers), and Hart is compared to Hitler by the film's Dr. Melnicker. The notion of anonymous psi-enabled individuals secretly using their mind-control abilities behind the scenes is a truly paranoid idea that harks back to medieval legends of witchcraft. The film's final scene suggests that even the morally upright Tanner may succumb to the temptations posed by his psychic powers.

John Farris' novel *The Fury*, published in 1976, was the first significant fictional treatment of the theme of psychic espionage. Taking the 1970 nonfiction book *Psychic Discoveries Behind the Iron Curtain* as a starting point, Farris concocted a psi-spy narrative that implicated the American intelligence establishment in dangerous parapsychological experiments. The possibility of deadly psychic powers being exploited by a covert group of government technocrats had great resonance in the post–Watergate era, and the book was quickly optioned for the big screen. Farris was assigned to write the screenplay and Brian De Palma, fresh from the psychic horrors of *Carrie* (1976), was in the director's chair.

Our story begins with a prologue set in an unnamed Arab country in the Middle East in 1977, where intelligence operative Peter Sandza (Kirk Douglas), his son Robin (Andrew Stevens) and his boss Ben Childress (John Cassavetes) are

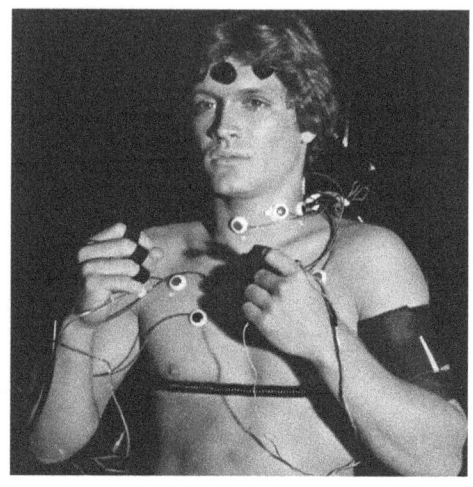

Super-psychic Robin Sandza (Andrew Stevens) is wired for an ESP experiment in Brian De Palma's *The Fury* (1978).

relaxing at a resort on the Mediterranean. Peter and Robin are discussing their impending return to the USA, with Robin expressing his misgivings about being considered a "freak" because he possesses psi powers. "You have a talent that would shock the hell out of people," Peter acknowledges while exhorting his son to study at the Paragon Institute in Chicago. Suddenly Arab terrorists attack the resort, but the event seems staged. Peter is apparently killed, and Robin is devastated and led away by Childress, who has had a cameraman film the entire attack. Peter emerges from the sea alive, however, and observes Childress's treachery, wounding his spymaster in the arm before disappearing.

A year later, teenager Gillian Bellaver (Amy Irving) is hanging out at a Chicago beach when she realizes she is being stalked by a geeky individual who looks like a homeless man. In reality, he is psychic Raymond Dunwoodie (William Finley), a down-and-out seer who is working for Peter Sandza. Peter is hiding from Childress and using Dunwoodie's ESP to search for another psychic who will have the power to find out where Childress has hidden Robin. Unfortunately, Childress's organization is monitoring Dunwoodie, whose call unwittingly leads them to Peter, who is forced to go on the run once more. Stalked through the tenements and back alleys of Chicago in a deadly game of cat-and-mouse, Peter eludes his captors while preparing to infiltrate a local outfit called the Paragon Institute that is conducting psychic research.

In the meantime, Gillian becomes aware of her own paranormal gifts and decides to enroll as a student at Paragon, where she undergoes ESP tests with Zener cards, feedback machines and the like. The institute, located in a Chicago townhouse, is obviously well-funded and fully equipped, and is run by the

Eight • Remote Viewing, Black Psi-Ops and Paranoia   185

Peter Sandza (Kirk Douglas, top) holds on to his son Robin (Andrew Stevens) for dear life at the conclusion of *The Fury* (1978).

agreeable, avuncular parapsychologist Dr. Jim McKeever (Charles Durning). The special potency of Gillian's psi abilities becomes apparent when she spontaneously experiences a frightening vision of Robin Sandza (whom she has never seen) that causes Dr. McKeever to have a severe nosebleed. McKeever theorizes that the psychic girl is able to generate an enormously powerful electromagnetic field, and ruminates, "There's no place for these kids in our culture ... and what a culture can't assimilate, it destroys."

In the wake of this psychic interlude, the sinister Childress pays a visit to McKeever at the Institute, where it becomes apparent from their conversation that Paragon is merely the happy-face front for Childress's clandestine, government-funded psi research program. Robin Sandza has been sequestered in Childress's main facility, located outside of the city in a palatial country estate, ever since his father's "death," where his abilities are being probed by a team of scientists. Robin's psychic talents are unique, according to Childress. "The Chinese don't have one," he tells McKeever, "the Soviets don't have one." But Robin has been showing signs of mental instability of late, and Childress wants to hedge his bets by using Gillian as a backup. "Will the girl be another Robin Sandza?" he asks McKeever, and when the parapsychologist equivocates, the spymaster insists that she be detained and sent to his psi facility the very next day.

Meanwhile, Peter is planning to infiltrate Paragon and spring Gillian, whose powers he hopes to utilize in locating his son. Toward this end he has established a romantic relationship with Hester (Carrie Snodgrass), a nurse who works at Paragon. During the botched rescue attempt, Hester is killed while Peter escapes with Gillian. Back at the psi facility, Robin's mental state continues to deteriorate as he is given mood-altering drugs and forced to watch films of his father's staged demise. He is further manipulated by project psychiatrist Dr. Susan Charles (Fiona Lewis), who has become Robin's lover in a bid to control the youth and channel his sexual energy. When one of the psi project scientists enthusiastically notes that Robin is "developing the power of an atomic reactor," Dr. Charles replies, "Or an atomic bomb." Robin displays his dangerous psychokinetic powers when he is allowed to visit an amusement arcade and observes a group of Arab men in traditional bedouin dress riding a ferris wheel. Flashing back to the scenes of Peter's death at the hands of Arab militants that he has been forced to relive, Robin destroys the ride in a fit of telekinetic rage, killing several of the Arabs.

That evening, Gillian leads Peter to the psi facility, where Robin telepathically senses Gillian's presence. Believing the girl has been brought to the facility to replace him and that he is to be killed, the paranoid youth turns on Dr. Charles, brutally spinning her around faster and faster until her internal organs burst. Peter and Gillian are apprehended by Childress, who forces Peter to confront his son. Brainwashed by Childress's extreme methods, Robin attacks his father, the two of them crash through a window and Robin winds up holding on to his father for dear life. The crazed psychic chooses to slip from his father's grasp in a suicidal plunge, and Peter, undone by Robin's demise, also opts to join his son in death. In an epilogue, Childress attempts to cozy up to Gillian and con her into being Robin's replacement, but an enraged Gillian tells him, "You go to hell." She then uses her psychokinetic powers to cause his body to explode, sending his severed head sailing through the room in a spray of blood and gore.

The Fury was the first attempt to mate the espionage thriller with the sci-fi horror film, and De Palma's film is a mixed bag that doesn't quite deliver the goods in either genre. Fresh from the paranormal horrors of *Carrie*, De Palma drops the ball in this lackluster directorial effort. One series of slo-mo, close-up reaction shots of Amy Irving emoting is downright embarrassing, for instance. In contrast to *Carrie*, the horror element in *The Fury* is understated and not particularly effective. Farris's screen version of his novel simplifies and eliminates many intriguing subplots in the book. Ultimately, the film fails to elicit interest in the characters due to uninspired performances by the principal actors, and also suffers from a bleak, downbeat ending in a cloud of gore. Veteran screen composer John Williams provides a moody, mysterioso score that is occasionally marred by the use of a hokey, theremin-style theme that plays whenever Gillian is having one of her psychic visions.

De Palma's paranormal espionage chiller would provide the template for a number of similarly themed sci-fi psi-spy movies that followed, including *Scanners* (1981), *Firestarter* (1984), *Dreamscape* (1984) and *The Lawnmower Man* (1992). In these films the post–Watergate U.S. government is the nefarious force behind the manipulation of the quasi-occult powers of psychic individuals. These psychics are brainwashed or otherwise constrained into cooperating with the military-industrial complex's corruption of their miraculous gifts for warfare or espionage purposes. Naturally, these government forces unwittingly open up a Pandora's Box of trouble and unleash deadly paranormal forces that give them their much-deserved comeuppance. Concepts of psi thus become further demonized and tainted by their association with anti-government paranoia and conspiracy theories that would ultimately provide inspiration for the popular paranormal TV series *The X-Files*. In *The Fury,* Uncle Sam's deep pockets provide lavish funding for parapsychological research projects: the lush Paragon Institute townhouse and Childress's secluded psi facility housed in a suburban mansion suggest a well-funded, well-organized effort to identify and recruit psychics. The Raymond Dunwoodie character would become the prototype for psychics in later films who would be portrayed as loners and misfits existing at the margins, alienated from society as a whole by their uncanny abilities yet pursued by a power structure that wishes to exploit these very same talents.

Psychic Black Ops

The horror/espionage trend in psi-oriented movie fare continued with Canadian cult director David Cronenberg's psychic thriller *Scanners* (1981). The film begins in a Toronto shopping mall, where grotty-looking Cameron Vale (Stephen Lack) is sleazing around tables at the mall's food court, grubbing uneaten food from the tables. When a middle-aged woman at a nearby table disses him, Vale uses mental power to cause her to have a nosebleed and then go into convulsions. Two trench-coated men have observed these events and begin chasing Vale around the mall, eventually subduing him with a tranquilizer dart.

Vale awakens inside "The Factory," an industrial building that has been converted into an ESP research facility. He is greeted by scientist Dr. Paul Ruth (Patrick McGoohan), who seems intimately acquainted with Vale's tragic backstory. "Why are you such a derelict," Ruth asks rhetorically, "such a piece of human junk?" Answering his own question, he continues, "You're a scanner. That has been the source of all your agony." The paternal scientist explains that Vale is a psychic "scanner," an individual in possession of telepathic and telekinetic powers. Vale is given an injection of a drug called ephemerol, which quiets the maddening telepathic babble inside his head for awhile.

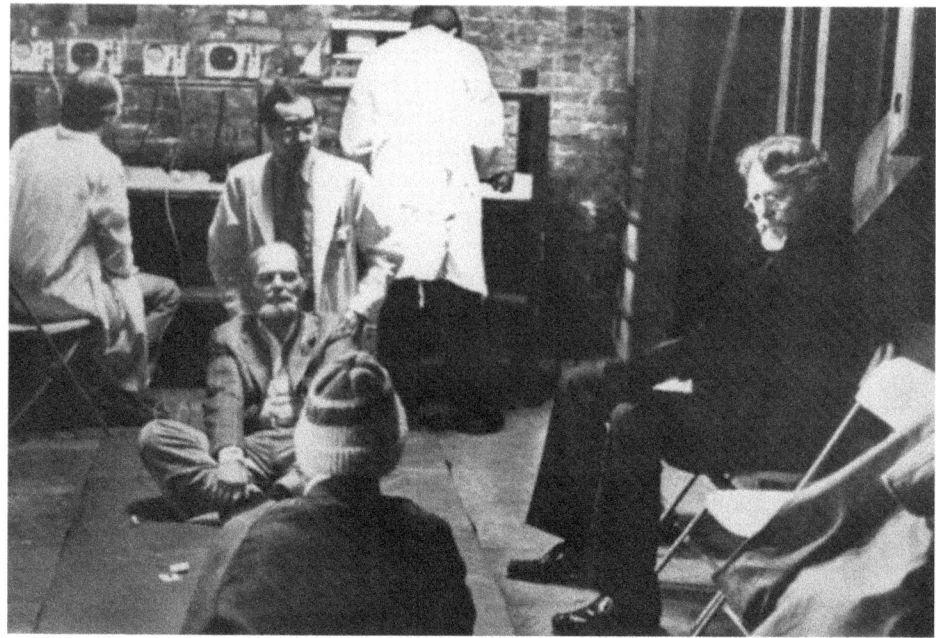

Dr. Paul Ruth (Patrick McGoohan, extreme right) presides over the parapsychology lab in *Scanners* (1981).

Cut to a lecture room at the headquarters of multinational corporation ConSec, a Blackwater–like private security firm, where a ConSec scanner is conducting a psychic demonstration. "I would like to scan all of you in this room one at a time," he announces, adding that "the scanning experience is usually a painful one," and may produce nosebleeds, stomach cramps, earaches, nausea and other symptoms. When the scanner asks for a volunteer from the audience, Darryl Revok (Michael Ironside) steps onstage, but during the ensuing telepathy demonstration, Revok literally blows the ConSec scanner's head off in the film's most outrageous and memorable sequence. Revok is taken into custody by ConSec security, but the renegade scanner uses his powers to make short work of the rent-a-cops and easily escapes.

At a ConSec meeting in the aftermath of the debacle, the new head of security, Braedon Keller (Lawrence Dane) recommends disengaging from corporate research into the "telepathic curiosities known as scanners." "Let us leave the development of dolphins and freaks as weapons of espionage to others," he suggests, advocating for the closure of the psychic research program. Dr. Ruth, citing the infiltration of ConSec in the deadly scanner attack, disagrees, noting that the corporation has a list of 236 known scanners with whom they've lost contact. The doctor theorizes that these psychics have joined a scanner underground of revolutionaries who pose a threat to ConSec's corporate interests.

Eight • Remote Viewing, Black Psi-Ops and Paranoia

He explains that he intends to use unaffiliated scanner Vale to infiltrate the rebel group and eliminate the threat.

Dr. Ruth preps Vale for his mission while teaching him how to maximize his psychic abilities. Ruminating on the "derangement of the synapses which we call telepathy," which, "could be a disease, possibly," Ruth observes that Vale's sense of self is fragmented by his uncontrolled psi sensitivities. "With all those other voices in your head," Ruth wonders, "how can you hear your own voice? How can you develop a self, personality?" The answer lies with ephemerol, the scan-suppressant pharmaceutical that prevents the flow of telepathy. The parapsychologist teaches Vale how to focus his scanning abilities, which combine telepathy, hypnotic mind domination and psychokinesis into a single package. "Telepathy is not mind reading," Ruth insists, "it is the direct linking of two nervous systems separated by space." Using a trained yogi as a psychic "sparring partner," Vale learns how to induce rapid heartbeat with his scan.

His psychic skill set sharpened, Vale is sent out to find Revok and infiltrate his organization. Vale makes contact with scanner sculptor Ben Pierce (Robert Silverman) in the artist's studio, located in a rural barn filled with weird, grotesque forms. Here Vale learns that Pierce uses his art to quiet the telepathic voices in his head. "My art keeps me sane," the eccentric sculptor explains to his fellow scanner. As they converse inside one of Pierce's works, an enormous human head, Revok, who wishes to remain hidden, sends a hit team out to murder them. Pierce is mortally wounded before Vale can use his psychic firepower to dispatch the assassins, but before dying Pierce gives Vale a line on a group of benevolent, unaffiliated scanners led by the elusive Kim Obrist (Jennifer O'Neill). Contacting the New-Agey scanner group, Vale participates in a séance-like telepathic meditation session with Kim and the other scanners, but their group mind-meld is interrupted by Revok's henchmen, who break in on a killing rampage from which only Vale and Kim manage to escape.

Seeking refuge at ConSec, Vale contacts Dr. Ruth in an attempt to "come in," but no one at the corporation knows that security chief Keller is secretly working for Revok. When Vale and Kim are brought in to headquarters, Keller isolates Kim and attempts to murder her. The couple manage to scan their way out of ConSec and eliminate Keller, but not before the security head murders Dr. Ruth in order to keep him quiet. On the run again, Vale uses his psychic powers to hack into ConSec's computer network and learns that ConSec subsidiary Biocarbon Amalgate, a pharmaceutical firm, has been taken over by Revok and is manufacturing ephemerol in large quantities. Vale and Kim pay a visit to one of the pediatricians who is prescribing the drug, and Kim experiences the unsettling feeling of being scanned by an unborn fetus in a pregnant mother's womb. In the final confrontation, Revok tells Vale the bitter truth: they are brothers and their father was Dr. Ruth, who experimented with ephemerol on his own wife decades earlier and unwittingly produced the first

Jennifer O'Neill and Stephen Lack as paranormal "scanners" in David Cronenberg's *Scanners* (1981).

two psychic children. Revok is using the ephemerol manufactured at Biocarbon Amalgamate to create a new race of scanners that will "bring the world of normals to its knees." Vale begs to differ, however, and the two psychic brothers engage in a telepathic/psychokinetic scanner duel, the outcome of which is uncertain at the film's conclusion.

The script for *Scanners*, penned by Cronenberg, recycles plot elements from both *The Power* and *The Fury* such as psi-induced nosebleeds and tachycardia, and *mano a mano* paranormal duels between warring psychics. As a horror-oriented director, however, Cronenberg's treatment of the theme is characteristically darker and more perverse. Makeup whiz Dick Smith concocted the film's shocking gore effects, including the money shot of the Con-Sec psychic's head exploding. While the screenplay is sometimes confusing and reportedly went through numerous rewrites during production, Cronenberg's directorial execution is masterful, creating an atmosphere of brooding dread that sets the nerves on edge. A moody 80s-era synth score by Howard Shore creates an eerie aural counterpoint to the horrific visuals.

Although a group of benevolent scanners is briefly depicted in the film, the main action in *Scanners* is driven by the psychopathic Revok as ably portrayed by Michael Ironside. In contrast, Stephen Lack's human-friendly Cameron Vale is bland whitebread, a sympathetic character but not particularly engaging, while Patrick McGoohan's Dr. Ruth is a remote, pathetic excuse for a father figure. Cronenberg accentuates the horrific aspects of psychic poten-

Eight • Remote Viewing, Black Psi-Ops and Paranoia   191

Mystic Native-American assassin John Rainbird (George C. Scott, center) brings down Charlie McGee (Drew Barrymore) with tranquilizer darts in *Firestarter* (1984).

tial in a heady brew of gore, murder and post–Watergate political paranoia, and psychic functioning is described as "a disease" and "a derangement of the synapses" in the screenplay. Scanner protagonist Vale is a victim of his own telepathy, unable to shut out the many voices in his head. His mind-reading sensitivities blur the boundaries of his personality and serve to make him dysfunctional. The film presents a mostly negative view of psi potential for society and deliberately exploits and exaggerates the more sensational and horrific implications of psychic functioning.

As *Scanners* acquired a cult audience over the years, it inspired a string of low-budget, Canadian–made sequels in the 1990s, none of which was directed by Cronenberg. *Scanners II: The New Order* (1990) featured more head-exploding scanner duels, and the psychic shenanigans continued with *Scanners III: The Takeover* (1991), *Scanner Cop* (1993) and *Scanners: The Showdown* (1994). These mediocre entries did little to expand ideas about psi as presented in the original film.

Stephen King, whose novels *Carrie* and *The Dead Zone* had both exploited and popularized parapsychological themes, generated his own novel of psychic espionage that was filmed under its own title as *Firestarter* (1984). Andy McGee (David Keith), a psychic with mind domination abilities, and his young daughter Charlie (Drew Barrymore), who has pyrokinetic powers, are on the run

The pyrokinetic Charlie (Drew Barrymore) burns it all down in *Firestarter* (1984).

from a super-secret psi research outfit known as the Department of Scientific Intelligence (DSI), or simply "The Shop." Pursued through a grim urban landscape by The Shop's agents, the down-and-out father-and-daughter pair are shown scrounging a marginal existence by using their psychic powers to get coins out of pay phones and the like. Given temporary shelter by kindly farmer Irv Manders (Art Carney) and his wife Norma (Louise Fletcher), their backstory unfolds in flashbacks. When they were in college Andy and his wife, Victoria (Heather Locklear), had participated as paid volunteers in experiments with a mind-altering drug called "Lot 6," which is described as "a synthetic copy of a pituitary extract, a powerful pain-killer hallucinogen." Exposure to Lot 6 made Andy and Victoria telepathic, and their offspring, Charlie, inherited a double dose of psychic power from her parents. After Victoria was murdered (for no apparent reason) by agents of The Shop, Andy and Charlie went on the run and have lived in the shadows ever since.

In the aftermath of a ham-handed attempt to acquire Charlie at the farm which leaves a number of his agents dead or incapacitated, The Shop's head honcho, Captain Hollister (Martin Sheen) calls in Native-American assassin John Rainbird (George C. Scott) to take the firestarter out. The ponytailed Rainbird, however, harbors some crackpot mystical notion about killing the girl and absorbing her psi power, which is "a force that belongs only to the gods themselves." DSI scientist Dr. Joseph Wanless (Freddie Jones), however, warns that the child may have talents beyond what they already suspect, theorizing she may be "capable of creating a nuclear explosion with the power of her will," that could "crack the very planet in two like a china plate in a shooting gallery."

Subdued by tranquilizer darts and transported to The Shop's bucolic scientific facility in Longmont, Virginia, father and daughter are separated from each other and maintained in isolation. Andy is forced to take a drug cocktail that nullifies his psychic powers, while Rainbird, donning an eyepatch, disguises himself as "John," a simple-minded orderly who befriends the girl and becomes her surrogate father. Gaining Charlie's trust over time, Rainbird persuades the young psychic to participate in a series of pyrokinetic experiments that showcase her fiery PK. In the meantime, Andy has secretly stopped taking his meds and has regained a measure of his mind-control powers. He manages to mentally dominate Hollister and plans to use him to spring Charlie and himself from The Shop, but Rainbird gets wind of the plot. In the finale, Rainbird shoots Hollister dead and mortally wounds Andy before being immolated by Charlie. Cradling his little girl in his arms, with his dying breath Andy tells her to destroy The Shop so that this will never happen again. "Burn it all down, Charlie," he pleads, "burn it all down." Her pyrokinetic rage unleashed, the girl creates a murderous firestorm that destroys The Shop in a fiery conflagration. In an epilogue, Charlie is shown returning to the Manders farm, where she will be cared for by the elderly couple and eventually reveal the story of the government's hideous psi experiments to the *New York Times*.

Stephen King rates *Firestarter* as one of the worst adaptations of his work. Directed by Mark L. Lester from a screenplay by Stanley Mann, the film recycles shopworn paranormal clichés from both *The Fury* and *Scanners*. Characters are killed off for no apparent reason or motive other than to demonstrate to the audience how evil the bad guys are. While David Keith and Drew Barrymore deliver solid dramatic performances as the principals, Martin Sheen's role as The Shop's steward is bland and throwaway, and the venerable George C. Scott is laughably miscast as the ponytailed American-Indian psychopath Rainbird. Director Lester does a workmanlike job but somehow the whole just doesn't hang together.

The plotlines of *The Fury, Scanners* and *Firestarter* share several common elements. All three films exploit the horror/fantasy aspect of paranormal phenomena in a mostly negative fashion. Nosebleeds are depicted as a feature of psychic functioning (something that does not typically occur in real life) in all of them, for instance. Psi talents serve to make people into dysfunctional, marginal characters with mental problems such as Raymond Dunwoodie in *The Fury*, Cameron Vale in *Scanners*, and Andy and Charlie McGee in *Firestarter*. Psychics are shown to be unhappy, neurotic persons, yet the protagonists of these films are sympathetic individuals who must confront the overwhelming oppressive might of government agencies that wish to exploit their powers before ultimately destroying them. In all of these films psi is tainted by asso-

Rival psychics Alex Gardner (Dennis Quaid, left) and Tommy Ray Glatman (David Patrick Kelly) square off in *Dreamscape* (1984).

ciation with the excesses of covert government in the post–Watergate era. In *Firestarter*, little Charlie McGee unleashes the forces of hell against the reactionary DSI headquarters, hurling fireballs at the plantation-like colonial structure that strongly resembles the White House. Both here and in King's psychic opus *The Dead Zone*, psi alters the physical brain and creates life-threatening tumors in the unhappy psychic individuals John Smith and Andy McGee. Furthermore, gentle little Charlie has been endowed with psi abilities that far surpass those of the homicidal psychics in *The Fury* or even the head-splitting powers of the telekinetic supermen in *Scanners*, and is theoretically capable of reducing the entire world to a burnt-out cinder — more cinematic "proof" of psi's horrific downside.

Psychotronic Technology

A new wrinkle in the psi game was the use of techno-devices to augment or amplify a person's natural psychic powers. This concept was first mentioned in *Psychic Discoveries Behind the Iron Curtain*, in which Soviet bloc scientists had reportedly constructed "psychotronic" machines that performed these functions. In *Dreamscape* (1984), a group of dream researchers have invented a machine that enables a psychic to enter the dreamworld of another person.

Psychic Alex Gardner (Dennis Quaid) leads an aimless, low-life existence playing the ponies and hustling women until he is kidnapped and brought to nearby Thornhill College, where dream researcher Paul Novotny (Max von Sydow) and his assistant, Jane DeVries (Kate Capshaw) are experimenting with a high-tech device that enables dream telepathy. Using this machine a psi-talented individual could "psychically project himself inside the dream of a sleeping person," Novotny explains to Alex, and once inside the dream "become an active participant in it ... even shape and alter the dream itself" in a process called "dreamlinking." Alex is dubious but Novotny threatens to expose his gambling profits to the IRS unless Alex cooperates.

Forced to participate in the program, Alex soon warms to the task when he tries to help a young boy named Buddy (Cory Yothers) overcome his debilitating nightmares. Projecting himself inside one of Buddy's dreams, Alex helps the boy confront his worst fears within this hallucinatory landscape and cures him. But the positive aspects of the dream project also have a sinister side, as funding is provided by government technocrat Bob Blair (Christopher Plummer), a secretive intelligence official of dubious morality. Alex is introduced to the project's star performer, fellow psychic Tommy Ray Glatman (David Patrick Kelly), an unpleasant, seemingly sociopathic individual whose sarcasm reveals a deadly jealousy over Alex's developing ESP abilities, which could one day rival his own dream powers.

The potentially deadly aspects of the new technology are demonstrated when Tommy Ray deliberately murders a woman during a session using a "dream knife" that induces a heart attack in his victim, proving the old wives' tale that "when you dream that you die, you die in life at the very same instant." It soon becomes apparent that Blair envisions using dreamlinking technology to commit covert assassinations; the victims will die of a "coronary" in their sleep after being killed within the dream by a psychic murderer. Blair's target is none other than the American President (Eddie Albert), who has been suffering from intense nightmares about an atomic holocaust and plans to launch a nuclear disarmament plan during an upcoming summit meeting. Anti-Soviet militarist Blair hopes to prevent this from happening by having Tommy Ray murder the Prez inside the dreamlink when the chief executive is brought to the Thornhill facility for sleep therapy. The final showdown takes place inside one of the president's nuclear nightmares, as Tommy Ray and Alex (who can now access the dreamlink without using the machine) square off in a psychic battle that may ultimately decide the fate of the entire world.

Dreamscape is much lighter in tone than earlier essays in psychic espionage like *The Fury, Scanners* and *Firestarter,* and departs from a horror-movie formula in favor of a breezy spy-spoof ambience. Quaid is engaging as the high-rolling, womanizing psychic protagonist and is ably supported by screen vets

Alex (Dennis Quaid, right) tries to prevent the assassination of the President (Eddie Albert, center) by psychic killer Tommy Ray (David Patrick Kelly) inside a dream in *Dreamscape* (1984).

Plummer and von Sydow, and by David Patrick Kelly's creepy portrayal of homicidal psychic rival Tommy Ray. The screenplay by Bruce Cohn Curtis, David Loughery, Joseph Ruben and Chuck Russell starts with an intriguing sci-fi premise that director Ruben's execution fails to develop adequately. Most of the action is staged at race track, college campus and laboratory locations, and the film's modest budget prevents a more exciting treatment of the film's dream sequences, which are flat and unconvincing and lack the vivid qualities of the dream reality we experience on a nightly basis. Interestingly, Wes Craven's much more effective approach to the shared dream theme, the horror classic *A Nightmare on Elm Street*, was released just a few months after *Dreamscape*.

Once again, psi powers are shown to have the potential to destabilize the existing order of society in the service of secret political elites. Covert political operatives could utilize the dream machine depicted in the film to selectively assassinate national leaders and usher in a new world order. On the other hand, the positive potential and psychiatric benefits of this psychic technology are also shown. Alex is portrayed as a likeable, essentially normal fellow in his role as the film's paranormal dreamer, and is drawn as a moral man who sincerely wants to help others with his talents. Dream telepathy is a recognized psychic phenomenon that goes back to shamanic prehistory, as depicted in Peter Weir's psi thriller *The Last Wave* (see Chapter Three). Extensive research on this subject was carried out at Maimondes Medical Center's dream laboratory in New York in the late 1960s and early 70s, with inconclusive results. The film *Petter Ibbetson* (see Chapter Two) is another cinematic treatment of this theme.

Films like *The Fury, Scanners, Firestarter* and *Dreamscape* reflect a post–Watergate cynicism about the evils and excesses of governmental power, but as the powers of the CIA and other agencies were reined in by congressional oversight, concerns about covert development of a new technology that could be used to assassinate undesirables, enslave entire populations or even "crack the very planet in two like a china plate" began to wane, and rightfully so. As revelations about the then-secret government remote-viewing programs were made public, it became obvious that the American psi-spy program was an extremely modest effort, poorly funded and facing severe opposition from within the power structure. The paranormal threats posed in these sci-fi/horror/espionage thrillers never materialized in reality, and the theme also became passé in popular cinema for a time.

As computers and PCs came into wide use beginning in the 1990s, Brett Leonard's *The Lawnmower Man* (1992), based on a Stephen King short story, sought to unite the psychic with the cybernetic. The "lawnmower man" of the title is Jobe Smith (Jeff Fahey), a small-town nitwit who is a ward of the local Catholic Church and mows lawns in the neighborhood for pocket change. One of his neighbors is Dr. Angelo (Pierce Brosnan), a brilliant scientist working on virtual reality technology for high-tech corporation Virtual Space Industries (VSI). Dr. Angelo has been boosting the intelligence of chimpanzee subjects using elaborate VR computer simulations in combination with an experimental drug in VSI's "Project 5" regimen. Trouble is, the Project 5 drug is optimized to cause aggression in its experimental subjects, and when one of Angelo's chimps goes berserk, gets out of its cage and kills two VSI employees, the scientist resigns from the project in disgust.

Watching Jobe mow his lawn one day, Dr. Angelo becomes inspired by the idea of trying his techniques on the lawnmower man, using a non-violent analog of the Project 5 drug in an attempt to boost Jobe's intelligence. Using the virtual reality rig installed in his basement lab, Angelo is gratified when Jobe responds to his treatments and his I.Q. is boosted significantly. Soon the former village idiot is leading a more normal lifestyle and becomes sexually mature, taking up with town strumpet Marnie (Jenny Wright) while befriending a local boy, Peter (Austin O'Brien). Angelo even convinces his former VSI project manager, Timms (Mark Bringleson), to allow him to train Jobe using the company's VR facilities. However, Timms is keeping a close eye on Angelo's experiments and reporting back to The Director (Dean Norris), head of the Department of Scientific Intelligence, a.k.a. "The Shop" a government intelligence group that wishes to exploit Dr. Angelo's discoveries for warfare and intelligence purposes. Unknown to the scientist, Timms substitutes the original Project 5 aggression drug for the therapeutic formula Angelo is currently using on Jobe.

Clad in tight-fitting "cyber suits" and suspended in rotating "gyrospheres," Jobe and Angelo enter the computer-generated virtual world inside the VSI mainframe, but Jobe's consciousness is inundated with flashing images of arcane occult symbols and kabbalistic mandalas from an unknown source. Soon Jobe's I.Q. is climbing off the charts while he begins to experience spontaneous bouts of ESP. During a visit to the local diner, for instance, he begins to hear the customers' voices talking inside his head en masse. When Jobe demonstrates his newfound abilities to Dr. Angelo in the VSI lab by levitating a chair using PK, Timms witnesses the event and reports it to the Shop, who now wish to use Jobe's powers for "covert sector applications."

As the experiment progresses, Jobe's intelligence begins to eclipse that of Dr. Angelo, and his psychic powers are augmented to the point that he can control people's will mentally. After blowing Marnie's mind permanently during a shared VR session, he begins using his godlike powers of psychokinesis to exact a terrible revenge on townsfolk who have humiliated him for years. Jobe explains to Angelo, "This technology is simply a route to powers that conjurers and alchemists used centuries ago," and he is merely "reclaiming it through virtual reality." The former lawnmower man is transformed into a psychic superman, a "Cyber-Christ" with the terrifying power to manipulate physical reality at will. Imprisoning Dr. Angelo in his home lab, Jobe tells the scientist that he intends to project his consciousness inside the VSI mainframe and ultimately into the worldwide computer net in order to discover "a new electric dimension" and obtain the power to "cleanse this diseased planet." In the climactic battle, Dr. Angelo must confront his Frankenstein–like creation inside the virtual reality of the VSI mainframe to prevent Jobe from escaping into cyberspace with the fate of the human race hanging in the balance.

Director Brett Leonard's bold use of computer animation enlivens this cautionary tale about the perils of an emerging virtual technology. Although state of the art circa 1992, the film's CGI animation looks a bit dated by today's exalted standards. The film's opening sequence, showing the point of view of Angelo's escaped chimp inside a prototype battle helmet, is particularly effective, the distorted infrared imagery and scrolling alphanumeric symbols and icons depicting a view of the animal's artificially induced sensorium. The screenplay by Leonard and Gimel Everett liberally borrows plot elements from a number of sources, including William Gibson's cyberpunk novel *Neuromancer*, King's *Firestarter* and the similarly themed 1968 sci-fi flick *Charly*, but remains fresh enough to transcend its source material. Jeff Fahey's performance as the intellectually challenged lawnmower man who becomes a mega-genius drives the film, and his gradual metamorphosis from childlike innocence to arrogant psychic supermind is entirely convincing. Leonard would go on to direct the sci-fi cyber-thriller *Virtousity* (1995).

The Lawnmower Man was the last film to utilize the "government versus psychics" plotline that started with *The Fury* in 1978. Paranoia about the U.S. intelligence community meddling with the paranormal shifted to another theme: the alleged cover-up of the retrieval of a crashed flying saucer in Roswell, New Mexico in 1947. Beginning with the broadcast of the Showtime cable channel's TV-movie *Roswell: The UFO Coverup* in 1994, public attention was drawn to this new and even more compelling narrative of covert administration malfeasance and manipulation. In *The Lawnmower Man*, the bad guys are from the same alphabet soup outfit (the DSI, a.k.a. "The Shop") that was torched in *Firestarter* back in '84. Some people just never learn. Predictably, as befits the established formula for this type of film, psi talents are portrayed as having both positive potential and negative drawbacks, but, as usual, the dark side of the force prevails. Jobe's psychic exploits, depicted using computer imaging technology, are visually compelling and even more outlandish than the paranormal feats accomplished by psychics in films like *Scanners* or *Firestarter*. Although there have been some studies in which psychics have tried to influence computers using what is termed "micro-PK," virtual reality technology has not been utilized in psychic research.

As details about the U.S. government's remote viewing program began to seep into public consciousness in the 1990s as a result of investigative journalism by newshounds like Washington columnist Jack Anderson, films and TV shows began to incorporate themes gleaned from the world of real-life RV into fiction films and TV shows. Popular television series such as *Columbo* and *The Dead Zone* ran episodes that featured military/espionage RV programs. The first film to reflect this new trend was E. Elias Merhige's psychic crime thriller, *Suspect Zero* (2004).

In present-day New Mexico, a murderer is stalking serial killers, and Benjamin O'Ryan (Ben Kingsley), a grim, enigmatic individual, is the culprit. When one of the victims' vehicles is found on the state line between New Mexico and Arizona, precisely placed there using the Global Positioning System, the crimes become an interstate matter and the FBI is called to investigate. Special Agent Thomas Mackelway (Aaron Eckhart), formerly of the Dallas office and recently demoted and reassigned to Albuquerque over a botched case, is handed the unwelcome assignment. Soon Mackelway is receiving mysterious faxes that contain inside knowledge about the killings from an unknown source. Erstwhile colleague and former girlfriend Fran Kulok (Carrie-Anne Moss) is dispatched to New Mexico to assist him in the investigation.

O'Ryan is shown undergoing a strange, self-hypnotic ritual. Seated at a table, he goes into an altered state while listening to a tape recording of a man's voice repeating cryptic phrases like "See it," "Draw the environment," and "Do not identify with the victim," accompanied by a droning, subliminal noise that sounds like the buzzing of insects. Once inside his trance, he writes down a series of numbers, then begins to draw faces and objects while writing down a list of descriptive words. While O'Ryan stays on the run, agents Mackelway and Kulok trace him to his former abode at a group home, where they discover rows of numbers obsessively scribbled on the wall of his room along with a series of drawings. "With these numbers and pictures he said he could find anybody," the house caretaker helpfully explains. Mackelway eventually learns that O'Ryan is a former FBI agent who participated in an experimental law enforcement program called "Project Icarus," an effort to utilize remote viewing techniques to apprehend criminals. The psi-ops project was disbanded when the FBI psychics became psychotic after having remote viewed so many scenes of murder and mayhem.

The former FBI viewer's real target is a hypothetical serial killer O'Ryan has named Suspect Zero, "a random killing machine that never leaves a clue" and targets only children. Obsessed with bringing this monster to justice,

O'Ryan brings all of his RV skills to bear in the hunt for the criminal. At the same time, Mackelway begins experiencing his own spontaneous psychic visions of Suspect Zero's crimes, and realizes O'Ryan has recognized Mackelway's psi abilities and that this is the source of O'Ryan's intense interest in him. Eventually, the FBI agent and the former remote viewer combine forces to take out Suspect Zero, but in the aftermath O'Ryan begs Mackelway to put him out of his misery because he can no longer live with the consequences of his visions. "We saw things men shouldn't see," the psychic explains, "agony, torture, evil." He also pleads for Mackelway to use his developing psi powers to continue his work. "We make the world a little safer, we make justice," O'Ryan tells the agent before forcing Kulok to shoot him dead, but it's unclear whether Mackelway will follow in the remote viewer's footsteps.

Obviously influenced by serial-killer thrillers like *The Silence of the Lambs* and *Se7en* as well as TV's *The X-Files*, *Suspect Zero* is a competently made murder mystery that recalls psychic crime detection movies like *Man on a Swing* and *Manhunter*. Shot on location in New Mexico, the film's color palette is drab and rust-colored, and director Merhige sometimes employs documentary film-making techniques in telling his story. The screenplay by Zak Penn and Billy Ray is derivative and predictable, but contains enough original material to make the plot intriguing. Leads Eckhart and Moss deliver decent performances, but Oscar–winner Kingsley clearly dominates the film with his intense portrayal of the tortured O'Ryan, a tormented soul who is driven to madness and murder by his psychic gift.

The first feature film to use remote viewing as a plot device, *Suspect Zero* nonetheless must demonize RV as being connected with extreme misery, insanity and violent death. The forbidding-looking Kingsley is shown viewing in a trance in several scenes, his features screwed up into an intense scowl as his hands sketch rapidly, nervously, while jotting down his paranormal impressions of the murder site. An electronic score by Clint Mansell creates the disturbing, ultra high-pitched timbres on the tape recordings the psychic uses to potentiate his viewing. Kingsley's O'Ryan is portrayed as an obsessive-compulsive personality who recalls the twisted serial murderers that inhabit many other popular crime melodramas.

The O'Ryan character is loosely based on the real-life military remote viewer David Morehouse, who claimed in his exposé of RV, *Psychic Warrior*, that being exposed to remote viewing led to his own mental breakdown. While there have been a small number of individuals connected to the government's RV program who reportedly suffered from psychological problems as a result of their psychic exploits, they are a tiny minority. On the other hand, psychically viewing scenes of violence or death can be profoundly disturbing to the seer. In the real world, military remote viewers were sometimes run against law enforcement targets, and reportedly provided accurate information in drug interdiction cases being investigated by the Drug Enforcement Agency. In 1989 a military viewer correctly located fugitive Charles Jordan in a small town in Wyoming when he was thought to be in the Caribbean, although the information was not acted on by officials.

Nonetheless, *Suspect Zero* is the only film to date to portray remote viewing techniques with any degree of verisimilitude. Former U.S. Army Major Ed Dames, who had been a participant in the military psi-spy project, acted as technical consultant on RV for the film and has a small cameo. The DVD version contains an informative and well-produced video documentary entitled "What Do You See When You Close Your Eyes," which explores the theory behind RV functioning and provides background on the history of the government's RV program and interviews with psi researchers Dean Radin, Paul H. Smith, Russell Targ and Jessica Utts. There's also a second featurette in which director Merhige successfully participates in a remote viewing demonstration.

The FBI got involved in psychic espionage once more in *Next* (2007). Nicholas Cage plays Cris Johnson, a two-bit stage magician who performs under the stage name "Frank Cadillac." Unlike most illusionists, however, Johnson's psi powers are authentic. "Sometimes, not often, but sometimes," he muses in voice-over, "it's the real deal masquerading as an act, hiding behind a few $50 dollar tricks, hiding in plain sight. Because if the magician doesn't do that, the alternative is impossible for others to live with." Cris has the ability to see only his own future about two minutes ahead in time, and uses his powers to win modestly at the gaming tables while staying one step ahead of casino security and the cops. "Here's the thing about the future," he philosophizes to the audience, "Every time you look at it, it changes, because you looked at it. And that changes everything."

Johnson can't stay hidden forever, though, because his precognitive abilities have come to the attention of FBI agent Callie Ferris (Julianne Moore). The Bureau is tracking a group of international terrorists who have smuggled a 10-kiloton Russian nuclear munition into the United States, and intelligence sources suggest that they intend to set it off in Los Angeles. When agent Ferris attempts to recruit Cris in the effort to locate the terrorists, he refuses, citing involuntary ESP probing conducted by the government in the past. While the fate of eight million Angelinos hangs in the balance, Cris is instead obsessed with meeting a woman he has seen in a precognitive dream. She is Elizabeth Cooper (Jessica Biel), who Cris finally meets in reality and persuades to give him a ride out of Vegas to Flagstaff, Arizona. The couple predictably slide into a romantic relationship on the road while being pursued by both the FBI and the terrorists, who have gotten wind of Cris's prescience and want to take him out before he can spoil their plans.

Tracked to a rural Arizona motel, Cris spoils his chances for escape by saving Callie's life when things go wrong during the attempt to take him into custody. Cris is transported to L.A. where he is strapped into a restraining chair and fitted with a device that keeps his eyes propped wide open and fixed on a cable-TV news program, from which the FBI hopes he will draw pre-knowledge of the impending nuclear attack. The psychic is still uncooperative, however, telling Callie of his fear that "If I do what you want, you'll keep me in this chair forever." He changes his tune when his ESP hones in on a news item that shows Elizabeth being blown up in a bomb blast by the terrorists, who have taken her hostage in an attempt to lure Cris to his death in trying to prevent her killing. Somehow Elizabeth's involvement in his vision has extended the range of his clairvoyance from two minutes to two hours, as Cris and Callie race to save her and the city of L.A. from extinction.

Like the similarly themed *Minority Report*, *Next* is based on a short story by sci-fi cult author Philip K. Dick. Director Lee Tamahori piles on the action and non-stop chase scenes to create a well-crafted but undistinguished thriller that uses the paranormal angle mainly to create a series of clever, minutely choreographed escape sequences for a droll Nick Cage to waltz through. Part of the problem is that the script by Gary Goldman, Jonathan Hensleigh and Paul Bernbaum is constructed as a star vehicle for Cage: after an intriguing setup in the first act, it devolves into standard romantic drama in the second as Cage and Biel wander through pastel landscapes in search of true love. The film's narrative emphasis is placed on rescuing the romantic female lead from danger at the expense of exploiting the potentially more dramatic situation of saving L.A. from an atomic holocaust. Julianne Moore seems to be reprising her earlier role as FBI tough mama Clarice Starling in the *Silence of the Lambs* sequel, Ridley Scott's *Hannibal* (2001). At one point Cris seems to split himself into three distinct people, representing the three paths of his possible future actions, but this is confusing to the viewer, as is the film's unusual ending.

Next reduces precognition to the level of a cinematic gimmick as its psychic hero deftly navigates through space-time aided by his second sight. In an early scene, Cris breezes past a bevy of security guards and closed-circuit video cameras to escape from a casino without breaking a sweat. His prescience, shown visually, appears more like time travel to the viewer as we see the future through Cris's eyes. The scene in which Cris is strapped to the restraining chair with his eyeballs propped open recalls a similar tableau in Kubrick's *A Clockwork Orange* (1971) in which an errant youth is "re-programmed" by being forced to watch violent films. *Next* offers little sympathy for either the government spooks or its amoral protagonist, and no backstory is provided for Cris's cryptic remarks concerning the 36-hour ESP card-guessing experiments he was involuntarily forced to endure in the past.

Chris Carter's popular TV series *The X-Files* usually dealt with UFOs and alien abductions, but occasionally dealt with parapsychological themes in episodes like "Beyond the Sea." *The X-Files: I Want to Believe* (2008) departs from the story arc of both the first movie (*The X-Files: Fight the Future*, 1998) and the television series, which centered around FBI agent Fox Mulder's search for his missing sister, thought to have been abducted by extraterrestrials years earlier. The second movie is set six years after the events of the final episode of the TV show, which ended in 2001.

In the film's eerie opening sequence, a psychic leads a cordon of police through a wintry landscape to discover a severed arm frozen in the ice. The clairvoyant is Father Joseph Crissman (Billy Connolly), a former priest who has been defrocked for molesting altar boys but is now assisting the police in the investigation of a series of bizarre murders and disappearances. The padre, known as "Father Joe," sports long, scraggly gray hair, a two-day growth of beard, and has a generally unkempt appearance in keeping with his depressed mental state. When a female FBI agent comes up missing in connection with the case, the Bureau is called in, and because of the paranormal connection seeks to bring the former members of the X-Files unit into the investigation.

Former FBI agent and paranormal skeptic Dr. Dana Scully (Gillian Anderson), now a physician practicing at the pediatric wing of a Catholic children's hospital, is persuaded to join the investigation and instructed to contact her former colleague Fox Mulder (David Duchovny), who has dropped out of sight, to solicit his cooperation. Scully manages to locate Mulder, who is living in a tiny, isolated country house where he seemingly does nothing but collect newspaper clippings of various paranormal phenomena, and convinces him to join the hunt for the missing agent. Teaming up with Father Joe, they travel to one of the crime sites, where the psychic experiences a vision so intense it makes his eyes bleed. The former priest insists that his visions come from God, but the skeptical Scully is repulsed by his history of pedophilia. In the course of investigating another disappearance, Father Joe leads the team to a cache of frozen body parts, including a horrific severed head, and insists that according to his clairvoyance, the killers are surrounded by barking dogs. Support for the veracity of the priest's visions emerges when traces of an animal tranquilizer are discovered on one of the severed limbs.

The trail eventually leads to Russian émigré Janke Dacyshyn (Callum Keith Rennie), a medical worker who transports human organs for a living. Dacyshyn operates an illegal medical facility where he is conducting human head-transplantation experiments designed to obtain a body for the severed head of his homosexual partner, Franz Tomczeszyn (Christopher "Fagin" Woodcock), who has been kept alive by bizarre Russian medical techniques. In the meantime, Father Joe has a seizure and is rushed to the hospital, where he is diagnosed with terminal lung cancer. Trailing Dacyshyn, Mulder is abducted by the wily Russian and taken to the facility, where he is tied down and watches helplessly as the Russkie medicos prepare to perform another transplant experiment on a young woman they have kidnapped. Not to worry, though, for in the last reel Mulder and the girl are rescued by Scully and the FBI and Dacyshyn and Tomczeszyn are killed. Father Joe dies at the exact moment Tomczeszyn's head expires, and it turns out that Tomczeszyn was one of the altar boys the priest had molested. In the aftermath of the horrific case, Scully tells Mulder she cannot stay with him if he continues to explore "the darkness," but the audience knows that there's little chance of that ever happening.

Designed to appeal primarily to fans of the TV show, the second X-Files movie plays like one of the so-called "Monster of the Week" episodes that focused on individual paranormal phenomena and departed from the show's "mythic arc" involving Mulder's search for extraterrestrials. This lends *The X-Files: I Want to Believe* a stand-alone quality that allows it to be viewed independently of the intricacies of the series. The film languished in development hell for several years after the demise of the show in November, 2001, reportedly due to legal squabbles between Carter and 20th Century–Fox. Carter's direction has a slow, plodding quality, while the screenplay by Carter and Frank Spotnitz is often confusing and overly complicated. The scenario is basically a variation of the timeworn "psychics vs. criminals" plot formula. Shot on locations in Vancouver and Pemberton, British Columbia, the film's wintry landscape is both forbidding and claustrophobic, while the parade of severed limbs and disembodied heads lend a horror-film ambience to the proceedings.

From a paranormal standpoint Father Joe is the film's most significant feature, and he is portrayed in typical Hollywood fashion as an oddball existing on the margins of society. In this case, however, the psychic individual is even more aberrant, being a despised pedophile and failed religious leader. The relationship between Father Joe's perversions and his psi abilities is unclear, yet the defrocked priest insists his clairvoyance constitutes miraculous visions that come from God. Like *Suspect Zero*, the film invokes the gritty horror-movie ambience of genre fare like *Se7en* as the psychic realm is demonized and painted in tones of black yet again. The film's ominous mood and grotesquerie of severed body parts is typical of the way the paranormal exists in the paranoid universe of *The X-Files*. Some critics noted elements of homophobia in the plot, including the bizarro notion of Dacyshyn keeping his lover's head alive and the molestation of altar boys by Father Joe. Like *Manhunter* and *The Silence of the Lambs*, the film plays on the notion of using insights provided by a criminal to catch other criminals. Underneath all of the movie's macabre mise-en-scène is a parable of faith and skepticism underlined by the portion of the film's title that proclaims, *I Want to Believe*.

Remote Viewing the Remote Viewers

In reality the government's remote viewing program was very poorly funded and limited in scope, nothing like the high-tech, big-budget enterprises depicted in Hollywood psi-oriented fare such as *The Fury, Scanners, Firestarter* or *The Lawnmower Man*. In fact, it was the extremely low cost of the RV projects (by Defense Department standards) that kept them going for so long. Multi-million dollar atom smashers, supercomputers, spacecraft or other exotic

Eight • Remote Viewing, Black Psi-Ops and Paranoia

scientific hardware were not required to study ESP; all that was needed to pierce the veils of time and space were quiet rooms equipped with couches, tape recorders, video cameras and stationery. The CIA itself officially disparaged the effectiveness and importance of remote viewing in their 1995 report, but there have been dark rumors about deeper black-RV projects that have been completely concealed from the public. Remote viewing theorist and trainer Ingo Swann has intimated that he trained a hush-hush group of viewers for the American intelligence community. "I can't really talk about this second group," he has stated. "I don't even know where they went. They were much more 'black' and much more covert. I don't think I ever had their right names. But they were smart as hell."[1] So the possibility exists that secret ESP research programs may still be functioning despite the CIA's disclaimers. And of course little is known about the current state of psi research in Russia, China or other countries.

One final curiosity: somehow the titles of science fiction films seem to replicate the government's code names for the remote viewing projects. For instance, beginning in 1972, SRI researchers initially code-named their RV effort "Project SCANNATE," a contraction of "scanning by co-ordinate." The title of David Cronenberg's 1981 psi-spy thriller was *Scanners*, yet the term Project SCANNATE was not revealed to the public until it appeared in a column by investigative journalist Jack Anderson in 1985. Likewise, the name STAR GATE was selected for the U.S. Army's RV project from a list of government codewords by project director Dale Graff in 1990, but this was not revealed to the public until years later. Roland Emmerich's sci-fi adventure *Stargate* was released in 1994, and although the film was not about the paranormal, it did feature a secret government project striving to unlock ancient secrets. Is all of this coincidence, or are filmmakers remote viewing the remote viewers?

Conclusion

In his 2005 memoir *Reading the Enemy's Mind: Inside Star Gate — America's Psychic Espionage Program*, former U.S. Army Major Paul H. Smith recounts details of his remote viewing training at the hands of psychic instructor extraordinaire Ingo Swann. In 1984, Smith and several other military trainees traveled to New York City to be initiated into the mysteries of RV. According to Smith, part of the training involved going to the movies as a group and watching films with science fiction or psychic themes. Aside from providing a welcome diversion from the rigors of training, Swann "felt some movies contributed to the overall atmosphere of our training, especially if they dealt with out-of-the-ordinary-world themes such as science fiction or the paranormal. Though such films might be considered escapist, it was the ambience Ingo was after."[1] The future psi-spies went to see movies about fictional psychic espionage such as *Firestarter* and *Dreamscape*, and also viewed other excursions into science fiction, including *Star Trek III*, *Brainstorm* and *The Terminator*. "One of our favorites, though," Smith intimates, "was *Ghostbusters*. We identified with the down-and-out parapsychologists who in the end had to save the day."[2]

This illuminating anecdote illustrates a functional relationship between psi and movie-making. Like remote viewing, filmmaking is primarily a visionary process in which the image-producing right hemisphere of the brain is engaged in the creative activity of seeking to render a desired target visible. Because cinema is a visual art form, both film directors and remote viewers must "think in pictures" in order to invoke the desired result. Viewers sometimes describe their exploits in cinematic terms, their psychic eye acting like a camera that records long shots and closeups, moves through space, fades and dissolves and goes backward and forward in time. Like a film director, the viewer visualizes scenes from afar with the inner eye. Thus, creativity and psychic functioning employ similar visionary methods.

Even after science has been brought to bear upon the mysteries of the psychic realm, the paranormal continues to be shrouded in mystery and the trappings of the supernatural. Throughout its existence, the RV program had to contend not only with scientific skeptics but also with a Judeo-Christian religious bias that saw psi as something ungodly. This prejudice also extends into the world of entertainment. After the release of the 2007 psychic thriller *Next*, articles on Christian web sites protested that the film violated tenets of their faith involving predestination and free will. As the Nicholas Cage character intimates in *Next*, the perception that psi is real "is impossible for others to live with."

In their 1984 book *The Mind Race: Understanding and Using Psychic Abilities*, SRI researcher Russell Targ and remote viewer Keith Harary decry the generally negative attitudes about the paranormal that are routinely promoted and exploited by the film industry. They write: "The images of psychic functioning that are depicted in mass-media fiction quickly lead you to believe that only very strange people have psychic experiences and abilities, or that psi is experienced by normal people only under the most bizarre circumstances. You might even mistakenly conclude that psi does not exist at all, except in the minds of science fiction writers and deluded fanatics."[3] They further note that psychic events are presented as "abnormal and frightening, as adversely affecting those who encounter them, or as only appropriate for odd or demented people, zombies, or beings from other planets."[4] The authors cite films such as *Carrie, Scanners, Resurrection, Fanny and Alexander, Poltergeist, The Exorcist, The Legend of Hell House* and *Don't Look Now* in support of their thesis.

Alas, little has changed since these words were written. Perhaps the atavistic fears of the unknown always trump the Apollonian logic of science. Filmmakers know well how to play upon these ancient beliefs that continue to fascinate mankind with equal measures of wonder and terror. Most cinematic explorations of the paranormal remain within the confines of the horror and science fiction genres, where the more sensational and terrifying aspects of psi are exploited to the max by producers and directors striving to reach a mass-audience. As a result, the movie biz has been primarily responsible for fostering negative stereotypes about psi in more recent films such as *The Lawnmower Man, Possessed, Minority Report, An American Haunting, The Mothman Prophecies* and *Suspect Zero*. Even the *Star Wars* series, which started out with such a light tone, collapsed into Wagnerian *sturm und drang* as the dark side of the Force triumphed in the last chronological entry in the multi-movie epic, *Revenge of the Sith*. Psi also continues to be associated with crime and murder in thrillers like *Hideaway, In Dreams* and *The Gift*. At best, the paranormal is presented as constituting a two-edged sword whose positive virtues are usually outweighed by their negative implications.

It's not all doom and gloom, though; paranormal themes have also been tapped for use in more light-hearted comedy fare in crowd-pleasers like *Ghostbusters* and *What Women Want*. Perhaps psi is shown in its most positive light in children's films such as *Matilda* or *The Last Mimzy*, where innocent, good-hearted kids wield psychic powers for good and for just plain fun. In the realm of the dramatic film, however, psi-enabled individuals are tortured souls who are frequently the victims of their own unsought and misunderstood talents.

Targ and Harary point out that "In the fictional world of movies and TV, psi is often depicted as a potentially destructive force in people's lives, or as a power most human beings cannot ethically or easily cope with."[5] "I'm sorry for what I am," laments psychic John Coffey (Michael Clarke Duncan) in *The Green Mile*, before he is executed for a murder he did not commit. Likewise, the psychic protagonists of *Powder* and *Phenomenon* are literally consumed by their psychic gifts. Psi is negatively associated with the use or abuse of drugs in *Dune*, *The Fury*, *Firestarter*, *Scanners* and *The Lawnmower Man*, while psychics suffer from life-threatening brain diseases that are connected to their ESP in *The Dead Zone*, *Firestarter* and *Phenomenon*.

Targ and Harary note that, "taken as a whole, television and film portrayals of psi in general and psychic people in particular constitute a mass of destructive stereotypes set against a backdrop of ill-conceived myths and misconceptions about the origins and effects of psychic experiences and abilities."[6] Paranormal powers are usually greatly exaggerated in order to make them more dramatic and to provide vehicles for expensive, eye-candy special effects. As a result, these quasi-supernatural powers are inflated out of all proportion to anything in the real world. Surely no one believes there are psychics as powerful as the little girl in *Firestarter*, who scientists in the film fear could "crack the very planet in two like a china plate in a shooting gallery," or Sith Lords who control entire galactic empires with their paranormal energies. There are no super-psychics who can explode people's heads as in *Scanners*, or create whirlwinds of psychokinetic force the way Jean Grey does in *X-3*.

There is one way, however, that these films are helping to disseminate more accurate information about the true nature of psi. A byproduct of the DVD revolution has been the proliferation of "special features" included with DVD features, which is made possible by the data storage capacity of the disk medium. The DVD versions of *The Entity*, *Possessed* and *Suspect Zero* all contain bonus documentary material on the paranormal events that inspired these movies, and for those with an avid interest in psi, these featurettes are perhaps more interesting than the films themselves.

Viewed from an artistic standpoint, the paranormal theme has provided inspiration for some of the most popular films in the history of cinema, including *E.T.* and the *Star Wars* series. The *Star Wars* phenomenon in particular has had an enormous effect on popular culture and mythology, to the point that thousands of fans seem to have adopted the film's psi-oriented Jedi creed as a kind of folk religion. *The Exorcist* also became a cultural phenom, not only in the United States but throughout Latin America and other Roman Catholic countries worldwide with its heady blend of the paranormal and religion. Popular blockbusters such as Spielberg's *Close Encounters* and *Minority Report*, Tobe Hooper's *Poltergeist* and the *X-Men* movies dazzled movie audiences while disseminating notions of psi to the masses.

In addition to these high-profile crowd-pleasers, a number of more serious and thoughtful excursions into cinematic psi by talented directors have enthralled movie audiences over the years. These include John Farrow's *The Night Has a Thousand Eyes*, Alfred Hitchcock's *Shadow of a Doubt*, Anthony Pelissier's *The Rocking Horse Winner*, Bryan Forbes' *Séance on a Wet Afternoon*, Robert Wise's *The Haunting*, Peter Weir's *The Last Wave*, Nicolas Roeg's *Don't Look Now*, Jerzy Skolimowski's *The Shout*, Eliseo Subiela's *Man Facing Southeast*, Daniel Petrie's *Resurrection*, Michael Mann's *Manhunter* and Jon Turteltaub's *Phenomenon*. On a less exalted level are competently-made psychic thrillers such as Roger Corman's *Not of This Earth*, Wolf Rilla's *Village of the Damned*, George Pal's *The Power*, David Cronenberg's *Scanners*, Brian De Palma's *Carrie*, Roger Donaldson's *Species* and Brett Leonard's *The Lawnmower Man*. And then there are guilty pleasures and cult faves like *Killers from Space, The Brain from Planet Arous, The Crawling Eye, Visit to a Small Planet, Psychic Killer, Exorcist II: The Heretic, The Medusa Touch* and *Dune* that make fun DVD viewing despite their paranormal shortcomings.

Psychic phenomena have been with humankind for all of civilization's recorded history, and surely for millennia before that. The paranormal will still be with us in the 21st century and beyond, as our horizons expand and our consciousness opens up to new paradigms of reality. Perhaps, as science fiction writers and proponents of psi have envisioned, we will be able to harness these latent powers to benefit society and discover new, entangled realities. Or perhaps civilization will someday fall victim to psychic mind control or other negative aspects of psi. Either way, the movies were there first.

Filmography

The Amazing Mr. X (a.k.a. The Spiritualist) (1948) Director: Bernard Vorhaus. Producer: Ben Stoloff. Screenplay: Crane Wilbur. Cast: Turhan Bey, Lynn Bari, Cathy O'Donnell, Richard Carlson. USA. B&W. 70 m. DVD: Alpha Video.

An American Haunting (2006) Director/Screenplay: Courtney Solomon. Producers: Christopher Milburn, Courtney Solomon, André Rouleau. Cast: Donald Sutherland, Sissy Spacek, James D'Arcy, Rachel Hurd-Wood. Canada (Freestyle). Color. 90m. DVD: Lions Gate.

The Brain from Planet Arous (1957) Director: Nathan Hertz (Nathan Juran). Producer: Jaques Marquette. Screenplay: Ray Buffum Cast: John Agar, Joyce Meadows, Robert Fuller. USA (Howco International) B&W. 71m. DVD: Image Entertainment.

The Butcher's Wife (1991) Director: Terry Hughes. Producers: Lauren Lloyd, Wallis Nicita. Screenplay: Ezra Litwak, Marjorie Schwartz. Cast: Demi Moore, Jeff Daniels, George Dzundza, Mary Steenburgen, Frances McDormand. USA (Paramount). Color. 107m. DVD: Paramount Widescreen Collection.

The Cabinet of Dr. Caligari (*Das Kabinett des Dr. Caligari*) (1919) Director: Robert Weine Producer: Uncredited. Screenplay: Carl Mayer, Hans Janowitz. Cast: Werner Krauss, Conrad Veidt, Lil Dagover, Fredrich Feher, Rudolf Klein-Rogge. Germany (Decla-Bioscop). B&W. Silent. 71m. DVD: Kino on Video.

Carrie (1976) Director: Brian De Palma. Producers: Paul Monash, Brian De Palma. Screenplay: Lawrence D. Cohen. Cast: Sissy Spacek, Piper Laurie, Amy Irving, John Travolta, Nancy Allen, Betty Buckley. USA (United Artists). Color. 98m. DVD: MGM.

Children of the Damned (1963) Director: Anton M. Leader. Producer: Ben Arbeid. Screenplay: John Briley. Cast: Ian Hendry, Barbara Ferris, Alan Badel, Alfred Burke, Clive Powell. MGM (UK). B&W. 90m. DVD: Warner Home Video.

The Clairvoyant (a.k.a. The Evil Mind) (1935) Director: Maurice Elvey. Producer: Michael Balcon. Screenplay: Charles Bennett. Cast: Claude Raines, Fay Wray, Ben Field, Jane Baxter. Gaumont (UK). B&W. 81m. DVD: Unavailable.

Close Encounters of the Third Kind (1977) Director/Screenplay: Steven Spielberg. Producers: Julia Phillips, Michael Phillips. Cast: Richard Dreyfuss, Teri Garr, Melinda Dillon, François Truffaut. USA (Columbia). Color. 137m. DVD: Columbia/Tristar Home Entertainment.

The Crawling Eye (1958) Director: Quentin Lawrence. Producer: Robert S. Baker. Screenplay: Jimmy Sangster. Cast: Forrest Tucker, Janet Munro, Laurence

Payne, Jennifer Jayne. UK (DCA). B&W. 84m. DVD: Image Entertainment.

The Dark (1979) Director: John (Bud) Cardos. Producers: Dick Clark, Edward L. Montoro. Screenplay: Stanford Whitmore. Cast: Cathy Lee Crosby, William Devane, Richard Jaeckel, Keenan Wynn, Vivian Blaine. USA (Film Ventures International). Color. 92m. DVD: Shriek Show.

The Dead Zone (1983) Director: David Cronenberg. Producer: Debra Hill. Screenplay: Jeffrey Boam. Cast: Christopher Walken, Brooke Adams, Tom Skerritt, Martin Sheen. USA (Paramount). Color. 103m. DVD: Paramount Widescreen Collection.

Doctor Mabuse, the Gambler (a.k.a. Dr. Mabuse, der Spieler, 1922) Director: Fritz Lang. Producer: Erich Pommer. Screenplay: Thea von Harbou, based on the novel by Norbert Jacques. Cast: Rudolf Klein-Rogge, Aud Egede Nissen, Gertrude Welcker, Alfred Abel, Bernhard Goetzke, Paul Richter. Germany (UFA). B&W. Silent. 242m. DVD: Image Entertainment.

Don't Look Now (1973) Director: Nicolas Roeg. Producer: Peter Katz. Screenplay: Allan Scott, Chris Bryant. Cast: Donald Sutherland, Julie Christie, Hilary Mason, Clelia Matania. UK-Italy (Paramount) Color. 110m. DVD: Paramount Widescreen Collection.

Dreamscape (1984) Director: Joseph Ruben. Producer: Bruce Cohn Curtis. Screenplay: David Loughery, Chuck Russell, Joseph Ruben. Cast: Dennis Quaid, Max von Sydow, Christopher Plummer, Eddie Albert, Kate Capshaw. USA (Image Entertainment). Color. 99m. DVD: Castle Hill Productions.

Dune (1984) Director: David Lynch. Producer: Raffaella De Laurentiis. Screenplay: David Lynch. Cast: Kyle MacLachlan, José Ferrer, Sean Young, Max von Sydow, Patrick Stewart, Sting. USA (Universal). Color. 137m. DVD: Universal Home Video.

8½ (1963) Director: Federico Fellini. Producer: Angelo Rizzoli. Screenplay: Ennio Flaiano, Tullio Pinelli, Federico Fellini, Brunello Rondi. Cast: Marcello Mastroianni, Claudia Cardinale, Anouk Aimée, Sandra Milo. Italy (Embassy) B&W 138m. DVD: The Criterion Collection.

The Entity (1983) Director: Sidney J. Furie. Producer: Harold Schneider. Screenplay: Frank De Felitta. Cast: Barbara Hershey, Ron Silver, David Labiosa, Margaret Blye. USA (20th Century–Fox). Color. 125m. DVD: Starz/Anchor Bay.

Escape to Witch Mountain (1975) Director: John Hough. Producer: Jerome Courtland. Screenplay: Robert Malcolm Young. Cast: Ray Milland, Eddie Albert, Donald Pleasence, Ike Eisenmann, Kim Richards. USA (Wlat Disney/Buena Vista) Color. 97m. DVD: Disney/Buena Vista.

E.T.: The Extraterrestrial (1982) Director/Producer: Steven Spielberg. Screenplay: Melissa Mathison, Steven Spielberg. Cast: Henry Thomas, Dee Wallace, Peter Coyote, Drew Barrymore. USA (Universal). Color. 115m. DVD: Universal Home Video.

The Exorcist (1973) Director: William Friedkin. Producer/Screenplay: William Peter Blatty. Cast: Linda Blair, Ellen Burstyn, Max von Sydow, Jason Miller, Lee J. Cobb. USA (Warner Bros.) Color. 132m. DVD: Warner Home Video.

Exorcist II: The Heretic (1977) Director: John Boorman. Producers: John Boorman, Richard Lederer. Screenplay: William Goodhart. Cast: Linda Blair, Richard Burton, Louise Fletcher, Max von Sydow, James Earl Jones, Paul Henreid. USA (Warner Bros.). Color. 117m. DVD: Warner Home Video.

Filmography

The Eyes of Laura Mars (1978) Director: Irvin Kershner. Producer: Jon Peters. Screenplay: John Carpenter, David Goodman. Cast: Faye Dunaway, Tommy Lee Jones, Brad Dourif, Raul Julia. USA (Columbia). Color. 104m. DVD: Sony Pictures Home Entertainment.

Family Plot (1976) Director: Alfred Hitchcock. Producer: Uncredited. Screenplay: Ernest Lehman. Cast: Barbara Harris, Bruce Dern, William Devane, Karen Black, Cathleen Nesbitt. USA (Universal). Color. 121m. DVD: Universal Home Video.

Fanny and Alexander (1982) Director/Screenplay: Ingmar Bergman. Producer: Jörn Donner. Cast: Pernilla Allwin, Bertil Guve, Börje Ahlstedt, Lena Olin, Harriet Andersson, Anna Bergman, Erland Josephson. Sweden. Color. 312m. DVD: The Criterion Collection.

Firestarter (1984) Director: Mark L. Lester. Producer: Frank Capra, Jr. Screenplay: Stanley Mann. Cast: David Keith, Drew Barrymore, Heather Locklear, Martin Sheen, George C. Scott. USA Color. 114m. DVD: Universal Home Video.

Five Million Years to Earth (a.k.a. Quatermass and the Pit) (1967) Director: Roy Ward Baker. Producer: Anthony Nelson Keys. Screenplay: Nigel Kneale. Cast: Andrew Keir, Barbara Shelley, James Donald, Duncan Lamont. UK (Hammer/Warner Bros.) Color. 97m. DVD: Starz/Anchor Bay.

Forbidden Planet (1956) Director: Fred McLeod Wilcox. Producer: Nicholas Nayfack. Screenplay: Cyril Hume. Cast: Walter Pidgeon, Anne Francis, Leslie Nielsen, Warren Stevens. USA (MGM). Color. 98m. DVD: Warner Bros. Home Video.

The Fury (1978) Director: Brian De Palma. Producer: Frank Yablans. Screenplay: John Farris. Cast: Kirk Douglas, John Cassavetes, Amy Irving, Carrie Snodgress, Charles Durning. USA (20th Century–Fox). Color. 117m. DVD: 20th Century–Fox Home Entertainment.

Ghostbusters (1984) Director: Ivan Reitman. Producers: Bernie Brillstein, Ivan Reitman. Screenplay: Dan Aykroyd, Harold Ramis. Cast: Bill Murray, Sigourney Weaver, Dan Aykroyd, Harold Ramis, Rick Moranis, Ernie Hudson. USA (Columbia). Color. 107m. DVD: Sony Pictures Home Entertainment.

The Gift (2000) Director: Sam Raimi. Producers: James Jacks, Gary Lucchesi, Tom Rosenberg. Screenplay: Billy Bob Thornton, Tom Epperson. Cast: Cate Blanchett, Keanu Reeves, Katie Holmes, Giovanni Ribisi, Greg Kinnear, Hillary Swank. USA (Paramount). Color. 112m. DVD: Paramount Widescreen Collection.

The Green Mile (1999) Director/Screenplay: Frank Darabont. Producers: David Valdes, Frank Darabont. Cast: Tom Hanks, Michael Clarke Duncan, David Morse, Bonnie Hunt, Barry Pepper. USA (UIP/Universal) Color. 188m. DVD: Warner Home Video.

The Haunting (1963) Director/Producer: Robert Wise. Screenplay: Nelson Gidding. Cast: Julie Harris, Claire Bloom, Richard Johnson, Russ Tamblyn. USA (MGM). B&W. 112m. DVD: Warner Home Video.

Hideaway (1995) Director: Brett Leonard. Producers: Jerry A. Baerwitz, Gimel Everett. Screenplay: Andrew Kevin Walker, Neal Jiminez. Cast: Jeff Goldblum, Christine Lahti, Alicia Silverstone, Jeremy Sisto. USA (Tristar). Color. 106m. DVD: Sony Pictures Home Entertainment.

In Dreams (1999) Director: Neil Jordan. Producers: Charles Burke, Stephen Wooley. Screenplay: Bruce Robinson, Neil Jordan. Cast: Annette Bening, Katie

Sagona, Aidan Quinn, Robert Downey, Jr. USA (Amblin/DreamWorks). Color. 98m. DVD: DreamWorks Home Entertainment.

Juarez (1939) Director: William Dieterle. Producer: Henry Blanke. Screenplay: John Huston, Aeneas MacKenzie, Wolfgang Reinhardt. Cast: Paul Muni, Bette Davis, Brian Aherne, Claude Rains. USA (Warner Bros.) B&W. 132m. DVD: Unavailable.

Killers from Space (1954) Director/Producer: W. Lee Wilder. Screenplay: Bill Raynor. Cast: Peter Graves, Barbara Bestar, James Seay, Frank Gerstle. USA (RKO). B&W. 71m. DVD: Alpha Video.

The Last Mimzy (2007) Director: Bob Shaye. Producer: Michael Phillips. Screenplay: Bruce Joel Rubin, Toby Emmerich. Cast: Rhiannon Lee Wryn, Chris O'Neil, Rainn Wilson, Timothy Hutton, Michael Clarke Duncan. USA (New Line Cinema). Color. 96m. DVD: New Line Home Entertainment.

The Last Wave (1977) Director: Peter Weir. Producer: Hal McElroy. Screenplay: Peter Weir, Tony Morphett, Petru Popescu. Cast: Richard Chamberlain, David Gulpilil, Olivia Hamnett. Australia (United Artists) Color. 106m. DVD: The Criterion Collection.

The Lawnmower Man (1992) Director: Brett Leonard. Producer: Gimel Everett. Screenplay: Brett Leonard and Gimel Everett. Cast: Pierce Brosnan, Jeff Fahey, Jenny Wright, Geoffrey Lewis. USA (New Line Cinema). Color. 108m. DVD: New Line Home Video.

The Legend of Hell House (1973) Director: John Hough. Producers: Albert Fennell, Norman T. Herman. Screenplay: Richard Matheson. Cast: Pamela Franklin, Roddy McDowall, Clive Revill, Gayle Hunnicutt, Ronald Culver. UK (20th Century–Fox). Color. 95m. DVD: 20th Century–Fox.

Man Facing Southeast (1986) Director/Screenplay: Eliseo Subiela. Producer: Lujan Pflaum. Cast: Lorenzo Quinteros, Hugo Soto, Inés Vernengo. Argentina (Starmaker). Color. 108m. DVD: Unavailable.

Man on a Swing (1974) Director: Frank Perry. Producer: Howard B. Jaffe. Screenplay: David Z. Goodman. Cast: Cliff Robertson, Joel Grey, Dorothy Tristan, Peter Masterson. USA (Paramount). Color. 109m. DVD: Unavailable.

Manhunter (1986) Director/Screenplay: Michael Mann. Producer: Richard Roth. Cast: William Petersen, Kim Griest, Joan Allen, Dennis Farina, Brian Cox, Tom Noonan, Stephen Lang. USA Color. 118m. DVD: MGM Home Video.

Matilda (1996) Director: Danny DeVito. Producers: Danny DeVito, Michael Shamberg, Stacy Sher, Liccy Dahl. Screenplay: Nicholas Kazan, Robin Swicord. Cast: Danny DeVito, Mara Wilson, Rhea Perlman, Embeth Davidtz. USA (Tristar). Color. 98m. DVD: Columbia/Tristar Home Video.

The Medusa Touch (1978) Director: Jack Gold. Producer: Denis Holt. Screenplay: John Briley. Cast: Richard Burton, Lee Remick, Lino Ventura, Harry Andrews, Alan Badel. UK/France (ITC) Color. 105m. DVD: Unavailable.

Minority Report (2002) Director: Steven Spielberg. Producers: Gerald R. Molen, Bonnie Curtis, Walter F. Parkes, Jan de Bont. Screenplay: Scott Frank, Jon Cohen, from the short story by Philip K. Dick. Cast: Tom Cruise, Colin Farrell, Max von Sydow, Samantha Morton. USA (20th Century–Fox/Amblin). Color. 146m. DVD: DreamWorks Home Video.

The Mothman Prophecies (2002) Director: Mark Pellington. Producers: Tom Rosenberg, Richard Hatem, Gary Lucchesi. Screenplay: Richard Hatem. Cast: Richard Gere, Laura Linney, Debra

Messing, Will Patton. USA (Sony Pictures). Color. 119m. DVD: Sony Pictures Home Entertainment.

Murder, My Sweet (1944) Director: Edward Dmytryk. Producer: Adrian Scott. Screenplay: John Paxton. Cast: Dick Powell, Anne Shirley, Claire Trevor, Mike Mazurki, Otto Kruger. USA (RKO). B&W. 95m. DVD: Warner Home Entertainment.

Next (2007) Director: Lee Tamahori. Producers: Nicolas Cage, Jason Koornick, Todd Garner, Norm Golightly, Graham King, Arne Schmidt. Screenplay: Gary Goldman. Cast: Nicolas Cage, Julianne Moore, Jessica Biel, Thomas Kretschmann, Peter Falk. USA (Paramount). Color. 96m. DVD: Paramount Widescreen Collection.

The Night has a Thousand Eyes (1948) Director: John Farrow. Producer: Endre Bohem. Screenplay: Barré Lyndon, Jonathan Latimer. Cast: Edward G. Robinson, Gail Russell, John Lund, Virginia Bruce. USA (Paramount). B&W. 81m. DVD: Unavailable.

Nightmare Alley (1947) Director: Edmund Goulding. Producer: George Jessel. Screenplay: Jules Furthman. Cast: Tyrone Power, Joan Blondell, Coleen Gray, Helen Walker. USA (20th Century–Fox). B&W. 110m. DVD: 20th Century–Fox Home Entertainment.

Not of this Earth (1957) Director/Producer: Roger Corman. Screenplay: Charles Griffith, Mark Hanna. Cast: Paul Birch, Beverly Garland, Morgan Jones, Jonathan Haze, Anne Carroll, Dick Miller. (Allied Artists). B&W. 67m. DVD: Unavailable.

Patrick (1978) Director: Richard Franklin. Producers: Anthony I. Ginnane, Richard Franklin. Screenplay: Everett De Roche. Cast: Susan Penhaligon, Robert Thompson, Robert Helpmann, Rod Mullinar. Australia (Australian International). Color. 96m. DVD: Elite Entertainment.

The People (1971) Director: John Korty. Producers: Gerald I. Isenberg, Francis Ford Coppola. Screenplay: James M. Miller. Cast: Kim Darby, William Shatner, Dan O'Herlihy, Diane Varsi. USA (ABC-TV). Color. 74m. DVD: Unavailable.

Peter Ibbetson (1935) Director: Henry Hathaway. Producer: Louis D. Lighton. Screenplay: John Meehan, Edwin Justus Mayer, Waldemar Young, Constance Collier, Vincent Lawrence. Cast: Gary Cooper, Ann Harding, Ida Lupino, John Halliday. USA (Paramount). 88m. DVD: Universal (on "The Gary Cooper Collection").

Phenomenon (1996) Director: John Turteltaub. Producers: Barbara Boyle, Michael Taylor, Charles Newirth. Screenplay: Gerald Di Pego. Cast: John Travolta, Kyra Sedgwick, Forest Whitaker, Robert Duvall. USA (Touchstone Pictures). Color. 123m. DVD: Disney/Buena Vista.

Poltergeist (1982) Director: Tobe Hooper. Producers: Frank Marshall, Steven Spielberg. Screenplay: Steven Spielberg, Michael Grais. Cast: Craig T. Nelson, Jo-Beth Williams, Dominique Dunne, Oliver Robins, Heather O'Rourke, Beatrice Straight, Zelda Rubinstein. USA (Warner Bros.) Color. 114m. DVD: Warner Home Video.

Possessed (2000) Director: Steven E. de Souza. Producer: Jane Bartelme. Screenplay: Michael Lazarou. Cast: Timothy Dalton, Henry Czerny, Christopher Plummer, Piper Laurie, Jonathan Malen, Michael McLachlan. USA (Showtime Entertainment). Color. 111m. DVD: Showtime Entertainment.

Powder (1995) Director/Screenplay: Victor Salva. Producer: Roger Birnbaum. Cast: Sean Patrick Flanery, Jeff

Goldblum, Mary Steenburgen, Lance Henriksen. USA (Caravan Pictures). Color. 111m. DVD: Disney/Buena Vista.

The Power (1968) Director: Byron Haskin. Producer: George Pal. Screenplay: John Gay. Cast: George Hamilton, Suzanne Pleshette, Michael Rennie, Nehemiah Persoff, Aldo Ray, Arthur O'Connell. USA (MGM). Color. 103m. DVD: Unavailable.

Premonition (2007) Director: Mennan Yapo. Producer: Ashok Amritaj. Screenplay: Bill Kelly. Cast: Sandra Bullock, Julian McMahon, Shyann McClure, Courtney Taylor Burness. USA (TriStar Pictures). Color. 110m. DVD: Sony Pictures Home Entertainment.

The Psychic (1968) Director/Producer: James F. Hurley. Screenplay: James F. Hurley, Herschell Gordon Lewis. Cast: Dick Genola, Robyn Guest, Arlene Banas, Elaine Blake. USA (Hurlon Productions) Color. 90m. DVD: Unavailable.

The Psychic (a.k.a. Sette Note in Nero, 1977) Director: Lucio Fulci. Screenplay: Lucio Fulci, Roberto Gianviti. Cast: Jennifer O'Neill, Gabriele Ferzetti, Marc Porel, Ida Galli, Gianni Garko. Italy (Group I) Color. 97m. DVD: Severin.

Psychic Killer (a.k.a. The Kirlian Effect, 1975) Director: Ray Danton. Producer: Mardi Rustam. Screenplay: Greydon Clark, Mike Angel, Ray Danton. Cast: Jim Hutton, Paul Burke, Aldo Ray, Neville Brand, Whit Bissell, Della Reese. USA (Avco-Embassy). Color. 90m. DVD: Elite Entertainment.

Resurrection (1980) Director: Daniel Petrie. Producer: Renée Misel, Howard Roseman. Screenplay: Lewis John Carlino. Cast: Ellen Burstyn, Sam Shepard, Eva Le Gallienne, Roberts Blossom. USA (Universal). Color. 103m. DVD: Sony Pictures Home Entertainment.

Return from Witch Mountain (1978) Director: John Hough. Producers: Ron Miller, Jerome Courtland. Screenplay: Malcolm Marmorstein. Cast: Christopher Lee, Bette Davis, Kim Richards, Ike Eisenmann, Jack Soo, Brad Savage. USA (Walt Disney/Buena Vista). Color. 95m. DVD: Disney/Buena Vista.

The Rocking Horse Winner (1949) Director/Screenplay: Anthony Pelissier. Producer: John Mills. Cast: Valerie Hobson, John Howard Davies, Ronald Squire, John Mills. UK (Two Cities Films) B&W. 91m. DVD: Home Vision.

Scanners (1981) Director/Screenplay: David Cronenberg. Producer: Claude Heroux.: Cast: Stephen Lack, Jennifer O'Neill, Patrick McGoohan, Michael Ironside, Lawrence Dane. Canada (Filmplan International). Color. 103m. DVD: 20th Century–Fox Home Entertainment.

Séance on a Wet Afternoon (1964) Director: Bryan Forbes. Producer: Richard Attenborough. Screenplay: Bryan Forbes, Mark McShane. Cast: Kim Stanley, Richard Attenborough, Nanette Newman, Mark Eden, Patrick Magee, Judith Donner. UK (Rank). B&W. 115m. DVD: Home Vision.

Shadow of a Doubt (1943) Director: Alfred Hitchcock. Producer: Jack H. Skirball. Screenplay: Thornton Wilder, Sally Benson, Alma Reville. Cast: Joseph Cotten, Teresa Wright, Macdonald Carey, Henry Travers, Hume Cronyn. USA (Universal). B&W. 108m. DVD: Universal.

The Shout (1979) Director: Jerzy Skolimowski. Producer: Jeremy Thomas. Screenplay: Michael Austin, Jerzy Skolimowski. Cast: Alan Bates, Susannah York, John Hurt, Tim Curry, Robert Stephens. UK (Rank Organization). Color. 87m. DVD: Unavailable.

The Silence of the Lambs (1991) Director: Jonathan Demme. Producers: Kenneth Utt, Edward Saxon, Ron Bozman.

Screenplay: Ted Tally. Cast: Jodie Foster, Anthony Hopkins, Scott Glenn, Ted Levine, Diane Baker. USA (Orion Pictures). Color. 118m. DVD: Image Entertainment.

The Space Children (1958) Director: Jack Arnold. Producer: William Alland. Screenplay: Bernard C. Schoenfeld. Cast: Johnny Crawford, Sandy Descher, Jackie Coogan, Russell Johnson. USA (Paramount). B&W. 69m. DVD: Unavailable.

Species (1995) Director: Roger Donaldson. Producers: Dennis Feldman, Frank Mancuso. Screenplay: Dennis Feldman. F/X: Richard Edlund, Steve Johnson. Cast: Ben Kingsley, Natasha Hentsridge, Forest Whitaker, Michael Madsen, Alfred Molina, Marg Helgenberger. USA (MGM/United Artists). Color. 108m. DVD: MGM DVD

Star Wars Episode I: The Phantom Menace (1999) Director/Screenplay: George Lucas. Producer: Rick McCallum. Cast: Liam Neeson, Ewan McGregor, Natalie Portman, Ian McDiarmid, Terrence Stamp. USA (20th Century–Fox). Color. 133m. DVD: Lucasfilm Ltd.

Star Wars Episode II: Attack of the Clones (2002) Director/Screenplay: George Lucas. Producer: Rick McCallum. Cast: Ewan McGregor, Natalie Portman, Hayden Christensen, Ian McDiarmid, Christopher Lee. USA (20th Century–Fox). Color: 142m. DVD: Lucasfilm Ltd.

Star Wars Episode III: Revenge of the Sith (2005) Director/Screenplay: George Lucas. Producer: Rick McCallum. Cast: Ewan McGregor, Natalie Portman, Hayden Christensen, Ian McDiarmid, Christopher Lee. USA (20th Century–Fox). Color. 140m. DVD: Lucasfilm Ltd.

Star Wars Episode IV: A New Hope (1977) Director/Screenplay: George Lucas. Producer: Gary Kurtz. Cast: Mark Hamill, Harrison Ford, Alec Guinness, Carrie Fisher, Peter Cushing. USA (20th Century–Fox). Color. 123m. DVD: Lucasfilm Ltd.

Star Wars Episode V: The Empire Strikes Back (1980) Director: Irvin Kershner. Producer: Gary Kurtz. Screenplay: Leigh Brackett, Lawrence Kasdan. Cast: Mark Hamill, Harrison Ford, Carrie Fisher, Billy Dee Williams. USA (20th Century–Fox) Color. 129m. DVD: Lucasfilm Ltd.

Star Wars Episode VI: Return of the Jedi (1983) Director: Richard Marquand. Producer: Howard Kazanjian. Screenplay: Lawrence Kasdan, George Lucas. Cast: Mark Hamill, Harrison Ford, Carrie Fisher, Billy Dee Williams, Ian McDiarmid. USA (20th Century–Fox). Color. 136m. DVD: Lucasfilm Ltd.

Starship Troopers (1997) Director: Paul Verhoeven. Producers: Alan Marshall, Jon Davison. Screenplay: Ed Neumeier. Cast: Casper Van Dien, Dina Meyer, Denise Richards, Neil Patrick Harris, Michael Ironside, Jake Busey. USA (Columbia). Color. 130m. DVD: Columbia/Tristar Home Entertainment.

Suspect Zero (2004) Director: E. Elias Merhige. Producers: Paula Wagner, E. Elias Merhige, Gaye Hirsch. Screenplay: Zak Penn, Billy Ray. Cast: Ben Kingsley, Aaron Eckhart, Carrie-Anne Moss. USA (Paramount). Color. 99m. DVD: Paramount Home Entertainment.

Svengali (1931) Director: Archie Mayo. Producer: Uncredited. Screenplay: J. Grubb Alexander. Cast: John Barrymore, Marian Marsh, Donald Crisp, Bramwell Fletcher, Carmel Myers. USA (Warner Bros.) B&W. 81m. DVD: Alpha Video.

The UFO Incident (1975) Director/Producer: Richard A. Colla. Screenplay: Lee Pogostin, Hesper Anderson. Cast: James Earl Jones, Estelle Parsons, Bernard

Hughes, Beeson Carroll. USA (NBC-TV). Color. 100m. DVD: Unavailable.

Village of the Damned (1960) Director: Wolf Rilla. Producer: Ronald Kinnoch. Screenplay: Sterling Silliphant, Wolf Rilla, George Barclay. Cast: George Sanders, Barbara Shelley, Michael Gwynne, Martin Stephens. UK (MGM). B&W. 78m. DVD: MGM Home Video.

Village of the Damned (1995) Director: John Carpenter. Producers: Sandy King, Michael Preger. Screenplay: David Himmelstein. Cast: Christopher Reeve, Kirstie Alley, Mark Hamill, Michael Paré. USA. Color. 99m. DVD: Universal.

Visit to a Small Planet (1960) Director: Norman Taurog. Producer: Hal B. Wallis. Screenplay: Edmund Beloin. Cast: Jerry Lewis, Joan Blackman, Fred Clark, Earl Holliman, Gale Gordon, John Williams. USA (Paramount). B&W. 85m. DVD: Unavailable.

What Women Want (2000) Director: Nancy Meyers. Producers: Susan Cartsonis, Bruce Davey, Gina Matthews, Nancy Meyers, Matt Williams. Screenplay: Josh Goldsmith, Cathy Yuspa. Cast: Mel Gibson, Helen Hunt, Marisa Tomei, Alan Alda, Bette Midler. USA (Paramount). Color. 127m. DVD: Paramount Widescreen Collection.

Wilder Napalm (1993) Director: Glenn Gordon Caron. Producer: Stuart Cornfeld. Screenplay: Vince Gilligan. Cast: Dennis Quaid, Debra Winger, Arliss Howard. USA (Tristar). Color. 109m. DVD: Sony Pictures Home Entertainment.

The X-Files: I Want to Believe (2008) Director: Chris Carter. Producers: Chris Carter, Frank Spotnitz. Screenplay: Frank Spotnitz, Chris Carter. Cast: David Duchovny, Gillian Anderson, Amanda Peet, Billy Connolly, Alvin Joiner, Mitch Pileggi, Callum Keith Rennie. Canada/USA. (20th Century–Fox). Color. 104m. DVD: Pending Release 2008/2009.

X-Men (2000) Director: Bryan Singer. Producers: Lauren Shuler Donner, Ralph Winter, Richard Donner, Avi Arad, Stan Lee, Tom DeSanto. Screenplay: David Hayter. Cast: Hugh Jackman, Patrick Stewart, Ian McKellen, Anna Paquin, Halle Berry, James Marsden, Famke Janssen. USA (20th Century–Fox). Color. 104m. DVD: 20th Century–Fox.

X2: X-Men United (2003) Director: Bryan Singer. Producers: Tom DeSanto, Avi Arad, Bryan Singer, Ralph Winter, Lauren Shuler Donner. Screenplay: Michael Dougherty, Dan Harris, David Hayter, Bryan Singer, Zak Penn. Cast: Hugh Jackman, Patrick Stewart, Ian McKellen, Anna Paquin, Halle Berry, James Marsden. USA (20th Century–Fox). Color. 133m. DVD: 20th Century–Fox.

X3: The Last Stand (2006) Director: Brett Ratner. Producers: Lauren Shuler Donner, Ralph Winter, Avi Arad. Screenplay: Simon Kinberg, Zak Penn. Cast: Hugh Jackman, Patrick Stewart, Ian McKellen, Anna Paquin, Halle Berry, Kelsey Grammer. USA (20th Century–Fox). Color. 104m. DVD: 20th Century–Fox.

Chapter Notes

One

1. Jim Schnabel, *Remote Viewers: The Secret History of America's Psychic Spies* (New York: Dell Books, 1997), 145.

Two

1. Raymond Chandler, *Farewell, My Lovely* (New York: First Vintage Crime/Random House, 1992), 103.

Three

1. Russell Targ and Keith Harary, *The Mind Race: Understanding and Using Psychic Abilities.* (New York: Ballantine Books, 1984), 145.

Four

1. Thomas Harris, *Red Dragon* (New York: Dell Books, 1980), 152.
2. Ibid., 152.

Five

1. Thomas B. Allen, *Possessed: The True Story of an Exorcism* (New York: Bantam Books, 1994) p. 236.
2. William Peter Blatty, *William Peter Blatty on The Exorcist* (New York: Bantam Books, 1974), 211.
3. Ibid., 24.

Six

1. Ann Druffel and D. Scott Rogo, *The Tujunga Canyon Contacts* (New York: Signet, 1988), 235.

2. John Mack, *Passport to the Cosmos: Human Transformation and Alien Encounters* (New York: Three Rivers Press, 1999), 18.
3. Jim Marrs, *Alien Agenda: Investigating the Alien Presence Among Us* (New York: Harper, 1997), 443.
4. Robert Heinlein, *Starship Troopers* (New York: Ace Books, 1987), 236.
5. David M. Jacobs, *Secret Life: Firsthand Accounts of UFO Abductions* (New York: Simon & Schuster, 1992) 87–88.
6. Ingo Swann, *Penetration: The Question of Extraterrestrial and Human Telepathy* (Ingo Swann Books, 1998) 173.

Eight

1. Jim Marrs, *Psi Spies: The True Story of America's Psychic Warfare Program* (New Jersey: New Page Books, 2007), 158.

Conclusion

1. Paul H. Smith, *Reading the Enemy's Mind: Inside Star Gate, America's Psychic Espionage Program* (New York: Tor Books, 2006), 237–238.
2. Ibid., 238.
3. Targ and Harary, *The Mind Race*, 141.
4. Ibid., 141.
5. Ibid., 145.
6. Ibid., 153.

Bibliography

Allen, Thomas B. *Possessed: The True Story of an Exorcism*. New York: Bantam Books, 1994.
Bartlett, Laile E. *Psi Trek*. New York: McGraw-Hill, 1981.
Bester, Alfred. *The Demolished Man*. New York: Vintage Books, 1996.
Blatty, William Peter. *William Peter Blatty on The Exorcist: From Novel to Film*. New York: Bantam Books, 1974.
Chandler, Raymond. *Farewell, My Lovely*. New York: Vintage Crime/Random House, 1992.
Clarens, Carlos. *An Illustrated History of the Horror Film*. New York: Capricorn Books, 1967.
Druffel, Ann, and D. Scott Rogo. *The Tujunga Canyon Contacts*. New York: Signet, 1988.
Everman, Welch. *Cult Science Fiction Films*. New York: Citadel Press, 1995.
Graff, Dale E. *Tracks in the Psychic Wilderness*. Element Books, 2000.
Harris, Thomas. *Red Dragon*. New York: Dell Books, 1980.
Heinlein, Robert. *Starship Troopers*. New York: Ace Books, 1987.
Jones, Marie D. *Psience: How New Discoveries in Quantum Physics and New Science May Explain the Existence of Paranormal Phenomena*. Franklin, NJ: New Page Books, 2007.
Mack, John. *Passport to the Cosmos: Human Transformation and Alien Encounters*. New York: Three Rivers Press, 1999.
Mandelbaum, W. Adam. *The Psychic Battlefield: A History of the Military-Occult Complex*. New York: St. Martin's, 2000.
Marrs, Jim. *Alien Agenda: Investigating the Alien Presence Among Us*. New York: Harper Paperbacks, 1997.
_____. *Psi Spies: The True Story of America's Psychic Warfare Program*. Franklin, NJ: New Page Books, 2007.
Mayer, Elizabeth Lloyd. *Extraordinary Knowing: Science, Skepticism and the Inexplicable Powers of the Human Mind*. New York: Bantam, 2007.
Morehouse, David. *Psychic Warrior*. New York: St. Martin's, 1996.
Ostrander, Shiela, and Lynn Schroder. *Psychic Discoveries Behind the Iron Curtain*. New York: Bantam Books, 1971.
Radin, Dean. *Entangled Minds: Extrasensory Experiences in Quantum Reality*. New York: Paraview Pocket Books, 2006.
Rhine, J.B., and William McDougall. *Extra Sensory Perception*. Whitefish, MT: Kessinger Publishing, 2003.

Roll, William, and Valerie Story. *Unleashed: Of Poltergeists and Murder: The Curious Story of Tina Resch*. New York: Paraview Books, 2004.
Schnabel, Jim. *Remote Viewers: The Secret History of America's Psychic Spies*. New York: Dell Books, 1997.
Sinclair, Upton. *Mental Radio*. New York: Collier Books, 1971.
Smith, Paul H. *Reading the Enemy's Mind: Inside Star Gate, America's Psychic Espionage Program*. New York: Tor Books, 2005.
Stanley, John. *Creature Features: The Science Fiction, Fantasy and Horror Movie Guide*. New York: Boulevard Books, 1997.
Stapeldon, Olaf. *Odd John*. Dover, 1972.
Sturgeon, Theodore. *More Than Human*. New York: Vintage Books, 1999.
Swann, Ingo. *Natural ESP: A Layman's Guide to Unlocking the Extrasensory Power of Your Mind*. New York: Bantam Books, 1987.
_____. *Penetration: The Question of Extraterrestrial and Human Telepathy*. Privately published, 1998.
Targ, Russell, and Harold Puthoff. *Mind Reach: Scientists Look at Psychic Ability*. New York: Delacorte Press, 1977.
Targ, Russell, and Keith Harary. *The Mind Race: Understanding and Using Psychic Abilities*. New York: Ballantine Books, 1984.
Van Vogt, A.E. *Slan*. New York: Orb Books, 2007.
Von Gunden, Kenneth, and Stuart H. Stock. *Twenty All-Time Great Science Fiction Films*. New York: Arlington House, 1982.
Weldon, Michael J. *The Psychotronic Encyclopedia of Film*. New York: Ballantine Books, 1983.
_____. *The Psychotronic Video Guide*. New York: St. Martin's Griffin, 1996.
Wilson, Colin. *Poltergeist: A Study in Destructive Haunting*. St. Paul, MN: Llewellyn, 1993.

Index

Academy Award 47, 61, 62, 66, 71, 73, 78, 88, 91, 97, 200
Adams, Brooke 100
Adams, Julie 66
Aeschylus 19
Agamemnon 19
Agar, John 112–114
Aherne, Brian 49
Alaska 140
Albert, Eddie 55, 195–196
Albuquerque 199
Alcatraz Island 175
Alda, Alan 53
Alien 94, 134, 136, 154
Alien abductions 138–140
Allen, Nancy 86
Allen, Thomas B. 79, 81
Alley, Kirstie 123
Almereyda, Michael 38
Alton, John 34
Amagula, Nandjiwarra 89
The Amazing Mr. X 2, 4, 34, 36
American Association for the Advancement of Science 3, 18
An American Haunting 75, 102–104, 207
American Society for Psychical Research 14
Ancient Near East 19
Anderson, Gillian 203
Anderson, Hesper 139
Anderson, Jack 179, 199, 205
Anderson, Jamie 74
Angel, Mikel 66
Annis, Francesca 163, 165
Antichrist 12

Antoon, Jason 168
Apports 16, 97
Argento, Dario 68
Arizona 199, 201
Arnold, Jack 114–116, 120
Arthurian Cycle 29
Attack of the Crab Monsters 109
Attack of the 50-Foot Woman 114
Attenborough, Richard 61–62
Augurs 12
August, Pernilla 156
Australia 157
Ayahuasca 166
Aykroyd, Dan 3, 50–52
Aykroyd, Peter 51

Babylon 11
Badel, Alan 120
Baker, Kenny 143–144
Baker, Roy Ward 129
Barclay, George 119–120
Bari, Lynn 34
Barron, Bebe 128
Barron, Louis 128
Barrymore, Drew 191–193
Barrymore, John 28–29, 30
Bartkowiak, Susan 134
Bates, Alan 38–39
Bava, Mario 68
Baxter, Jane 29
BBC-TV 129
Bell, Richard 103–104
The "Bell Witch" 103–104
The Bell Witch — An American Haunting 103
Beloin, Edmund 124
Bening, Annette 71–72

Bennett, Charles 30
Benson, Sally 61
Bergman, Ingmar 49–50
Bernbaum, Paul 202
Berry, Halle 171, 173
Bestar, Barbara 108
Bester, Alfred 20, 24–25, 59
Bey, Turhan 34
"Beyond the Sea" 202
Biel, Jessica 201–202
Binder, Mike 168
Bingen 16
Birch, Paul 110–111
Bissell, Whit 66
Bither, Doris 100
Black, Karen 67
The Black Hole 154
Blackman, Joan 123
Blackwater Corporation 188
Blade Runner 154, 167
Blair, Linda 17, 80, 82–83
Blanchett, Cate 73–74
Blatty, William Peter 78–80
Blithe Spirit 13–14, 62
Blondell, Joan 32
Blood Feast 63
Bloom, Claire 76–77
The Body Snatcher 75
Boston 14
Boston Strangler 59
Boulton, Davis 122
Bowdern, Father 81
Boyd, Russell 89
Brackett, Leigh 146
The Brain from Planet Arous 112–114, 209
Brainstorm 206
Brainwashing 107

Brand, Neville 66
Brestoff, Richard 99
Briley, John 93 120–121
Bringleson, Mark 197
Bronze Age 9
The Brood 100
Brookes, Jacqueline 99
Brosnan, Pierce 197
Brown, Gaye 103
Bruce, Virginia 35
Bruyere, Rosa 41
Bryant, Chris 84
Bubb, Karl W., Sr. 80
Buckley, Betty 86
Buddhism 57, 150
Buenos Aires 125
Bullock, Sandra 47–49
Burram, Ray 114
Burbank 59
Burke, Paul 66
Burstyn, Ellen 39–41, 43, 80
Burton, Richard 3, 82–83, 92–94
Burton, Tim 53
The Butcher's Wife 51–53, 58, 74

Cabaret 66
The Cabinet of Dr. Caligari 26
Caesar, Julius 12
Cage, Nicholas 201–202, 207
California 115, 125
California Healing Light Center 41
Cambridge 14
Campbell, Joseph 141
Canada 101, 138
Canning, Victor 68
Cardos, John "Bud" 133
Carey, Macdonald 60
Carlson, Richard 34, 180
Capshaw, Kate 195
Caribbean 201
Carney, Art 192
Caron, Glenn Gordon 53
Carpenter, John 91–92, 123
Carrie (movie) 2, 3, 43, 47, 75, 85–88, 104, 184, 186, 191, 207, 209
Carrie (musical) 88
Carrie (TV remake) 88
Carroll, Anne 110
Carter, Chris 202, 204

Carter, Jimmy 3, 179
Casella, Martin 96
Cassavetes, John 184
Castandea, Carlos 142–143, 150
Catholic Church 78–79, 197, 208
Chamberlain, Richard 89
Chandler, Raymond 31
Changeling 120
Charly 198
Chicago 32–33, 184
Children of the Damned 120–123
China 9, 121, 205
Chong, Rae-Dawn 102
Christensen, Hayden 157, 159
Christianity 11–13, 207
Christie, Agatha 13
Christie, Julie 83
Church, Sen. Frank 179
CIA 18, 178–180, 196, 205
Ciccolella, Jude 49
Clairvoyance (definition) 2
The Clairvoyant 6, 29–31, 35
Clark, Greydon 66
Clark, William A. 64
Clarkson, Patricia 47
Clayton, Jack 120
A Clockwork Orange 202
Close Encounters of the Third Kind 94, 95, 106, 129–130, 167, 178–179, 208
Clownhouse 44
Cohen, John 169
Cohen, Lawrence D. 88
Cold War 116, 123, 177
Cole, Gary 73
Collinge, Patricia 59
Colombo 199
Columbia University 50
Communism 107
Conan Doyle, Sir Arthur 14
Condon, Richard 107
Connolly, Billy 203
Constantine 12
Cooper, Gary 31
Co-ordinate Remote Viewing (CRV) 178
Copenhagen's Psychic Lovers see *The Psychic*, 1968
Coppola, Francis Ford 124

Corbett, Tom 78
Corman, Roger 109–111, 114, 209
Cotten, Joseph 59–61
Cowan, Jerome 35
Coward, Noel 13, 62
Cox, Brian 69, 173
Craven, Wes 196
The Crawling Eye 107, 131–133, 134, 209
The Creature from the Black Lagoon 115
Croesus 9–10
Cro-Magnon 20
Cromwell, James 47
Cronenberg, David 40, 100–101, 105, 187, 190, 205, 209
Crookes, Sir William 14
Crosby, Cathy Lee 133
Cruise, Tom 167, 169
The Crying Game 72
"Crystal Children" 116
Culver City 100
Cummings, Constance 14
Curse of Frankenstein 132
Curse of the Cat People 75
Curse of the Demon 62
Curtis, Bruce Cohn 196
Czechoslovakia 177

Dagover, Lil 27
Dahl, Roald 56
Dallas 199
Dallas, Ian 49
Dalton, Timothy 81
Dames, Ed 201
Dan Aykroyd Unplugged on UFOs 51
Dane, Lawrence 188
Daniel 10
Daniels, Anthony 144
Daniels, Jeff 52
Danton, Raymond 66
Darabont, Frank 46, 47
Darby, Kim 124
D'Arcy, James 103
The Dark 5, 107, 133–134
Darnton, John 20
Davidtz, Embeth 56
Davies, John Howard 37
Davis, Bette 49, 55–56
Davison, Bruce 171
The Day the Earth Stood Still 107, 182

Index

The Day the World Ended 109
The Dead Zone (movie) 2, 40, 47, 63, 100–102, 191, 194
The Dead Zone (novel) 59, 63, 100, 104, 208
The Dead Zone (TV show) 102, 199
The Deadly Mantis 114
DeFilitta, Frank 100
De Laurentiis, Dino 162
Della Sorte, Joseph 66
Delphic Oracle 9–10, 12
Delsol, Gerald 122
Demarest, William 35
The Demolished Man 20, 24–25, 59
Demonic Possession 17, 78–83
De Palma, Brian 3, 43, 83, 85, 87–88, 105, 184, 186–187, 209
Dern, Bruce 67
Destination Moon 180
Deuteronomy 11
Devane, William 67, 133–134
Devil's Tower 130, 178–179
DeVito, Danny 56–57
Diary of a Mad Housewife 66
Dick, Philip K. 167, 169, 202
Dieterle, William 49
Dillon, Melinda 130
DiPego, Gerald 45
Director's Guild 95
Divination 12
Dmytryk, Edward 32
DNA 57, 135, 158
Dr. Mabuse the Gambler 26, 183
Doll's Eyes 72
Donald, James 129
Donaldson, Roger 135, 209
Donner, Judith 61
Donovan's Brain 107
Don't Look Now 2, 83–85, 104, 207, 209
Don't Torture a Duckling 68
Douglas, Kirk 184–185
Dourif, Brad 91
Downey, Robert, Jr. 71–72
Dracula (movie) 27, 107

Dracula (novel) 26
The Dream Play 50
Dream Telepathy 31, 89, 196
Dreamscape 4, 6, 187, 194–196, 206
Dreyfuss, Richard 130, 178
Drug Enforcement Agency 74, 200
Duchovny, David 203
Dugway 135
Duke University Parapsychology Lab 15–16, 20, 70, 73
Du Maurier, Daphne 83
Du Maurier, George 28, 31
Dunaway, Fay 90–91
Duncan, Michael Clarke 46–47, 57, 208
Dune (movie) 4, 5, 162–166, 170, 208, 209
Dune (novel) 142, 162
Dunne, Dominique 95, 98
Durning, Charles 185
Duvall, Robert 45–46
Dzundza, George 52

E! Channel 98
Earth vs. the Flying Saucers 108
Easy Rider 20
Eckhart, Aaron 199–200
Eddas 19
Edlund, Richard 51
Edwards, John 54
Egypt 9
8½ 6, 49, 50
Eisenmann, Ike 54–55
Ekblad, Stina 49
Elisha 11
Elvey, Maurice 29–30
Emmerich, Roland 205
Emmerich, Toby 57
Enemy from Space 108
England 123
The Entity (movie) 75, 98–100, 104, 208
The Entity (novel) 100
"The Entity Files" 100
Epic of Gilgamesh 19
Epperson, Tom 73
Escape to Witch Mountain 6, 55, 58, 124
ESP (Extra Sensory Perception) (definition) 2
E.T.: The Extraterrestrial 5,

55, 94, 95, 116, 125–127, 154, 167, 208
Everett, Gimel 198
Exodus 11
The Exorcist 17, 75, 78–82, 88, 99, 104, 120, 207, 208
Exorcist II: The Heretic 17, 82–83, 209
Expressionism 26
Ezekiel 11

Fahey, Jeff 197–198
Family Plot 2, 4, 36, 60, 67–68, 74, 134
Fanny and Alexander 6, 49–50, 207
Farewell, My Lovely 32, 36
Farina, Dennis 69–70
Farrell, Colin 167
Farris, John 183–184
Farrow, John 31, 34–35, 209
Faulds, Andrew 132
FBI 57, 69–71, 108, 199–200, 201, 202–204
Feldman, Dennis 135
Fellini, Federico 49, 50
Ferrer, Jose 162–164
Ferris, Barbara 121–122
Ferris, Pam 56
Film noir 4, 31–36, 59, 134
The Final Countdown 154
Finley, William 184
Firestarter 6, 24, 47, 187, 191–194, 195, 196, 198, 199, 204, 206, 208
Fisher, Carrie 144
Five Million Years to Earth 106, 128–129
Flagstaff 201
Flanery, Sean Patrick 42–44
Fletcher, Bramwell 28
Fletcher, Louise 82, 192
Focus (poltergeist) 17
Fonda, Peter 20
Forbes, Bryan 62, 209
Forbidden Planet 106, 107, 127–128, 129, 176
"The Force" 4, 141, 144–146, 159–160

Ford, Harrison 144
Forever 31
Fort Meade 18, 179
Fosse, Bob 66
Foster, Jodie 71
Fowler, Ray 139
Fox, Catherine 13
Fox, Margaretta 13–14
Francis, Anne 127–128
Frank, Scott 169
Frankenstein 27, 43
Franklin, Pamela 77
Franklin, Richard 94
Frederick, John 109
The French Connection 81
Friedkin, William 75, 81
Frowling, Ewa 49
Fulci, Lucio 68, 91
Fuller, John 139
Fuller, Robert 112
Furie, Sidney J. 99
The Fury (movie) 4, 6, 24, 88, 183–187, 190, 193, 194, 195, 196, 198, 204, 208
The Fury (novel) 183

Garko, Gianni 68
Garland, Beverly 110–111
Garmes, Lee 33
Garson, Henry 124
Gaumont Studios 30
Gay, John 182
Geller, Uri 2, 178
General Electric Corporation 177
Genola, Dick 62
Georgetown University 78
Georgia 72–73
Gere, Richard 130–131
Germany 26–27
Ghostbusters 3, 6, 15–16, 50–52, 206, 207
Ghosts 75–78
Giallos 68
Gibson, Mel 53–54
Gibson, William 198
The Gift 2, 4, 5, 73–74, 207
Giger, H.R. 136
Gilligan, Vince 53
The Girl on the Volkswagen Floor 64
Global Climate Change 57
The Godfather 124
Gold, Jack 93

Goldblum, Jeff 42–43, 102–103
Golding, William 20
Goldman, Gary 202
Goldsmith, Josh 54
Gondola Wish 179
Goodhart, William 83
Goodman, David 91
Goulding, Edmund 32–33
Graff, Dale 31, 205
Grais, Michael 97
Grammar, Kelsey 174
Graves, Peter 108–109
Graves, Robert 39
Gray, Colleen 32–33
"Gray Aliens" 139–140
Greece 1, 9–10
The Green Mile 2, 6, 46–47, 57, 58, 208
Greenwich Village 52
Gresham, William Lindsay 33
Grey, Joel 63–64, 66
Griffith, Chuck 111
Grill Flame 179
Groundhog Day 48
Guilfoyle, Paul 72
Guinness, Sir Alec 143–146
Gulpilil, David 89
Guve, Bertil 49
Gwynne, Michael 118

Hall, Anthony Michael 102
Halliday, John 31
Hamilton, George 180–183
Hammer Studios 78, 132
Hammill, Mark 123, 143–146, 147–148, 150–151
Hammond, Kay 13–14
Hanks, Tom 46–47
Hanna, Mark 111
Hannibal 69, 202
Hannibal Rising 69
Harary, Keith 41, 207–208
Harding, Ann 31
Harris, Barbara 67
Harris, Julie 76–77
Harris, Neil Patrick 136–137
Harris, Thomas 69–70
Harrison, Rex 13
Haruspices 12
Harvard University 106
Haskin, Byron 180, 183
Hathaway, Henry 31
Haun, Lindsey 123

The "Haunted Boy" 78–79
Haunted houses 17, 75–78
The Haunting 75–77, 81, 88, 122, 209
The Haunting of Hill House 77
Hayter, David 173
Heinlein, Robert A. 136–137
Helgenberger, Marg 135
Helpmann, Robert 94
Henderson, Zenna 124
Hendry, Ian 121
Henriksen, Lance 42–43
Henry, Thomas Browne 113
Hensleigh, Jonathan 202
Herbert, Frank 142, 162, 166
Herbert, Victor 60
Herodotus 9
Hideaway 102–103, 207
Hill, Barney 138–139
Hill, Betty 138–139
Himmelstein, David 123
Hitchcock, Alfred 30, 59–61, 66, 67, 74, 134, 209
Hitler, Adolf 182, 183
The Hobbit 142
Hobson, Valerie 37
Holliman, Earl 180
Holmes, Katie 73–74
Hooper, Tobe 94–95, 97, 133, 208
Hopkins, Anthony 70–71
Hopkins, Budd 139
Hopper, Dennis 20
Horror of Dracula 132
Houdini 14
Houdini, Harry 14
Hough, John 78
Howard, Arliss 53
Howco International 112, 114
Hudson, Ernie 51
Hughes, Terry 52
Hugo Award 24
Hume, Cyril 125
Hunnicutt, Gale 77
Hunt, Helen 53–54
Hurdwood, Rachel 103
Hurkos, Peter 59, 63, 101
Hurley, James F. 62
Hurt, John 38–39
Hutchison, Doug 47
Hutton, Jim 65–66
Hutton, Timothy 57

Index

Hybrid Children 118–120
Hyde, Jacqueline 133
Hydesville 13
I Ching 9
Id 127
In Dreams 5, 71–73, 74, 89, 207
In the Company of Wolves 73
The Incredible Shrinking Man 115
Independence Day 5
India 9, 121
"Indigo Children" 116
Indovino, Mary 49
Industrial Light & Magic 97, 153, 169
The Inheritors 20
The Innocents 120
The Interrupted Journey 139
Invaders from Mars 108
Invasion of the Body Snatchers 108, 119
The Invisible Invaders 114
The Invisible Man 29
Ironside, Michael 3, 188, 190
Irving, Amy 86, 184, 186
Isaiah 10
Israel 10–11
It Came from Outer Space 107, 115

Jackman, Hugh 171–173
Jackson, Samuel L. 156
Jackson, Shirley 77
Jacobs, David 139
Jaeckel, Richard 133
Janssen, Famke 171
Jayne, Jennifer 131
Jedi 1, 4, 5, 17, 88, 143–146, 147, 149–162, 166, 176, 208
Jeepers Creepers 44
Jeremiah 10
Jiminez, Neal 102
Joan of Arc 13
Joash 10
Jodorowsky, Alejandro 162
Johnson, Ashley 54
Johnson, Richard 76
Jones, Freddie 192
Jones, James Earl 82, 139, 144

Jones, Morgan 110
Jones, Tommy Lee 91
Jordan, Charles 201
Jordan, Neil 71–73
Journal of Parapsychology 16
Juarez 6, 49
Julia, Raul 91
Julius Caesar 12
The Jungle 15
Juran, Nathan 114
Jurassic Park 167

Kansas 39–40
Karen, James 97
Kasdan, Lawrence 146, 153
Katt, William 86
Keel, John 130
Keir, Andrew 128–129
Keith, David 191, 193
Kelly, Bill 48
Kelly, David Patrick 194–196
Kennedy, John F. 85
Kershner, Irvin 91, 146
Key, Alexander 55
Killers from Space 106, 108–109, 209
King, Stephen 46, 47, 59, 63, 75, 85–86, 100–101, 102, 191, 193–194, 197, 198
King Kong 30
Kingsley, Ben 3, 134–136, 199–200
Kinnear, Greg 73–74
Kirby, Jack 170
The Kirlian Effect see *Psychic Killer*
Kirlian Photography 67
Kittanning 130
Klein-Rogge, Rudolf 26, 27
Kneale Nigel 129
Kogan, I.M. 177
Koontz, Dean R. 102
Korean War 107
Korty, John 124
Krauss, Werner 26–27
The Kremlin 177
Kronos 108
Kruger, Otto 32
Kubrick, Stanley 146, 202
Kulagina, Nina 94
Kuttner, Henry 57

Lack, Stephen 187, 190
LaGallienne, Eva 39, 43

Lahti, Christine 102
Lang, Fritz 26, 183
Las Vegas 112, 201
The Last Mimzy 6, 57–58, 59, 207
The Last Wave 2, 9, 39, 89–91, 104, 196, 209
Laurie, Piper 86, 88
The Lawnmower Man 6, 187, 197–199, 204, 207, 208, 209
Lawrence, D.H. 37–38
Lawrence, Quentin 132
Lawson, Richard 96
Leader, Anton M. 122
Lean, David 13, 62
Lee, Christopher 55–56, 157–158
Lee, Stan 170
Lee, Yuke-Moon 122
The Legend of Hell House 77–78, 207
Lehman, Ernest 68
Lenin Prize 177
Leonard, Brett 102, 197–198, 209
Leonidas 10
Lester, Mark L. 193
Lewis, Fiona 186
Lewis, Herschell Gordon 63
Lewis, Jerry 123–124
Lewton, Val 75, 78
The Leyden Papyrus 9
Liberty Island 173
Linney, Laura 130
The Little Rascals 56
Litvak, Ezra 52
Lloyd, Jake 155
Locklear, Heather 192
Lodge, Sir Oliver 14
Lom, Herbert 100
London 61–62, 128
The Lord of the Rings 142
Los Angeles 55, 110, 134, 135, 140, 201–202
Loughery, David 196
LSD 180
Lucas, George 141–143, 146, 153–155, 162
Lugosi, Bela 27
Lund, John 35
Lydia 10
Lynch, David 142, 162, 166

Mack, John 106, 139
MacLachlan, Kyle 162–163, 165
Madsen, Michael 135
Magic Mushrooms 143, 166
Maimondes Medical Center 196
Malmsjo, Jan 49
Man Facing Southeast 125, 209
Man on a Swing 2, 5, 36, 63–64, 66, 74, 200
The Manchurian Candidate 107
Mangano, Sylvana 162
Manhattan 83
Manhattan Project 80
Manhunter 69–71, 74, 200, 204, 209
Mann, Michael 69–70, 209
Mann, Stanley 193
Mansell, Clint 200
Marin County 123
Marmorstein, Malcolm 56
Marquand, Richard 153
Marrs, Jim 131
Marsden, James 171
Marsh, Marian 28, 30
Marvel Comics 173
Maryland 18, 179
Mason, Hilary 84
Massachusetts 138
Mastroianni, Marcello 49
Matania, Clelia 84
Mathen, Mahdu 122
Matheson, Richard 78
Matilda 6, 56–57, 58, 207
Mayer, Elizabeth Lloyd 31
Mayhew, Peter 144
Mayo, Archie 29
McCrindle, Alex 144
McDiarmid, Ian 151–152, 156
McDonell, Gordon 61
McDowell, Roddy 77–78
McGoohan, Patrick 187–188, 190
McGregor, Ewan 154–155
McKay, Michael Reid 174
McKellan, Ian 172–173
McMahon, Julian 48
McMillan, Kenneth 162, 164
McShane, Mark 62
Mead, Margaret 18
Meadows, Joyce 112–114

Mediterranean 184
The Medusa Touch 2, 3, 4, 35, 75, 92–94, 101, 104, 114, 209
Merhige, E. Elias 199–200
Memento 48
Men in Black 130
Mental Radio 15
Menzies, William Cameron 108
"Merry Widow Waltz" 60–61
Mesmer, Franz 13
Mesmerism 13, 26
Mesopotamia 9
Metrosexual 54
Mexico 166
Meyers, Nancy 53–54
Miami Vice 70
Micro-PK 178, 199
"Middle Earth" 142
Middle East 184
Midler, Bette 54
Midnight in the Garden of Good and Evil 73
The Midwich Cuckoos 116, 120
Midwich Main 120
Milland, Ray 55
Miller, Jason 81
Mills, John 37
"Mimsy Were the Borogoves" 57
The Mind Race 41, 207
Mind-Reach:Scientists Look at Psychic Ability 178
Mind to Mind 15
"Mindscan" 138–139
Minority Report 2, 5, 59, 167–170, 176, 202, 207, 208
"The Minority Report" (story) 167
Mitchell, Warren 132
MK-ULTRA 179–180
Molina, Alfred 102, 134–135
Monahan, Brent 103
Moore, C.L. 57
Moore, Demi 51–52
Moore, Julianne 201
Moranis, Rick 51
More Than Human 23–24
Morehouse, David 18, 200
Mormons 124
Morphett, Tony 90

Morris, Brett 171
Morrison, Temuera 158
Morse, David 46
Morton, Samantha 168–169
Moses 10–11
Moss, Carrie-Anne 199–200
The Mothman Prophecies (book) 130
The Mothman Prophecies (movie) 106, 130–131, 207
Mount Ranier 78
Moyers, Bill 141
Mundy, Meg 91
Muni, Paul 49
Munro, Janet 132–133
Murder, My Sweet 32, 34, 59
Murnau, F.W. 26
Murray, Bill 3, 15–16, 50–52
Mutual UFO Network (MUFON) 51
Myers, Carmel 28
Myers, F.W.H. 14
Mystery Science Theater 132

Nautilus 177
NBC-TV 139
Neanderthal 21
Neanderthals 20–21
Near-Death Experience (NDE) 49, 102
Nelson, Craig T. 95
Nesbitt, Cathleen 67
Neumeier, Ed 137
Neuromancer 198
New Hampshire 138
New Mexico 198, 199–200
New Testament 11–12
New York 50–51, 172, 173, 180, 196, 206
New York Times 193
Newman, Paul 11
Next 201–202, 207
Nicasio 124
Nicholson, Jack 114
Nielsen, Leslie 127–128
Nigeria 121
The Night Has a Thousand Eyes 2, 31, 34–35, 36, 209
Nightmare Alley 2, 4, 32–34, 36, 59

Index

A Nightmare on Elm Street 196
Nimoy, Leonard 125
Nixon, Richard 179
Njal's Saga 19
Nobel Prize 14, 20
Noonan, Tom 69–70
Norris, Dean 197
North Carolina 15, 51
Norton, Edward 70
Nosferatu 26, 27
Not of This Earth 106, 110–111, 209

O'Brien, Austin 197
O'Connell Arthur 180
Odd John 21–22, 24, 121–122, 176
O'Donnell, Cathy 34
O'Herlihy, Dan 124
Ohio 64
Old Testament 1, 4, 10–11
Olson, Frank 180
The Omen 120
O'Neil, Chris 57
O'Neill, Jennifer 68, 189–190
O'Rourke, Heather 95, 98
Ostrander, Sheila 177
Our Town 61
The Outer Limits 139
Outland 154
Oz, Frank 147, 153

Padgett, Lewis 57
Pal, George 14, 180, 182, 209
Palance, Jack 11
Paleolithic 9
Palo Alto 3, 18, 178
Papapetros, Maria 53
Paquin 173
Paramount Studios 31
Parapsychological Association 3, 18
Paris 28–29
Park, Ray 156
Parsons, Estelle 139
Patrick 4, 75, 94, 101
Patrick Still Lives 94
PBS 141
Pelissier, Anthony 37–38, 209
Pellington, Mark 130
Pemberton 204

The People 124
Pendelton, Steve 108
Penetration: The Question of Extraterrestrial and Human Telepathy 140
Penhaligon, Susan 94
Penn, Zak 200
Pennsylvania 130
Perlman, Rhea 56–57
Perry, Frank 64, 66
Persian Empire 10
Persoff, Nehemiah 66, 180
Peter 11
Peter Ibbetson 31, 35, 89, 196
Peters, Jon 90–91
Petersen, William 69–70
Petrie, Daniel 41, 209
Peyote 143, 166
Phenomenon 44–46, 58, 74, 208, 209
Phillips, Sian 162–164
Picnic at Hanging Rock 89
Pidgeon, Walter 127–128
Pierce, Stack 66
Pittsburgh 130
Plan 9 from Outer Space 114
Pleasence, Donald 55
Pleshette, Suzanne 180–183
Plummer, Christopher 195–196
Pogostin, S. Lee 139
Point Pleasant 130
Poltergeist 17, 75, 94–98, 100, 104, 105, 133, 207, 208
Poltergeist II: The Other Side 98
Poltergeist III 98
"Poltergeist Curse" 98
Poltergeist Phenomenon (definition) 2, 4, 16–17
Popescu, Petru 90
Porel, Marc 68
Portman, Natalie 155
Possessed 81–82
Possessed: The True Story of an Exorcism 78–79, 81–82, 207, 208
Powder 42–44, 45, 58, 74, 208
Powell, Clive 121–122
Powell, Dick 32
The Power (movie) 3, 4, 180–183, 190, 209
The Power (novel) 180

Power, Tyrone 32–33
Precognition (definition) 2
Premonition 6, 47–49
Presentiment 20
Price, Pat 59
Prochnow, Jurgen 162–163
Project Scannate 18, 305
Prophets 10–11
Prowse, David 144–145, 148, 151
Psi (definition) 1–2
The Psi Factor 51
Psionics 20
Psychedelic drugs 18, 180
The Psychic (1968) 62–63
The Psychic (1977) 5, 68, 74, 91
Psychic Discoveries Behind the Iron Curtain 29, 177, 183, 194
Psychic Friends Network 2
Psychic Killer 4, 65, 65–67, 74, 94, 134, 182, 209
Psychic Warrior 200
Psychics (definition) 1
Psycho 67
Psychokinesis (definition) 2
Psychometry 62
Psychotronics 177
Pullman, Bill 5
The Purple Monster Strikes 108
Puthoff, Hal 18, 178
Pyle, Denver 55
Pythia 9–10

Quaid, Dennis 53, 194–196
Quatermass and the Pit 129
Quinn, Aidan 71

Rabid 100
Race to Witch Mountain 55
Radin, Dean 201
The Rage: Carrie 2 88
Raiders of the Lost Ark 94
Raimi, Sam 73
The Rainbird Pattern 68
Rains, Claude 29–30, 49
Ramis, Harold 3, 50–51
Ramm, Haley 174
Rand Corporation 177
Ray, Aldo 66
Ray, Michael 115
Rea, Stephen 71

Reading the Enemy's Mind... 138, 206
Recurring spontaneous psychokinesis (RSPK) 4, 17
Red Dragon (movie) 70
Red Dragon (novel) 69–70
The Reds 70
Reese, Della 66
Reese, Jeffrey 133
Reeve, Christopher 123
Reeves, Keanu 73–74
Reitman, Ivan 51
Remick, Lee 92
Remote Viewers 14
Remote viewing 3, 18–19, 59, 107, 123, 131, 138, 177–180, 199–201, 204–205, 206
Rennie, Callum Keith 203
Rennie, Michael 3, 180, 182
Resurrection 2, 4, 5, 6, 39–42, 43, 44, 45, 58, 74, 102, 207, 209
Return to Witch Mountain 55–56, 58
Revill, Clive 77, 147
Reville, Alma 61
Rex, Roberta 122
Rhine, J.B. 15–16
Rhine River 16
Richards, Denise 137
Richards, Kathy 133
Richards, Kim 54–55
Richardson, Joely 57
Richet, Charles 14
Richmond, Anthony 84
Rilla, Wolf 119–120, 209
Robertson, Cliff 63–64, 66
Robins, Oliver 95
Robinson, Bruce 72
Robinson, Edward G. 34–35
Robinson, Frank 180
The Rocking Horse winner 37–38, 58, 209
Rockwell, Sam 47
Roeg, Nicholas 83–84, 89, 105, 209
Roerick, William 110
Rogo, D. Scott 106
Rome 11–13
Romijn, Rebecca 174
Rosemary's Baby 120
Ross, Chelcie 73
Roswell 198

Roswell: The UFO Coverup 198
Rubenstein, Zelda 96–97
Rubin, Bruce Joel 57
Rubini, Michael 70
Russell, Chuck 196
Russell, Gail 35
Russia 121, 177, 201, 205
Rutherford, Margaret 13

Sagona, Katie 71
Saint Louis 79
Salva, Victor 44
Salvati, Sergio 68
Samuel 10
San Francisco 175
Sanders, George 118–120
Sangster, Jimmy 132
Santa Monica 133
Santa Rosa 59–60
Saunders, Stuart 132
Scannate 178, 179, 205
Scanner Cop 191
Scanners 2, 3, 6, 24, 100, 101, 187–191, 193, 194, 195, 196, 198, 199, 204, 205, 207, 208, 209
Scanners: The Showdown 191
Scanners II: The New Order 191
Scanners III: The Takeover 191
Schnabel, Jim 14
Schoenfeld, Bernard 116
Schroeder, Lynn 177
Schultze, Rev. Luther 81
Schwartz, Marjorie 52
Science and Life 177
Scott, Allan 84
Scott, George C. 191–193
Scott, Ridley 134, 162, 202
Seance on a Wet Afternoon 2, 4, 36, 61–62, 68, 78, 209
Seattle 57
Seay, James 108
Secombe, Andrew 155
Secret Life 139
"The Secret of the Nautilus" 177
Sedgwick, Kyra 44, 46
September 11 attacks 85
Serling, Rod 7
SETI 134

Se7en 200, 204
Seven Notes in Black see *The Psychic*, 1977
Shadow of a Doubt 6, 59–61, 67, 74, 209
Shakespeare, William 12
Shamanism 9, 40, 150, 182–183
Shatner, William 124
Shaye, Bob 57
Sheen, Martin 101, 192
Shelley, Barbara 118, 129
Shepard, Sam 39
Shore, Howard 190
The Shout 38–39, 58, 90, 209
Showtime Cable Network 81
Shyamalan, M. Night 48
Sidgwick, Henry 14
Siegel, Don 119
The Silence of the Lambs (movie) 70–71, 72, 200, 202, 204
The Silence of the Lambs (novel) 69
Silliphant, Stirling 119
Silver, Ron 99
The Silver Chalice 11–12
Silverman, Robert 189
Silverstone, Alicia 102
Simmons, J.K. 73
Simon Magus 11–12
Sinclair, Hugh 37
Sinclair, Mary Craig 15
Sinclair, Upton 15, 178
Singer, Bryan 170, 173
Singer, Raymond 99
Sisto, Jeremy 102
Skerritt, Tom 100
Skolimowski, Jerzy 38–39, 90, 209
Slan 22–23
Small, Jim 62
Smith, Brandon 43
Smith, Dick 190
Smith, Lois 168
Smith, Paul H. 138, 201, 206
Snodgrass, Carrie 186
Society for Psychical Research (SPR) 14, 20
Solomon, Courtney 104
Somnabules 13, 26
Soto, Hugo 125
Southall Studios 132

Index

Soviets 177, 179, 182, 185, 194, 195
The Space Children 114–116, 120
Spacek, Sissy 3, 86–88, 103–104
Sparta 10
Species 107, 134–136, 209
Spencer, Bobbi 62
Spider-man 73
Spielberg, Steven 55, 59, 94–95, 97, 105, 116, 125–127, 134, 167, 169, 178, 208
Spinotti, Dante 70
Spiritualism 13–14, 62, 78
Spotnitz, Frank 204
Squire, Ronald 37
Stanford Research Institute (SRI) 3, 18, 140, 178–180, 205
Stanley, Kim 61–62
Stapeldon, Olaf 21–22, 121, 176
Star Gate 179, 205
Star Trek (TV show) 5, 125
Star Trek: The Motion Picture 154
Star Trek III: The Search for Spock 206
Star Trek IV: The Voyage Home 125
Star Wars (series) 4, 5, 88, 123, 141–143, 153, 154–155, 159, 161–162, 166, 170, 176, 179, 207, 208
Star Wars Episode I: The Phantom Menace 150, 154–157, 159, 161
Star Wars Episode II: Attack of the Clones 157–159, 161, 162
Star Wars Episode III: Revenge of the Sith 159–161, 162, 207
Star Wars Episode IV: A New Hope 2, 94, 143–146, 157
Star Wars Episode V: The Empire Strikes Back 146–151, 153, 159
Star Wars Episode VI: Return of the Jedi 151–154, 161
Stargate 179, 205

Starman 5
Starship *Enterprise* 5, 125
Starship Troopers (movie) 107, 136–138
Starship Troopers (novel) 136–137
Statue of Liberty 173
Steenburgen, Mary 42–43, 52
Stephens, Martin 117–118, 120
Stevens, Andrew 4, 184–185
Stewart, Athole 29
Stewart, Patrick 162, 171–173
Sting 162, 164
Stockwell, Dean 164
Stoker, Bram 26
Straight, Beatrice 96
Striesand, Barbra 91
Strindberg 50
Sturgeon, Theodore 23
Subiela, Eliseo 125, 209
Summerscale, Frank 122
Sun Streak 179
Sunset Boulevard 134
Superman: The Movie 154
Suspect Zero 3, 199–201, 204, 207, 208
Sutherland, Donald 83–85, 103–104
Svengali 28–29, 107
Swank, Hilary 73–74
Swann, Ingo 131, 140, 178, 205, 206
Swanson, Gloria 134
Sydney 89
Syria 10–11

Taff, Barry 100
Tamahori, Lee 202
Tamblyn, Russ 77
Tarantula 114
Targ, Russell 18, 41, 178, 201, 207–208
Tarot cards 34
Tate, Sharon 59
Taurog, Norman 124
The Teachings of Don Juan 142–143
Telepathine *see* Yage
Telepathy (definition) 2, 14–15
Temple of Apollo 12
Temple University 139

Tennessee 103
The Terminator 206
The Testament of Dr. Mabuse 27
The Texas Chainsaw Massacre 94
Thermopylae 10
They Came from Within 100
The Thing 154
The Thing from Another World 107
The 39 Steps 30
This Island Earth 108
Thomas, Henry 125–126
Thompson, Robert 94
Thornton, Billy Bob 73–74
300 10
Tolkein, J.R.R. 142
"Tonalities" 128
Toronto 187
Tourneur, Jacques 62
Tracks in the Psychic Wilderness 31
The Transatlantic Tunnel 30
Travers, Henry 60
Travolta, John 44–46, 87
Trilby 28
The Trollenberg Terror see *The Crawling Eye*
Tron 154
True Hollywood Stories 98
Truffaut, François 130
Tucker, Forrest 131
Tujunga Canyon 106
Turpin, Gerry 62
Turtletaub, Jon 45, 209
20th Century Fox Studios 142, 204
The Twilight Zone 7, 97, 139
2001: A Space Odyssey 146
Two Thousand Maniacs! 63

The UFO Incident 139
UFOs 51, 106–107, 120, 127, 129–131, 138–140, 178
UNESCO 121
United Nations 121, 131, 132, 173
United States 121, 208
U.S. Air Force 177, 181
U.S. Army 18, 179, 205
U.S. Army Intelligence and

Index

Security Command (INSCOM) 18
U.S. Congress 179
U.S. Defense Department 204
U.S. Government 178, 182, 187
U.S. Navy 177
Universal Studios 27, 28
University of California–Irvine 96
University of California–Los Angeles 142; parapsychology department 98–100
Urecal, Minerva 60
Urim and Thummin 11
Utah 135
Utts, Jessica 201

Vancouver 204
Van Dien, Casper 137
Van Vogt, A.E. 22
Varsi, Diane 124
Vasiliev, Leonid 177
The Vatican 161
Veidt, Conrad 26–27
Venice 83–85
Ventura, Lino 92
Verhoeven, Paul 137–138
Vertigo 60
Victor, Mark 97
Vidal, Gore 123–124
Videodrome 101
Village of the Damned (1960) 107, 116–120, 124, 140, 209
Village of the Damned (1995) 107, 123
Virginia 193
Virtuosity 198
Visit to a Small Planet 123–124, 209
Von Sydow, Max 81, 162, 168, 195–196
Vorhaus Bernard 34
Voskovec, George 64
"Vulcan Mind-Meld" 5, 125

Wain, Charles 89
Walkabout 89
Walken, Christopher 100–101
Walker, Andrew Kevin 102
Walker, Helen 32–33
Walt Disney Studios 55
The War of the Worlds 107–108, 180
War on Terror 57, 169
Warcollier, Rene 15, 178
Warner Brothers Studios 28
Washington, D.C. 83, 171, 199
Washington Post 78, 130
Washington University 80
Watergate 93, 179, 184, 187, 191, 194, 196
Weaver, Sigourney 51
Weine, Robert 26
Weir, Peter 9, 39, 83, 89, 91, 105, 196, 209
Wellington, Larry 63
Wells, H.G. 29
West Virginia 130
Westchester 172
Westinghouse Corporation 177
Whale, James 29
"What Do You See When You Close Your Eyes?" 201
What Women Want 6, 53–54, 207
When Worlds Collide 180
Whitaker, Forest 44, 46, 134–136
The White House 131, 173, 194
The Wicker Man 93
Wilder Napalm 6, 53, 58
Wilbur, Crane 34
Wilcox, Fred 128
Wilcox, Mary Charlotte 66
Wilder, Billy 108, 134
Wilder, Myles 109
Wilder, Thornton 61
Wilder, W. Lee 108–109
Williams, Adam 115
Williams, Billy Dee 149
Williams, JoBeth 95
Williams, John (actor) 123
Williams, John (composer) 169, 186
Williams, Michelle 135–136
Wilson, Mara 56–57
Wilson, Rainn 57
Winger, Debra 53
Wise, Robert 75, 77, 81, 105, 122, 209
The Witches 56
Woman in a Lizard's Skin 68
Wood, Bari 72
Wood, Ed, Jr. 114
Woodcock, Christopher "Fagin" 203
Woolrich, Cornell 34
World War I 26
World War II 80, 81
Wray, Fay 29–30
Wright, Jenny 197
Wright, Teresa 60–61
Wryn, Rhiannon Leigh 57
Wyndham, John 116, 119–120
Wynn, Keenan 133
Wyoming 130, 178, 201

Xerxes I 10
The X-Files (TV show) 130, 187, 200, 202, 204
The X-Files: Fight the Future 202
The X-Files: I Want to Believe 202–204
X-Men (comic book) 170
X-Men 2, 170–173, 208
X-Men 2: X-Men United 173–174
X-Men 3: The Last Stand 174–176, 208

Yage 166
Yapo, Mennan 48
Yeats, William Butler 14
York, Susannah 38–39
Yothers, Cory 195
Young, Sean 162, 164
Yuspa, Cathy 54

Zaire 18, 179
Zener cards 15–16, 51, 73, 184

www.ingramcontent.com/pod-product-compliance
Ingram Content Group UK Ltd.
Pitfield, Milton Keynes, MK11 3LW, UK
UKHW041945140426
5217IPUK00014B/658